JN114758

日英二言語版
Japanese-English Bilingual Version

人類の選択→
繁栄か、それとも、滅亡なのか？

Humanity's Choice →
Prosperity or Destruction?

岡本浩作

Kosaku Okamoto

東京図書出版

人類の選択→
繁栄か、それとも、滅亡なのか？

ハイライト

01　人類の総意

　核兵器を人間界から廃絶すること及び人間界が平和であることは、全世界全人類全ての個の総意（人類の総意）であると考えて良いと思います。

　然るに、核兵器は廃絶されず我が人間界に居座り、人間界は平和ではなく紛争や戦争が絶えません。

　人間が統べる人間界でありながら、人類の総意が通らず実現できないなどという愚かでおかしな事態がなぜ生じているのでしょうか？

　この絶対矛盾が生じているメカニズムを解消しない限り、核兵器廃絶も恒久的平和も実現することはありません。夢のまた夢です。

02　一蓮托生

　地球上に在る全人類の存亡も幸・不幸も一蓮托生です。仲良くしなければならないとか愛し合わなければならないということは当然のことであって、神や宗教や美徳に関係していることではありません。そのようなことができなくて、人間同士が争っていたのでは、人類は滅亡することになります。幸福にはなれません。

03　底に穴の開いた泥船

　数多の主権国家が存在する形の中で国家間に必然的に生じる争いを含め、次から次へと起こる様々な負の出来事や現象に対処するため、何を考え何を為しても、それは底に穴の開いている泥船の水を掻い出しているようなもので、根本的解決にはなりません。何れ、穴が拡がり沈没を免れることはできません。

根本的解決のためには、この船を離れ、新しい丈夫な船に乗り換えなければなりません。この船とは、国家間の争いはなく、負の出来事や現象が生じることを極小化できる「世界国家」という名の船のことです。

04　根本的矛盾とその解消

「数多の主権国家ありき」の中にあって、国際秩序や国際安全保障など、どのように議論をしても努力を重ねても、それが真なるそして恒久的平和を担保することにはなりません。なぜなら、それは「争いを必然とする主権国家間の中の平和」という「根本的な矛盾」の中にあるからです。

従って、我々が議論するべきことは、「数多の主権国家ありき」の下での議論ではなく、その既存の前提から離れて、「争いのない世界国家」という「新しい前提への移行」についての議論でなければなりません。

地球上に在る唯一の国である世界国家には敵対国は存在しませんから、戦争は（したくても）成立しません。従って、世界国家の下では、国際秩序や国際安全保障を含め国際に関わる一切の見解も議論も学問も無用になり、人類はそのような悩みから未来永劫に亘って解放されることになります。

05　主権国家 vs 世界国家

主権国家間に争いが生じる主権国家体制という名の木には、平和という花も自由という花も咲くことはありませんから、幸福という実を結ぶこともありません。従って、主権国家と人間のセットで成っている人間界から争いを消滅するためには、主権国家か人間かのいずれかを消去しなければ収まらないことになりますが、人間を消去するわけには参りませんから、消去するべきは主権国家であるということになります。

そもそも、国家とは人間が創出した実体のない幻想の産物です。然るに、同じ幻想の産物であっても、様々な難点のある数多の主権国家群という世界に比

べ、地球上にある唯一の国としてある世界国家は、敵対国が存在しないことにより、自動的に争いのない平和な世界になるという観点から格段に優れています。

06 世界国家＝国の最終形

　我々人間界は「国々ありき」から「世界国家ありき」へと心のパラダイムを転換しなければなりません。なぜなら、人間界に生じている問題・紛争・戦争は国々が存在しているがゆえに必然的に生じているからです。この国々がそれぞれ自国の主張を通し自国を守るために費やしている物心両面のエネルギーの総和を人間界は、人間の幸福のためにではなく不幸にするために、無駄に費やし失っています。毎日毎日世界に報道されている憂慮すべき様々な不幸な出来事を思う時、人類の存在意義とは相争うためにあるのか、と錯覚しそうになります（錯覚であればいいのですが…）。

　然るに、現状の「国々ありき」というパラダイムは絶対ではなく幻想にすぎません。地球上に存在する数多の主権国家は国の最終形ではありません。国の最終形は人類を一つの群れとし、地球に唯一の国として存在する地球国すなわち世界国家でなければなりません。なぜなら、この国には敵対国は存在しませんから、恒久的な平和の実現が約束されるからです。つまり、我々人間の個々の主権の負託先は国々の中の国ではなく、世界国家がより良い選択肢であるということになります。幻想は捨てなければなりません。

　主権国家の数多ある世界においては、個の命題が「平和」であることに対し、国家の命題が「戦争」であるという矛盾が必然的に生じますが、世界国家の下では個と国の命題は「平和」で一致します。

07 人間の自然状態vs科学の発達vs平和

　トマス・ホッブス（17世紀のイギリスの哲学者）は「人間の自然状態は、

万人が富や権力を求めて戦う戦争状態である」という見方をしていますが、仮にこの見方が正鵠を得ているとしても、人類を絶滅する兵器を製造できる科学の発達という条件が登場した今、我々はホッブスの言う人間の自然状態のままでいることはできません。争い戦えば人類は絶滅するからです。我々が「平和と自由に包まれて末永く存続する幸福を希望する生命体である」ということであるならば、我々は賢きに就き知恵により、ホッブスの言う「自然状態」から脱却しなければなりません。争わないために我々に課せられる必要最小限の要求は、争いの三大根源を断つこと、すなわち、敵対国家の存在しない世界国家をめざすことに加え、宗教という妄想そして人種・民族の差別を去ること、にあります。

　神仮説に基づき、穿った見方をすれば、神は「人間の自然状態と科学の発達とのセット」という障害物を設えて、人類がこの試練を乗り越えて自らの絶滅を回避し、平和と理想郷と幸福を手にすることができるかを試されておられるのやもしれません。そうであれば、我々は神にも負けてはなりません。

　人間は、闘争と博愛という対立する遺伝子を持っているようですが、人間性が志向する幸福の概念である「人間界至高の理念」（付録2-01）の実現をめざすのであれば、理性の働きにより、争い殺すことよりも許し助け合う遺伝子の方を発動するよう心掛けねばなりません。闘争の遺伝子は、対人間に向けて発動するのではなく、この世に理想郷を築くためにいかなる難関をも克服するという難関突破の闘争のために発動されるべきことになります。

　人間界から争いが消え平和でありさえすれば、人類は思いのままに幸福になることができます。争いのために費やされていた計り知れない物心両面のエネルギーの全てをこの地上、宇宙船地球号の中、にこの世における理想郷を築くために充当することもできます。理想郷の２つの条件である自然環境と人為環境を我々の望むように磨き上げて行くことが可能になり現実になるということです。

08 非現実を現実に

　人類の末永い平和と自由と幸福のために人類の理想郷を建設するという希望、そしてそのための必要条件となる人類滅亡の回避、は現実から見れば遠い非現実です。この非現実を実現するためには、現実を以てしてはその実現は困難です。つまり、非現実の実現は非現実によるしかないということになります。

　その非現実の取っ掛かりに「兵器の廃絶」と「世界国家の樹立」があります。従って、この地上を人類の理想郷とするために、我々には今この非現実の実現に向かう決意と行動が要求されることになります。

　これに対して、理想ではあってもこのような非現実を語ることは、現実を無視した不可能極まりない「たわごと」であるという批判はあるものと思います。しかし、その批判は成立しません。なぜなら、真なる論点は、現実を踏襲すれば人類の滅亡が論理的必然として推論されるのですから、非現実に向かいそれを実現するよりほか人類が助かる道がない、ということにあるからです。つまり、非現実の実現に向かうことは、「できるか、できないか」の問題ではなく、人類の滅亡を回避し、末永い未来に亘る栄光のためには、それ以外の選択肢のない人類に残された唯一の道である、ということです。

09 負のスパイラルから正のスパイラルへ

　軍備をして戦争をすることで、戦争の原因を増やしています。そのための財物及び心身のエネルギーを人間界の幸福のため、すなわち、人々の日常と未来の生活の安心、に振り替えて使用すれば、それだけでも戦争をする原因を少なくすることができます。

　戦争という負のスパイラルを脱し、平和という正のスパイラルをめざさなくてはなりません。

10 精神世界の向上

　我々人類が、国や、宗教や、人種・民族差別に固執して争っている限り、人間界が平和にも幸福にもなることはありません。これは100％の保証付きです。

　人類は、人間同士で相争い、科学を悪用した兵器を作り戦争をしながら、平和と幸福を神に祈るという笑い話のような愚の骨頂は止しにしなければなりません。そのように迄愚かで身勝手で恥じらいのない生命体であっては助かる者も助かりません。この場合、たとえ我々人類が滅亡しても、それは自業自得ですから、分相応にして仕方がありません。

　従って、我々万人（ホモ・サピエンス）にとって、滅亡を回避し、恒久的平和と自由と幸福のための理想郷をこの地上に築くためには、精神世界の向上をめざさなければならないことが必須条件になります。

目 次

序文

本書の趣旨

　我々人類はどのような未来の世界を思い描いているのでしょうか？

　本書は「人類の選択→繁栄か、それとも、滅亡なのか？」という、いささか過激な題名になっていますが、繁栄を希望するものとしても、今ある世界の実情は、その逆に、滅亡をめざしていると見受けられる憂いのあることをそのように表現したものです。

　繁栄とは、この世に生を受け今現在生活している全ての人々そしてその子子孫孫の末永き未来に亘る栄光のことであり、それは「人類全ての個が、平和で自由である人為環境と全ての生物に好都合な生態系である自然環境の中で、その生を全うできる幸福」を意味するものとします。

　本書は、この認識のもと、我々人類が、滅亡へと向かう臨界点に立つリスクを回避し、その希望を実現するためには何を考え何を為すべきか、について思いをめぐらしているものです。従って、筆者は、本書が（拙いものですが）世界の全ての個が「人類とこの宇宙船地球号の今と未来」についてあらためて考えるための一つの機会として捉えられることを期待したいと思います。

現状の世界

　今ある世界を踏襲して行けば、近未来に自滅による人類滅亡のリスクが推論されます。我々人類の希望が「平和と自由に包まれて末永く幸福に存続する」ということであるとしますと、我々の構築している今ある世界はこの希望の実現に調和しているとは言えません。

　なぜなら、我々は我々人類を含む動植物の存在基盤である自然環境・生態系

（自然環境）を損壊し続けており、それはもういつ全滅に向かって止められない進行を開始してもおかしくない状況にあります。又、人間社会（人為環境）においては、人間同士の争いが絶えず、そのため発達した科学を悪用して人間を殺傷する様々な兵器を造り、戦争やテロ行為に使用しているからです。人間界の争いに果てがなく、科学の発達に果てがなく、人間の愚かさに果てがなく、科学の厄災化に果てがないとすれば、人類は自らが手にした科学により絶滅することは論理的必然になります。

　人間界の争いの三大根源には(イ)数多の主権国家の存在、(ロ)宗教、(ハ)人種・民族差別、があります。

　(イ)各主権国家は領土や経済などの利害紛争から戦争という命題を必然的に具有することになり、それは主権国家を構成している全ての個の持つ平和という命題を蹂躙するという矛盾に結果しています。つまり、主権国家の存在そのものが人間界に争いを創造するメカニズムの中枢にあり、我々人間界はそのメカニズムの中で悶え苦しんでいることになります。(ロ)宗教は、人々を救うという高い志の光で始まったことに疑いはありませんが、遺憾にもその成り立ちは虚構から変貌した妄想でしかなく、その妄想で無垢で自由な存在として生を受けている人間を裁き罰するという神をも畏れぬ極悪非道・悪逆無道を為し、宗教間では妄想の僅かな違いを言い募り、聖とは真逆の血で血を洗う争いを為しその反省はなく、人間・人間界を幸福にしないばかりか不幸にし、さらに人類滅亡のリスク因子の一つとなる事態をも招来しています。又、(ハ)人種・民族差別は人間界を不和にしています。

　本書は、上記の争いの三大根源の内、(ロ)宗教、そして(ハ)人種・民族差別、は一旦横に置き（付録1にそれらの概説）、主たる範囲を(イ)主権国家の存在、に焦点を絞り、それが創造する争いとその解消を、そしてこの地上に人類の理想郷を築くことを論じているものです。

地上の理想郷

　人間界から争いがなくなり全人類が仲良くしている人為環境にある世界においては、損壊した自然環境である地球の自然・生態系の原状回復からさらに改善に向かって全人類が協力一致して勤しむことが可能になります。この理想的な人為環境と全ての生物に好都合な自然環境が実現している世界とは、宗教が説く来世に在るという天国、楽園、浄土などではなく、現世における人類の理想郷であると言えます。

本書の成り立ち

　本書は、特に昨今の数々の憂えるべき世界情勢に鑑み、拙著「神からの自立、Independence from God、㈱幻冬舎メディアコンサルティング、2020年9月発行」の「第8章 地上の理想郷」を骨子としそれを再編集したもの及び新たに付け加えたもの多少から構成されているものです。

　その拙著は、今ある世界を踏襲して行けば、近未来に自滅による人類滅亡のリスクが推論されるところ、この世界をどのように修正すれば人類は滅亡を回避し栄光ある未来を手にすることが可能なのか、をテーマとした「子供の為すつぶやきのようなもの」です。人類の滅亡を回避し栄光ある未来のために、我々人類は、主権国家の存在、宗教、人種・民族差別から必然する争いを解消し、自然環境・生態系の安定を確保し、科学を厄災化することなく専ら人類の幸福にのみ役立てること、又宇宙に冠たる知的生命体をめざし精神文明の発達を図らなければならない、ということを論じているものです。

　その内、宗教につきましては「神と宗教を考える、Thinking of God and Religion、㈱幻冬舎メディアコンサルティング、2021年12月発行」として本書に先立ち上梓しております。従って、「神からの自立、Independence from God（母体書）」、本書に先立ち上梓したその書、そして主権国家に関わる今回の本書の3冊は母子の書であり、後者の2冊は母体書の中の思想の一部を特化して

それぞれ1冊の書として著したものということになります。

　この母子の書は、拙いものであっても、人類の幸福な未来を願うという筆者の切なる思いに端を発しているものです。従って、全人類一人一人に捧げる書に位置づけたいと思います。その内、特に、「神と宗教を考える、Thinking of God and Religion」は、全ての宗教・宗教者の方々に、そして本書「人類の選択→繁栄か、それとも、滅亡なのか？　Humanity's Choice→Prosperity or Destruction?」は、全ての主権国家そして国際連合へ捧げさせていただきたいと思います。筆者の思想が人類の幸福という命題に照らして正鵠を得ているものかどうかはともかく、それをあらためて考える上での「手掛かり」にしていただくことがあればと願ってのことです。

本書の構成

　本書は、本文とその付録から成っています。付録は、本文に言及されている筆者の思想や用語の内必要と思われる項目について解説しているものです。これらは、本書の母体書「神からの自立、Independence from God」および/又は「神と宗教を考える、Thinking of God and Religion」に詳細ですが、本書をお読みいただく際に、それらを参照せずに済むように、一応概略的な解説を添付してあるものです。

　本書の構成は下記のようになっています。

第1章　序論

第2章　主権国家から世界国家へ

第3章　主権国家 vs 科学の発達

第4章　地上の理想郷

第5章　理想郷、その夢の世界

第6章　世界国家樹立への道

第7章　非現実な希望と非現実な決断

付録：本文中の思想及び用語の解説
1　主権国家を除く争いの二大根源
　1．宗教
　2．人種・民族の差別
2　様々な思想及び用語

本書の言語

　日本文が原典で、それを筆者が英文にした日英二言語から成っています。そうしたのは、本書の論点が我々全人類の存亡に関わっているものですから、読者が日本国内外すなわち世界に拡がることを願ってのことです。

　英語を選んだ理由の一つは、世界には英語を解する数多の人々がおられること、そして、二つには、日本語のほかに筆者が解する言語は英語しかなく、英語であれば拙くても、本書の大要を判読していただける程度にはお伝えすることができるのではないかと思ったことによります。

　日本語版と英語版を別冊ではなく1冊の書の中に収めたのは、例えば、本書の論点や思想について語り合っていただけるようなことがある場合、両言語版が参照できるように1冊の書としてまとまって手許に在ることが何かと望ましいのでは、という筆者の考えによるものです。

本書の記述に関わる注記

　多くの文献等によりその分野で周知となっていると判断される事柄につきましては、その出典を表示してありません。なお、周知の事柄であっても、文言や表現などをそのまま使わせていただいたものにつきましてはその出典を表示してあります。辞書とあるのは広辞苑第六版のことです。

　様々な人の言葉を本書の中に採り入れていますが、その内のいくつかはオリジナルのままぐはなく、筆者が消化して作成したオリジナルの意味あるいは内

容になっています。

特別のノート

　日本語版が原典で、英語版は原則原典の内容を一応忠実になぞったものです。しかし、筆者の英文が拙いため、英文の中に不適当な箇所や用語が発見されることがあるかもしれませんが、それは筆者の責に帰するもので、出版社を始め、他のどの方にも責任のあることではありません。

第1章　序論

1　主権国家の世界に必然する紛争

　我々人間は、「この我々は何処から来て何処へ行くのか、我々が此処に存在している理由は何か、そして、我々は何者なのか?」という問いを持ちますが、今現在その答えを知りません。しかし、実在している我々という実際に即して、「我々人間は、仮の自我でしかない自我を持ち、一瞬も止まることなく移ろい行き、己を己のものともできぬ夢幻のごとき実在者である」という認識は持てています。生まれて、成長して、老いて、然る後に死する生命体です。この移り変わりは、意識の外で、粛々と進行して行きます。その一生は、永遠に照らせば、一瞬の光芒で夢のようなものでしかありませんが、この実在者は、生ある限り、平和や自由の中での幸福を希望する生命体のようです。本書は、この希望は全人類全ての個に時と場所を問わず普遍的であるという前提に立っています。従って、人間一人一人の主権に属するこの希望は何人もみだりに侵害してはならないものです。

　さて、現状の世界においては、この希望の実現を阻害しているのみならず人類の滅亡迄もたらすリスク諸因子が存在しますが、本書はその内の主因子の一つである「数多の主権国家の存在」に焦点を絞って論じているものです。

　国の主権は国の構成員の主権の負託により生じているものです。全ての人間の希望は平和と自由を享受することのできる幸福にあります。従って、国はその希望の実現を委託されているというのが基本的構図になります。このため、国はその構成員の幸福を守るため、国を守るという命題を持つことになります。そして、ここまでは、一応納得できるように見えます。

　しかしながら、国というものは他国（又は他国集団）との間に領土や経済などに関わる紛争が必然的に生じますが（宗教や人種・民族差別も絡んできま

す）、対話により解決できなければ、戦争に行き着くことになります。そうしますと、国は、国防の名の下に、国の構成員を領有しているがごとく、軍事訓練や兵役を強い、戦争が生ずれば戦闘員として使用することになります。又言論統制・弾圧を行い、個の主権を無視し自由を奪い、従わない者には死をも含む罰を科すという理不尽が行われます。又、戦争では、軍人も民間人も害され殺され、多くの避難民が生じ、幸福とは全く逆のありとあらゆる不幸が人間・人間界を覆います。

　これは、驚くことに、国の構成員の主権の負託により成立している国の主権が、あろうことか、国の構成員の主権を侵害し支配するという招かれざるおかしな転倒が生じていることになります。絶対矛盾の構図とも言うべきものです。

　そして、悲劇物語はそこで止まりません。発達した科学を際限なく厄災化して製造される強力な兵器を使用して為す戦争は人類の滅亡迄もたらすことは論理的必然になります。愚かにも、今既に世界が保有している核兵器にしてもそれを用いての戦争が生ずることがあれば、人類は明日にも滅亡するリスクを抱えています。

　このように、主権国家間に争いが生じる世界という名の木には、平和という花も自由という花も咲くことはありませんから、幸福という実を結ぶこともありません。従って、主権国家と人間のセットで成っている人間界から争いを消滅するためには、主権国家か人間かのいずれかを消去しなければ収まらないことになりますが、人間を消去するわけには参りませんから、消去するべきは主権国家であるということになります。

　そもそも、国家とは人間が創出した実体のない幻想の産物です。然るに、同じ幻想の産物であっても、様々な難点の在る数多の主権国家という世界に比べ、地球上に唯一の国としてある世界国家は敵対国が存在しないことにより自動的に争いのない平和な世界になるという観点から格段に優れています。

2　栄光の未来へ

　本書は、上記の認識に基づき、平和、自由そして幸福という人類の希望の実現をめざして、我々人類は、来世のことは来世のこととして、生ある間に我々が幸福を享受できる理想郷をこの地上、宇宙船地球号の中、に築きましょうというお話です。

　理想郷の構築は人類が滅亡せず存続していることが前提になります。

　然るに、我々人間界の現状を見渡しますと、この前提とは真逆である「人類自滅へのリスク街道を驀進中」という様相を呈しています。

　本書はそのため、人類に滅亡のリスクをもたらす諸因子の中の主たる因子の一つである「数多の国々の存在」とそのリスクを解消するために、国々を発展的に解消し「人類を一つの群れとし、地球全域を一つの国とする世界国家構想」をお話しすることにしました。とんでもない非現実なことのように思われるかもしれませんが、至極真面目なお話です。なぜなら、この「地球一国」の実現なくして人類が自滅による滅亡から逃れる道は残されていないからです。世界国家の実現こそが人類滅亡のリスクを回避し、人類の存続を可能とする要求を満たすことになり、これは又我々人類が理想郷の門内に入ったことを意味することにもなるからです。

　我々が理想郷の門内に入った後は、全人類が協力一致してこの理想郷にさらに磨きをかけ、宗教が来世にあるという天国、楽園、浄土（極楽など）に勝るとも劣らないこの世における理想郷に仕上げて行くことができます。平和でありさえすれば、人類の物心両面のエネルギーは紛争や戦争という自らを不幸にするために費やし失うことはなく、その全てを人類が幸福になるための理想郷をこの宇宙船地球号の中に構築する目的に振り替えて使用できることになります。

第2章　主権国家から世界国家へ

　我々人類は、そして個としての全ての人間は、平和で自由で幸福な世界を希望しています。従って、この希望を踏みにじる戦争がなくなることを願っています。これは「人類の総意」であると考えて良いものと思います。

　然るに、人間界は平和ではなく紛争や戦争が絶えません。人間が統べる人間界でありながら、人類の総意が通らず実現できないなどという愚かでおかしな事態がなぜ生じているのでしょうか？　それはこの矛盾が生じる原因が存在しているからです。その原因は何かということになりますが、その主たる因子の一つに、戦争を命題に持つ数多の主権国家の存在があります。つまり、「今ある世界」が「国々ありき」というパラダイムを受け容れ凝り固まっている限り、その中で平和を模索してどのような議論をしても努力を重ねても、その実現は不可能であるということです。このことは人類史上において既に十二分に証明されています。個が平和と幸福を希望しているにもかかわらず個の集合である国が戦争をなし個の希望を蹂躙している、という絶対矛盾の状態です。従ってこの絶対矛盾が生じている原因を解消しない限り人間界から戦争がなくなることはありません。

　ここでは、物事の根底に関わる発想の転換が要求されます。

　国々が存在しているがゆえに戦争が生じているのですから、議論の赴くところは明らかです。それは、国々を統合して、敵対する国のない世界で唯一の国を作ることが要請されることになります。この小さな宇宙船地球号をさらに数多の小部屋に間仕切りしてその小部屋同士が相争い、その結果人類が宇宙船地球号から消滅するなどは涙が出るほどおかしく愚かなことです。現状の数多の国々が存在する形は、国の最終形である地球上唯一の国に至る過程にあり、その現在形が人類に災いするものであるからには、我々人間界はその形から早々に離れ最終形に向かうべきという理になります。

　これは突飛なことに思えますが、理屈の上ではそうなります。実現できるか
どうかは別の問題です。しかし、先ず理想を把握しなければ何事も前には進み
ません。そして理想に向かってその実現をめざすことになります。不幸にし
て、理想が実現できないことがわかれば、その次善をめざすことになります。
これが正しい手順です。然るに、数多の主権国家が存在する現状の世界を踏襲
する限り、この地上から戦争をなくすことのできる良策があるようには思われ
ず、そうであれば、我々は理想である地球一国すなわち世界国家を実現する
以外に助かる道はなさそうです。なぜなら、国々が存在し紛争・戦争を止めら
れなければ、益々発達する科学を厄災化した強力な兵器を使用しての戦争は、
我々に不幸の中に生きることを強いるだけではなく、人類の滅亡迄もたらすか
らです。

1　主権国家が数多ある難点と世界国家

1．戦争の生じるメカニズム＝主権国家の存在

　主権在民とは、「国家の主権が国民に存すること」です。辞書には、国の主
権とは、「①その国家の意思によるほか、他国の支配に服さない統治権力。国
家構成の要素で、最高・独立・絶対の権力。統治権。②国家の政治のあり方
を最終的に決める権利」であり、主権国家とは、「他国に従属せず、自らの国
内・国際問題を独立して決定できる国。国際法の基本主体」と解説されていま
す。国家の3要素は主権・領土・国民で、国家存続の第1条件に国防・安全保
障があります。

　さて、「主権在民、主権国家とその主権、国家の要素、国防と安全」、これら
一連の思想は無理なく納得できるように見えます。主権在民が第一の優位にあ
り（現状、そうなっていない「ように見える」国もありますが）、主権国家の
主権は国民により負託される形にもなっており、一見非の打ちどころがないよ
うに見えます。

27

しかし、この一連の思想こそが人間社会に戦争を創造する根源そのものであることに注意しなければなりません。

　そもそも、この思想は、「主権国家ありき」すなわち「宇宙船地球号を間仕切りした小部屋ありき」という前提に立っており、その前提の中で平和が約束されるという条件下においてのみ妥当に見える思想です。然るに、小部屋は数多存在しており、小部屋間には領土や経済を始め様々な利害関係が生じます。この時、それぞれの小部屋が国家の主権を行使し合えばどうなるかは火を見るより明らかです。話し合いで解決できなければ戦争になります。これが複数の主権国家の存在により戦争の生じることが必然となる簡明なメカニズムです。つまり、我々人類は、人間界に戦争を起こすメカニズムを創造してその存在を許容していることになります。そうしておいて、戦争の悲惨さを様々に語り訴えて平和を望んでも、「戦争絶滅」、「核兵器廃絶」、「全ての兵器の廃絶」、「軍隊の解散」は永遠に実現することのない「夢の又夢」でしかありません。

　それゆえに、人間界から戦争を絶滅するために我々人類が採ることのできる唯一の選択肢は、この宇宙船地球号の中に、複数の国々ではなく唯一地球国のみが存在しているという国の概念の最終形に迄、穏やかにかつ速やかに移行しなければならないことになります。この地球国には敵対国は存在しませんから、この地球上から戦争が消滅し人間界には恒久的平和が訪れることになります。理屈は簡明です。

「国々ありき」から「唯一の地球国ありき」へと心にあるパラダイムを転換しなければならないということです。

２．主権国家の暴走

　国際間には領土や経済などに関わり利害関係が生じます。この場合、料簡が狭い偏執により、自国の利益の最大化をめざして、掠奪主義を根本思想に持つ覇権主義あるいは帝国主義を採る国が暴走することがあります。

　この主義を実現するためには、その目的に向かって、国内体制を整えなけれ

ばなりませんが、強力な軍事力を持つこと及び全体主義国家体制を敷くことが
要求されることになります。このような全体主義を原理とする国家は、多くは
一国一党主義をとるか、あるいは一部の者が権力を掌握することになります。
権力者は言論を統制・弾圧し、又個人の自由を奪うことになりますが、これは
国の構成員の主権を「ないがしろ」にしていることにほかなりません。

　国内はこのような惨状となり、外国では、侵略を仕掛けられた国のみなら
ず、その他の国々にも計り知れない負の影響を及ぼすことが必定になります。
その上に、一国の権力者は、国内外の情勢を利用して、自身の権力の保持と保
身に執心する挙に出ることもないではありません。それは、偏執から生じる妄
想を正義と位置付けること、侵略を防衛と偽ること、自国の不幸は外国の責任
に転嫁するなど、知的生命体には程遠い意識の低さに由来することを唱えるこ
とが含まれます。世界の平和、自由、幸福そして人類の今と未来は乱されま
す。

　このような望ましくないことは、そもそもが、数多の主権国家が存在してい
るがゆえに生じて来る現象です。対して、世界国家の下では、国際間利害が生
じることはなく、掠奪する国もされる国も存在しませんから、戦争が生じるこ
とも、このようなおかしなこと一切もが生じる余地も憂いもありません。

3．国の最終形

　そもそも、数多の国が存在する現状は国の形の最終形ではありません。

　人は群れます。人類の歴史を見ても明らかですが、群れは小さな群れからよ
り大きな群れへと変遷して来ています。群れは集落に始まり、村となり、市と
なり、州となり、国となっています。この国が数多存在しているのが現状で
す。

　一つの地域で数多の群れが争っていたのでは平和や人々の幸福は望めません
が、争いの後それらの群れが統合して大きな群れとなり平和が訪れます。その
後に起こることは、この群れと他の地域の群れが争い統合しさらに大きな群れ

となります。このように、群れは統合を繰り返すことにより大きくなって行きますが、現在の群れの単位である国にはまだ他の国という争いの相手が存在していますから、群れの最終形ではありません。最終形へ向かう途中で停滞している未完成な形です。

　最終形とは全人類が一つの群れになることであり、そして地球全域が一つの国になった時に完成します。この群れには敵対者は存在しませんから、その時この地上、すなわち宇宙船地球号の中に恒久的な平和が実現することになります。

　従って、地球を一つの国にするという思想は何も奇異な思想ではなく、水が高きから低きに流れるように自然な思想です。対して、現状の国々の存在こそが、平和と人々の幸福の実現という目的に照らして最適ではなく、むしろ奇異であるということになります。

4. 国の最終形に対する逆行

　このように、我々人類が向かうべき方向は国の最終形である地球一国すなわち世界国家であるということになりますが、近年この大河の流れに逆行して、国をさらに細断しその数を結果的に増やす方向へ向かう動きが生じている事実があります。これは、第二次世界大戦後に大国の植民地が独立して行ったことを言っているのではありません。そうではなく、その後に生じている人種・民族や宗教というアイデンティティーの旗の下に集結した国を作りたいという動きのあることを指しているものです。

　しかし、この動きの志向するところは国の最終形である世界国家という思想に矛盾するものではありません。なぜなら、その動機は現状の国において少数派の人種・民族や宗教徒が差別や冷遇から逃れようとすることにありますが、世界国家の概念とは、人種・民族や宗教の違いに対する差別は一切なく、全ての個は平等に遇され、敬愛と融和をめざす世界であるからです。つまり、世界国家においては、そのような差別に由来する動機が生じることはないというこ

とです。

　又、そのようなアイデンティティーの旗の下に集結して独立できたとしても、経済的・統治的にそして国防・安全保障面などについて独立独歩できる国家としての体制を整えることができなければ、再び大国に飲み込まれることになるかもしれません。中々思うようには参りません。世界国家とは少数派にもやさしく、このような悩みが解消されている世界です。

２　国際間紛争の存在

　現在における国際間紛争は、国々の間で過去から続く利害関係から生じた紛争・戦争から結果し蓄積された恨みや憎しみが複雑に絡む解きほぐせない事情に基づくものが大方です。従って、表面に形になって出ている紛争もその理由である過去から引きずる諸問題の解決が伴わなければ真なる解決にはなりませんが、それは至難のことです。なぜなら今まで解決できていないから紛争が生じているからです。（なお、紛争には国に加えて、人種・民族や宗教も絡んで来ます）

　しかし、話し合いで解決できないまま、武器を取って長期間戦っていたのでは敵味方共に軍人・民間人に死傷者が生じ、難民が生じ、経済も生活も民心も疲弊します。これは争いの当事国のみではなく周辺諸国、支援国家、国際社会（国連など）に亘る問題になりますから、色々な形で仲裁が入り、とにもかくにも一旦武器を置き休戦しようという気運が生じ、緊急避難的に休戦することはあります。然るに、基本的には紛争の理由そのものは解決できているわけではありませんから、両陣営共に納得の行かぬままの状態であることに変わりはありません。

　その際、紛争の当事国のみではなく色々な意味での関係国が介入して、紛争の理由の一時的あるいは暫定的な解決が図られることはあります。しかし、これは最終解決完成計画図のない、パッチワークのような、その場限りの思想によるその場限りの修復をしているというのが一般的です。しかも、その場限り

の思想も紛争当事者のみではなく関係国の思惑をも多かれ少なかれ反映することになりますから、その思想そのものが当事者間では必ずしも納得できていないものになることは否めません。かくして、当然にそのような思想でなされた紛争の一時的・暫定的な解決は当事者間に納得感はなく従って尊重されず、不満や恨みや怒りが燻火のように残り、燃え上がり、再び武器を取っての戦いが繰り返されるという悪循環を形成することになります。当然の帰結とも言える元の木阿弥です。このように、今日では、この地上で生じているどの紛争も、当事者間のみの問題ではなく、世界の国々が直接的、間接的、有機的に関係しているのが一般ですから、この納得感が持てず、不満、恨み、怒りが澱となって世界に蔓延していることが常況になっています。お互いの"正義"が通らないことから生じているものです。

　世界の首脳が一堂に集まり会合しても解決できない紛争は数限りなく存在しています。それでも、たとえ緊急避難的であれ休戦できれば一応ヒートアップした争いに水をかけるくらいの意味はあり、それなりの効果のあることは否定できませんが、それさえもできず、武器を取りゲリラ活動もテロ活動も絶えることなく継続している現実があります。通常兵器による戦争なら、急な人類の滅亡に迄には至らないと考えられますが、核保有国間の戦争となりますと、通常兵器で戦況不利になった側は核兵器を使用することになることは否定できません。核戦争になれば、人類滅亡の危機を招来することになることは言う迄もありません。

　これが、世界の現況であり、それは戦争を命題に持つ主権国家の存在に由来していることであることは明白です。

3　世界国家移行への必要性

1. 世界国家の自然成立は期待薄

「国の最終形である世界国家は理想であるが非現実的な思想である。代えて、

世界国家については、今追い求めなくとも、熟すればいずれ自然にそうなる」という考え方はあります。しかし、我々はその考えを選択することはできません。

　その第1の理由は、現状の主権国家のある世界とそれから生ずる諸般を考慮すれば、自然成立の可能性があるとしても、その時期は今から何百年かあるいはそれ以上の未来のことであると考えられるところ、人類はその遥か前に戦争か又は世界がなおざりにした地球自然環境・生態系の崩壊により絶滅してしまっているであろうと思われることにあります。第2の理由は、人類が絶滅しないまでも、世界国家が自然成立するまでの長期間、人類は希求していることとは違う様々な負の人為環境及び自然環境の不幸の中での生存を強いられることになります。

　もう、これ以上人類は不幸であってはなりません。

　世界国家は、自然成立を座して待つ、という消極的な手法で手にすることはできません。それを達成するという積極的な強い意志と綿密な計画とその実行によってのみ手にすることのできる（かもしれない）世界です。

　数多の主権国家の存在により結果する過去から現在に続く紛争と戦争、そしてそれらの国々はあるべき国の最終形ではないこと、これらをこのまま放置すれば、未来にも継続する戦争により人類の不幸はもとより滅亡のリスク迄もが推論されます。我が人間界において毎日毎日生じている主権国家間のどうしようもない様々な紛争やそのため生じている人々の不幸を思う時、今が世界国家へ向かうべく精神のパラダイムの入れ換えをするべき時であり、そして、その方向へ向かっての一歩を踏み出すべき、もしかすると人類に残された最後の機会であるように思えることです。

２．世界国家の概念

　世界国家とは何か、ということを改めて概括しますと、世界国家とは、人類を一つの群れとし地球全域を一つとする国のことです。

この国には敵対国は存在しませんから、戦争のない恒久的平和が実現しています。この国の目指すところは、人間という生命体に由来する「人間界至高の理念」（付録2-01）に矛盾せず調和している世界であり、全ての個は差別されることなく、人権は守られ、自由で平等であり、それぞれの幸福を追求することが可能な世界であることです。つまり、今ある世界において、平和と戦争ということで対立している個とその集合である国の命題が、世界国家の中では「平和」で一致していることになります。又、衣食住は足り、自然環境は保全されさらに修復・改善されている世界、少なくともそのようなことに全ての個が協力一致して勤しんでいる世界です。この平和な世界は、人間同士が国々に分かれて争うことで無駄と不幸な形で費消されていた人、もの、金、そして人の精神などのエネルギーの全てを人類の幸福のためにのみ振り替えて使用することが可能となっている世界のことです。

4　唯一の選択肢としての世界国家

「国々をなくして、地球全域を一国とする世界国家にする」という命題につきましては、その構想および実現可能性に関連して様々な反論が湧出することは承知しています。

　しかし、どのような反論も、下記の「前提1」と「前提2」の関係に対する考えを明らかにした上でなければ意味のあるものではありません。

　　「前提1」数多の主権国家の存在とその結果必然的に生じる戦争を、科学
　　　　　　を厄災化し益々発達する兵器を以て戦う過去と同じ道を踏襲す
　　　　　　る。
　　「前提2」人類は、滅亡ではなく、平和と自由に包まれて幸福に存続する
　　　　　　ことを希望する。

　　(イ)　「前提1」を選択することは、「前提2」は放棄することになりますか

ら、自滅による人類滅亡のリスクを受け容れるということになります。阿修羅のごとく戦争を派手にドンパチやって太く短く生きて滅亡することになるかもしれませんが、これも人類の選択肢の一つです。

(ロ)　「前提１」の否定を選択し、戦争の消滅を希望しますと「前提２」へ向かう道は残されていることになります。このことは数多ある主権国家を解消し統合して世界国家樹立に向かうことを考えなければならないことを意味します。

(ハ)　「前提１」の数多の主権国家の存在は肯定するが主権国家間の戦争は否定する、ということが成立すれば、世界国家が人類の唯一の選択肢ではなくなることは考えられます。しかし、このような手品のようなことは、主権国家体制が成立している理屈の上からも成立せず現実的にも実現しそうにありません。

　ただ、(ハ)につきましては、「成立・実現しそうにない」と言っても、それを100％断定することはできず、何かのブレイクスルー（突破できないと思われるような難関を突破する手立てのようなこと）により「成立・実現する」ということも否定し切れません。しかし、そのような形で主権国家間の戦争がなくなり恒久的な平和が実現したとしますと、これは実質的に世界国家が実現した状態であると考えても良いことになります。

　人の世は、人が先に生まれ、その後に人が集合し集落に始まり現在の国々へと変遷して来ています。然るに、この今ある国が人の希望を負託することのできる唯一の形であるという思い込みは幻想にすぎません。より理想的負託先である世界国家があります。(ハ)が実現することがあるならば、その時数多ある主権国家を発展的に解消し統合して、名実共に世界国家に手直しすることは容易であろうと考えられます。しかし我々は、このことを期待することはできません。そのようになるという確信が持てないからです。

　なお、この(ハ)の「数多の主権国家の存在を肯定するが、主権国家間の戦争は否定する」という思想を実践しているように見えるものに、「国際の平和と

安全の維持のための普遍的国際機構」として機能する国際連合があります。しかし、国際連合は主権国家間に争いが生ずれば平和と安全の維持を模索するという形で機能するもので、あくまでも「"主権国家ありきの中の平和"という矛盾」を抱えているものですから、世界国家とは似て非なるものであり、この矛盾がある限り、国際連合からなしくずし的に世界国家が誕生することは期待薄であるというほかありません。

　因みに、国際連合教育科学文化機関憲章（ユネスコ憲章）を見てみますと（下に掲載）、世界の人々の相互理解、無知と偏見を去り民主主義の原理の人間の尊厳である平等・相互の尊重、正義・自由・平和、互譲の精神、人類の知的及び精神的連帯等がその目的となっています。これらを普遍するためには、客観的真理が拘束を受けず探究され、かつ思想と知識を自由に交換することを可能とする教育が必要であることが主張されています。世界の人々の教育、科学及び文化の関連を通じて、国際平和と人類共通の福祉という目的を促進することがこの憲章のめざすところである、という宣言です。

　然るに、国際連合はやはり「主権国家ありき」の中のものですから、この憲章にももどかしいものがあることは否めません。教育が必要でありそれが平和に貢献することに否やはありませんが、数多の主権国家が存在する限り、教育が平和に直結することはありません。教育があろうとなかろうと、世界の人々全ての個が平和を願っていることに変わりはありません。又、当憲章の冒頭にも、「戦争は人の心の中で生れるものであるから、人の心の中に平和のとりでを築かなければならない」と記されていますが、「平和のとりで」は人の心の中に既に久しく築かれています。しかし、戦争は起きるのです。数多の主権国家が存在する限り戦争が生じるメカニズムは前述した通りです。すなわち、個の命題が平和であることに対して個の集合である国の命題が戦争であるという矛盾が生じているからです。さらに、この矛盾は個の命題を国が守ろうとすることから生じる、という奇妙さにあります。すなわち、国は国民と国民の利益を守るためにその究極的手段として戦争をするということであり、戦争は国民をあらゆる意味で苦しめる、という矛盾です。

　この国民と国との間に生じる必然にして奇妙な矛盾を解消するためには、人間か国かのどちらか一方を消去しなければ収まらないことになりますが、人間を消去するわけには参りません。そうしますと、議論の赴くところ、消去するべきは国であるということになります。

　このようなことですから、「前提2」を選択する限り、やはり人類に残された選択肢は㈹の世界国家へ向かわなければならないということになります。

国際連合教育科学文化機関憲章（ユネスコ憲章）

前文

　この憲章の当事国政府は、その国民に代って次のとおり宣言する。

　戦争は人の心の中で生れるものであるから、人の心の中に平和のとりでを築かなければならない。

　相互の風習と生活を知らないことは、人類の歴史を通じて世界の諸人民の間に疑惑と不信をおこした共通の原因であり、この疑惑と不信のために、諸人民の不一致があまりにもしばしば戦争となった。

　ここに終りを告げた恐るべき大戦争は（第二次世界大戦 ― 筆者注）、人間の尊厳・平等・相互の尊重という民主主義の原理を否認し、これらの原理の代りに、無知と偏見を通じて人間と人種の不平等という教義をひろめることによって可能にされた戦争であった。

　文化の広い普及と正義・自由・平和のための人類の教育とは、人間の尊厳に欠くことのできないものであり、且つすべての国民が相互の援助及び相互の関心の精神をもって果さなければならない神聖な義務である。

　政府の政治的及び経済的取極のみに基く平和は、世界の諸人民の、一致した、しかも永続する誠実な支持を確保できる平和ではない。よって平和は、失われないためには、人類の知的及び精神的連帯の上に築かなければならない。

　これらの理由によって、この憲章の当事国は、すべての人に教育の充分で平等な機会が与えられ、客観的真理が拘束を受けずに探究され、且つ、思想と知

識が自由に交換されるべきことを信じて、その国民の間における伝達の方法を
発達させ及び増加させること並びに相互に理解し及び相互の生活を一層真実
に一層完全に知るためにこの伝達の方法を用いることに一致し及び決意してい
る。

　その結果、当事国は、世界の諸人民の教育、科学及び文化上の関係を通じ
て、国際連合の設立の目的であり、且つその憲章が宣言している国際平和と人
類の共通の福祉という目的を促進するために、ここに国際連合教育科学文化機
関を創設する。（文部科学省インターネットサイトから）

5　世界国家の実現可能性

　それでは、世界国家の実現可能性はどのようになるのでしょうか。

　それはわかりません。

　わかっていることはこの宇宙船地球号の中に現存する全ての国を解消し統合
して地球国一国にしない限り、人類は近未来に滅亡するリスクが高いというこ
とと、滅亡しないまでも、我々人間は不幸の中に生きていかなければならない
ということです。対して、世界国家地球国は地球全域において国々による争い
のない理想的国家になります。従って、問題は現状を踏襲して人類滅亡のリス
クと不幸を選択するか、あるいは人類の平和と幸福という希望が約束される世
界国家へ向かう挑戦を選択するか、という二者択一になります。どちらを選択
するのも人類の自由裁量です。前者を選択するならともかく、後者を選択する
のなら、「できるか、できないか」すなわち「実現可能性の如何」は問題では
ありません。人類は今存亡の瀬戸際に立たされていますが、幸いにも存続を希
望できる道筋は残されています。この難関を突破し栄光の未来をめざして、人
事を尽くすしかないことになります。

　上述のように、国際連合の延長線上に自然に世界国家が誕生することは考え
にくいことですが、世界国家へ至る道程や世界国家が実現した暁の初期の統治
につきましては、国際連合を有効に活用することが一つの有力なアプローチで

あると考えられます。

　この「世界国家への移行」の手順につきましては、その一つの例として、「第6章 世界国家樹立への道」と「第7章 非現実な希望と非現実な決断」の中に、筆者の考えを概説してあります。

第3章　主権国家vs科学の発達

1　主権国家を否定する科学の発達

　何千年も昔から数多の主権国家が存在しています。それらは、滅びそして新たに建国され、敵対者を意識して同盟・連合を結んだり解いたり、あるいは別の国と又結んだり、と本質的には同じことが相も変わらず今日に至る迄連綿と繰り返されています。数多の主権国家の下では、国々が、潜在化していようと顕在化していようと緊張・戦争状態にあることが常態ですから、平和があったとしても、それは真なるそして恒久的な平和ではなく、いつ崩れるかもしれない、束の間の平和でしかありません。戦いが生ずる度に、その悲惨や不幸が様々に語られ、様々な論文や小説などが書かれ、平和を希求する悲痛な声や思いが人間界を覆います。何千年も昔から同じことが繰り返されています。然るに、戦争は今まででもそしてこれからもなくなりません。

　この状況を評価しますと、人類は、自らが希望する平和や自由や幸福に調和していない世界を構築しそれに固執していることになりますから、単に愚かなだけではなく、愚かを自覚していながら目の前の現実に流されてその修正に挑戦しなかったのであれば、愚かに輪をかけた愚かであり、しかも怠惰な生命体であるということになります。人類がこれほど愚かであり怠惰であるならば、滅亡してもそれは自業自得であり仕方もないか、という風に思わないでもありません。

　これは、しかし、済んでしまったことですから、ただ悔やんでいても始まりません。大切なのは、人類が未来の栄光を希望するのであれば、過去を反省し、それを未来の糧とすることです。

　幸いに（などと言うのは、主権国家間の争いのため、生を全うできなかった無数の人々、そして心身の障害を始め様々な不幸を被った無数の人々には申し

訳ありませんが）、数千年の間、大小無数の様々な戦争があったにもかかわら
ず、人類は滅亡することなく何とか今日まで生き長らえています。

　その最大の理由は兵器が人類の滅亡をもたらす程に強力ではなかったことに
あります。ところが、第二次世界大戦以後兵器は様変わりしました。それは科
学の発達に依拠しています。つまり、科学を悪用して益々強力な兵器を次から
次へと開発・製造することになりました。現状その最強のものは核兵器です。
第二次世界大戦の終わり前に広島と長崎に投下されて以降そのレベルの核兵器
は使用されていないとは言え、世界が保有している既存の核兵器のみでも人類
を幾度も絶滅させるに足る威力を持つと言われています。人間を殺傷する兵器
など、現存のものだけでも「もう、沢山だ」という強い思いがありますが、主
権国家間の争いに果てがないとすれば、発達に果てのない科学を悪用してなす
際限なき強力な兵器の開発・製造にも果てがないことになります。戦争を命題
に持つ主権国家と科学の関係から生じる負のスパイラルというべきものです。

　このスパイラルを解消し人類の滅亡を回避するためには、科学の発達を断つ
ことはできませんから、断つべきは争いを創造する主権国家であるということ
になります。このことは、すなわち、科学の発達は、今日までぐずぐずと既存
の現実に流れ容認してきた主権国家の存在をこれより以降は容認できない事態
が到来したことを雄弁に物語っています。

　このように、科学は人類の幸・不幸そして存亡に迄深く関わっています。こ
の認識に基づき、本章では以下、「2　科学の厄災化」、「3　科学と不幸、そし
て幸福」そして「4　科学文明と精神文明」についてお話ししています。

2　科学の厄災化

　科学の厄災化には、「1．科学の非平和的使用」と「2．科学の平和的利用の
蹉跌」があります。前者が科学の厄災化であることは明白ですが、後者が科学
の厄災化になるのは、平和的利用をめざしたものが、こと志とは違い人間界に
害を及ぼす結果を招くもののことを言います。

1．科学の非平和的使用

　科学の非平和的使用の最たるものには、人間殺戮器である⑴核兵器と⑵通常兵器があります。

⑴ 核兵器

①核兵器の歴史

　核兵器は最初にアメリカ合衆国が開発製造し、第二次世界大戦の末期に日本の広島と長崎に使用しました。人類は、その歴史の中で、戦うためにより強力な兵器の開発に勤しんで来ました。特に、第一次世界大戦から第二次世界大戦中は敵国を制圧するために圧倒的な兵器の要求が高じましたが、発達した科学がその要求に応えられることを悪用し、遂に最終兵器とも言われる核兵器を手にするに至っております。広島と長崎に使用された原爆の威力は TNT 火薬に換算すれば16キロトンほどのものでしたが、以後核兵器は核分裂による原爆から核融合による水爆へと進みその威力は急激に膨張し、広島・長崎型の何十倍、何百倍もの威力を持つものが開発されています。

　第二次世界大戦後の世界は、アメリカとソビエト連邦（現在のロシア連邦）の二つの大国による世界の二極化が進み、世界は、大きくは、アメリカ側（西側）とソ連側（東側）に分かれて緊張が高まり冷戦時代に突入して行きました。アメリカに核兵器の威力を投影されたソ連は、アメリカに対抗するために、速やかに大量の核兵器を具備するに至っております。大戦後の四半世紀を越える期間、アメリカとソ連はあたかも核兵器開発合戦の様相を呈していました。ここに至り、核兵器を使用しての戦争となれば、人類の滅亡ということになり戦争の勝者も敗者もなくなりますから、どちらも核兵器は持てども使用できない事態となり、お互いが核に拠って相手の核を抑止するという恐怖のバランスが形成されております。アメリカとロシアが前面に出て直接戦うという世界大戦のような大きな戦争はなくこの意味では平和と言えば平和ですが、心か

ら納得できる積極的平和には程遠い、仕方もない消極的平和が危うく保たれているという構図です。

　アメリカとソ連に続き、第二次世界大戦の戦勝国であるイギリス、フランス、中国が核保有国になり、そして大戦後に2000年近くもの時を経て再建国が実現したイスラエルに加え、領土問題や宗教の違いが絡み長い緊張状態にあるインドとパキスタンの両国も核を持つに至っております。さらに、近年には北朝鮮も保有国になりました。

②核兵器の恐怖

　第二次世界大戦後のアメリカを中心にした西側とソ連を中心にした東側の緊張は、1962年のソ連によるキューバへの核兵器配備画策に代表される一触即発の状況にまで高まったこともありました。核兵器を持たない主な西側諸国は、核攻撃を受けた場合はアメリカが代わって核報復をする、というアメリカの核の傘に入ることで自国に対する核攻撃が抑止されるという構図に依拠することになりました。核を導入し、西側と東側のお互いがその威力を相手方へ投影し合い、恐怖し合っている愚かで嘆かわしい構図です。

　自国が開発した核兵器ではありませんが、ニュークリア・シェアリング（Nuclear Sharing）という核抑止における政策上の概念が生じ実施されています。ソ連やその衛星国に配備された核兵器に対抗するため、北大西洋条約機構（NATO）の内のドイツ、イタリア、ベルギー、オランダは自国内にアメリカが所有する核を置いていて、各国の政府がそれぞれ使用権限を持っています。（フリー百科事典ウィキペディアより）

　第二次世界大戦後四半世紀以上が過ぎ、ソ連も中国も、共産主義という名目は保ちながら、実質的には資本主義経済を採り入れています。ソビエト連邦は1980年代半ば以後ソ連社会主義の改革をめざしゴルバチョフがペレストロイカを展開し、1991年のソ連邦崩壊で終わっています。ソビエト連邦の幾つかの国は遊離して独立し、ソ連はその国名をロシア連邦に改名しています。その間、中国が経済や国際政治で台頭し、第二次世界大戦後のアメリカとソ連の二

極化世界という明確な枠組みは薄まり、経済活動のグローバル化と相まって、世界の緊張は緩くはなりました。しかし、西側と東側という大きな枠組みが消滅したわけではなく、その枠組みに由来する国際間の紛争が消滅したわけではありません。紛争が存在する以上、核に拠り相手の核の使用を抑止するという要求が消滅したわけではありません。又、近年には、北朝鮮による核武装に対する懸念も世界を覆っています。

③絶対悪である核兵器による人類の滅亡

通常兵器とは違い、戦略爆撃機、弾道ミサイル搭載原子力潜水艦、大陸間弾道ミサイル（ICBM）などの戦略核兵器による全面戦争は、人類の文明の終わりはおろか人類の絶滅につながります。

一旦核兵器が使用されますと、多数の人々の命が一瞬にして奪われ、あるいは一生治癒されることのない後遺症に苦しむという、人道に悖る筆舌に尽くし難い、理不尽な不幸・悲惨をもたらします。

又、核兵器は、爆心地の壊滅的な破壊はもとより、核爆発の熱、爆風、長期間消えない放射能により悲惨な被害をもたらします。さらに、核兵器の恐ろしさはその間接的被害にもあります。地球全域における生物の存続を不可能にする生態系の破壊です。核兵器は海洋も地表も大気も放射能で汚染し、巻き上がった灰で日光が遮られて気温が低下し、生物が生存できない環境になります。有機物である栄養分を自家生産できる独立栄養生物である植物は枯れ、その結果、有機物を自家生産できず植物の生産した栄養分を消費し食する従属栄養生物である動物も生存することはできなくなります。食物連鎖の壊滅による食料不足を原因とする絶滅です。食物連鎖の頂点にいる人類も例外ではありません。人類は最も悲惨な情況になります。

このように、核兵器は絶対悪です。科学を厄災化したものの最たるものであり、「人間界至高の理念」に矛盾する最たるものですから、人間界から可及的速やかにかつ完璧に駆逐するべきものです。従って、全世界から核兵器を無条件に断固廃絶しなければなりません。核による核の抑止などという愚かの極み

を蘊蓄するその道の専門家と言われる愚かな大人より、小学校の子供にもわかる疑う余地のない明らかなことです。

　④核兵器削減と廃絶への取り組み

　戦いのため、より強力な兵器を求めて来たのが兵器の歴史ですから、アメリカがその延長線上で核兵器を導入したことは不思議なことではありません。歴史に“もし”はありませんが、アメリカでなければ、どこかほかの国が最初の核兵器導入国になったことは論を俟ちません。しかし、導入してみると、そのあまりにも強力な威力のため、アメリカとソ連は言うに及ばず世界はその恐怖におののきました。そのため、核兵器削減と廃絶への取り組みが生じています。

　主な取り組みは以下の通りです。

国際連合

＊1963年に国連総会で「核拡散防止条約（NPT）」が採択され、1968年に署名され、1970年に発効されています。これは、アメリカ、ソ連、イギリス、フランス、中国（第二次世界大戦の戦勝国で国連常任理事国の5カ国）のみを国際的に認められた「核兵器保有国」として核軍縮義務を規定し、他の「非核兵器保有国」の核兵器保有を禁止し、「核は平和利用」に限定するものです。

＊1994年から毎年日本は世界で唯一の核被爆国として「核兵器廃絶決議案」を提出し採択されています。2009年には、アメリカのバラク・オバマ大統領の「核なき世界」の提唱により、アメリカが初めて共同提案国となっています。2012年には、核兵器廃絶決議案は184カ国という多数の国により決議されています。2017年に採択された決議案にはアメリカ、イギリス、フランスを含む156カ国が賛同国となっていますが、その数はその前年の167

カ国から11カ国減少しています。減少の主な理由には、当年の7月にNGOのICAN（International Campaign to Abolish Nuclear Weapons）の努力により国連で「核兵器禁止条約」が採択されましたが、核兵器廃絶決議案提出の日本がその反対に回ったということで、核なき世界に対するダブルスタンダードを持つ国という悪いイメージが生じたことにあることが否定できません。反対したのは、核使用が禁止されるとアメリカの核の傘に依拠している日本や他の国の安全保障のバランスが崩れるというのがその主たる理由です。

日本が「核兵器廃絶決議案」を提出しながら、ICANの「核兵器禁止条約」に核保有国と共に反対したのは自己矛盾以外の何物でもありませんが、このことはさて置きます。2016年と2017年そして2021年の「核兵器廃絶決議案」の採択状況は下記のようになっています（日本外務省報道発表）。

（核兵器廃絶決議案）

	2016年	2017年	2021年
賛 成 国	167	156	158
反 対 国	4	4	4
棄 権 国	16	24	27
会議参加国	187	184	189

反対国は僅か4カ国で、ロシア、中国、シリア、北朝鮮です。賛成国の中にはアメリカ、イギリス、フランスの3カ国は含まれていますから、反対国の中のロシアと中国が賛成国に回りますと、国連常任理事国であり、「核拡散防止条約（NPT）」において「核兵器保有国」として国際間で認められている5カ国すべてが賛成したことになります。そうなりますと、残った反対国も棄権国も、関連する諸般の事情が解消することも期待され、「核兵器廃絶決議案」は満場一致で採択される期待が持てることになります。

　全人類の現在と未来の栄光のために、ロシアと中国には賛成国に回る大英断が切に望まれます。

＊2009年、アメリカのバラク・オバマ大統領は「核兵器のない世界（核なき世界）」を演説し、ノーベル平和賞を受賞しています。しかし、他国が核を保有する限り、アメリカは核兵器を保有し続けることを言明しています。ロシア、中国も核廃棄を否定しています。

アメリカとロシア（ソ連）

＊1969年から戦略兵器制限交渉（SALT）が開始され、1972年には弾道弾迎撃ミサイル制限条約（ABM条約）が締結されたが、2002年にはミサイル防衛を推進するアメリカにより当条約は破棄された。

＊1982年からアメリカとソ連両国間の戦略核戦力削減のための戦略兵器削減条約（START）が開始され、1991年に第一次戦略兵器削減条約（START I ― 戦略核弾頭数保有の上限を米ロ各6,000発に制限）が締結され2001年に履行された。しかし、1993年に締結された第二次戦略兵器削減条約（START II ― 上限は米ロ各3,000〜3,500発）は、上述のように2002年にミサイル防衛を推進するアメリカにより弾道弾迎撃ミサイル制限条約が破棄されたため、ロシアはSTART IIを実行しないことを表明した。なお、予定されていた第三次戦略兵器削減条約（START III ― 上限は米ロ各2,000〜2,500発を予定していた）は未締結に終わっている。

＊START IIとIIIが潰れたため、START Iに続く新START（上限は米ロ各1,550発）が2010年に締結されその翌年に発効した。核弾頭数削減は未履行のままであるが、2021年2月に、両国は本条約の延長を発表している（日本外務省報道発表）。（2023年春現在、ロシアはその履行を停止状態にしている）

＊双方がその力を放棄すれば軍拡を招くことはないであろうという哲学によ

り、1987年に中距離核戦力全廃条約（INF）が締結され条約が定める期限の1991年の半ば迄に米ソ合わせ2,500発超の核弾頭および通常弾頭を搭載した中距離ミサイルが廃棄された。この条約はロシアに引き継がれたが、2019年2月にアメリカが破棄を通告し半年後の8月に失効した。

ストックホルム国際平和研究所（SIPRI）によると、2021年1月時点の世界の核兵器数は13,080発です（除く、北朝鮮の推定保有数40〜50発）。アメリカとロシアの両国がその90％強を半分ずつ保有し（アメリカ5,550発、ロシア6,255発の計11,805発）、残りの10％弱を他の6カ国（イギリス、フランス、中国、インド、パキスタン、イスラエル）が保有しています。アメリカとロシアの保有合計の11,805発は、1980年代後半の数万発をピークとして、両国が主として第一次戦略兵器削減条約（START I）を通して、減少したものです。然るに、今世紀に入った頃からその削減は停滞し、他の国を含め、むしろ「歯止め」がなくなり核軍拡へ逆戻りする恐れさえある憂いが拭い切れません。

NGOによるもの

＊核兵器の非合法化と廃絶を目指して活動するICANの略称を持つNGOは各国の平和団体と連携して各国政府や市民社会に働きかけ、核の非人道性を訴え続けています。ICANには世界101カ国と468のNGOなどが参加し、2017年7月国連で「核兵器禁止条約」の形で具現化しました。これによりICANはノーベル平和賞を受賞しています。

2021年1月時点では、本条約の署名国数は86カ国で（その他加入国2国）、批准国数は66カ国となっている。2020年10月に発効に必要な50カ国の批准に達したため、その90日後の2021年1月に発効した。（フリー百科事典ウィキペディア）

　対して、当条約には肝心の核保有国や核抑止力に依拠する日本を含む諸国は参加しておらず、北朝鮮の核武装などを引き合いに、「核抑止による安全保障を無視している」とか、「核保有国が条約に加わっていないので意味がない」という愚かな批判があります。

　しかし、そのような批判は当たっておりません。なぜなら、「核抑止による安全保障を無視している」などは、核兵器が禁止され消滅すれば核抑止の必要性も消滅しますから心配の種ではなくなるからです。また、「核兵器保有国が条約に加わっていないので意味がない」ということについては、それゆえに当条約の権威も実効性も薄弱なものであることは否めませんが、それでも核兵器を廃絶しようとする方向に向かって一歩前に進めているだけでも十分に意味のあることです。対して、当条約について批判を受けなければならない張本人は、第1には反対に回った核保有国や日本などであり、第2には自身は何もせず座しているのみで当条約には意味がないなどと批判をし、何か良識ある正論を語っていると勘違いをしている人たちです。良識や正論とは「人類の滅亡をもたらす核兵器を直ちに断固廃絶せよ」と主張することであり、これよりほかのことではありません。核兵器の廃絶は「核兵器ありき」というパラダイムの中の議論から実現することはありません。

⑤時代に逆行
　前項のように、1980年代後半から核兵器に「歯止め」を掛ける機運が高まり核兵器は1980年代の半ばの米ソ両国合わせた核弾頭数万発から11,805発に迄削減されましたが、今世紀に入った頃からその歯止めが消え核兵器削減の時流が逆行している感が払拭できません。不安定な国際情勢・紛争の存在にその理由が求められるのでしょうが、そのことと核を保有することに理知的なつながりがないことは今は世界に共通の認識となっている筈です。なぜなら、核戦争をすれば、人類の滅亡につながるからです。仮に、核戦争で相手方を全滅させ此方に多少が生き残ったとしても、この"戦勝者"も核による生態系の壊滅により続いて"生物的敗者"となり滅亡することになります。つまり、核を保

有することに戦略上の意味はありません。幸福のために使用できる人類の心身および財物という資産を人類を不幸にするために投資しているにすぎないことになります。

　従って、核は増強を図るべきものではなく、現存するものを温存するべきものでもなく、恐る恐るちびちびと削減をするべきものでもありません。可及的速やかに人間界から一挙にそして完璧に有無を言わせず駆逐するべきものです。

　願わくは、世界のリーダーたるアメリカとロシアには人類の未来の確保と栄光のため、是非とも率先して核廃絶という人類史上第１の英断と善処をお願いしたいものです。

⑥核の不拡散および廃絶

　核の不拡散は、人類にとって望ましいことですから、何がどうであれどのような場合も、肯定するべきものであることに異論はありません。

　さて、「核拡散防止条約（NPT）」の重要な点は、核保有５カ国（アメリカ、ロシア、イギリス、フランス、中国）には保有を認めるが、核をこれ以上拡散しないために、今迄に核を保有していない国の核保有は禁止するということです。しかし、「私たちは保有するが他の国は核を持つな」というのは筋の通らない話です。これでは非核保有国は、心の底から納得できるものではありません。なぜなら、人間とはそのような不公平な考えや物言いは基本的には受け容れられないと感じ考える生命体だからです。

　核のない時代においても、第二次世界大戦の戦勝国である核保有国は非核保有国に比べ通常兵器に限っても既に軍事大国でした。主権国家の安全保障という観点からは、軍事小国の方こそ可能であれば核のような強力な兵器を手にして軍事大国に対する安全保障を確保すると共に国際間における十分な発言権をも確保したいと願っていたことは当然であると考えられます。然るに、現実には核を手にすることになったのは通常兵器においても軍事大国の方で、そのため軍事においても国際間の発言権においても主導権は軍事大国に把握されて

いる形になっています。これでは、軍事小国の中に核を保有する軍事大国を恐れ、自国も核を保有し核抑止力による自前の安全保障をめざすことを考える国が出て来ることがあってもそれは自然と言えば自然なことで何らおかしなことではありません。核を導入しさえしなければ、核を以て核に対抗する必要性の諸々が生じることはありませんでした。この場合、どちらに理がないかと言えば、核保有国の方です。

　核不拡散という最終目標と上記の議論から見えてくることは明らかです。核不拡散の究極は核廃絶です。「核拡散防止条約（NPT）」は必要ではありませんでした。すなわち、非核保有国は核保有をめざすなというような条約を作ることに換えて、その時核保有国のなすべきであったことは、「我々は核を完璧に廃絶します」という非核保有国に向けて行う宣言でした。その時、人類は核の廃絶を決意し実行するべきでした。

　それができなく核が人間界に居座ったため、その後に生じていることは目を覆いたくなる色々様々な愚かな事柄です。核保有国の姿勢が、我々が核を持っていることでそれが抑止に働くので相手国から核攻撃を受けることはあるまい、従って、核保有は必要である、というような餓鬼の喧嘩とさして変わらない愚かで幼稚な考えに立っている限り、核は人類滅亡のその日迄廃絶されることはありません。自国に人類を滅亡する悪魔を導入しておいて、他国も悪魔を導入しているから、悪魔を以て悪魔を制御するために悪魔を手放せないという理屈ですが、自ら招いた自業自得の抜き差しならぬ事態下における、下らない愚の骨頂たる理屈です。このいわゆる「悪を以て悪を制する」というのが一つの理屈というのなら、ここは人類の英知を結集して、もう一つの理屈である「理外の理」を以て、この人類共通の悪魔を人間界から消滅するために人類は協力一致団結して当たらなければなりません。

　このことは「人類共通の願い」として全ての個人そして全ての国が、理解を深め喜び勇んで実行に移すことです。この「願い」が欠落したままに、仮に何か強要されたことのように疑念と共に「完全で検証可能かつ不可逆的な核廃棄」が実現できたとしても、それは今保有する核兵器についての物理的なお話

に過ぎません。核兵器の科学的知識も技術も、不可逆的ではなく、人間の文明には残ります。「人類共通の願い」が保たれなければ、核兵器はいつでも再製作できるのです。

核の知識やエネルギーそのものは基本的には善なるもので悪なるものではありません。それを厄災化している人類が愚かなのです。核の知識やエネルギーの平和的かつ安全な利用は人類の未来にとっては必要なものです。例えば、多くの例の内の一つとして、地球に衝突して来る小惑星の軌道をずらすことに使えるかもしれません。全てはそれを扱う我々人間の「心」にかかっていることです。

広島と長崎以降そのレベルに達する核兵器は使用されたことはありませんが、これ以後そのレベル以上の核兵器が戦争で使われる事態が発生した場合、それは高い確率で人類の滅亡をもたらすことが憂慮されます。なぜなら、それはドミノ倒し（将棋倒し）を誘発する可能性が高いからです。一度でも不使用の箍が外れれば、後はもう何が起きるかわかりません。人間の狂気や愚かさが瞬間的には良識や理性を押し流し、その結果我々は自身の滅亡という終着点にまで行き着くことを止めることができないという事態が起こりうるということです。それは過去に生じた大方の戦争を見れば明らかです。ただ、過去の戦争と核兵器戦争との決定的な違いは、前者においては戦後の世界が"あった"ことに対し、後者においては戦後の世界は"ない"という点です。つまり、人類は核戦争により滅亡するからです。

⑦悪魔の支配下にある世界から人類は自らを解放すべし

我々人類はつい最近まで、何を考えることもなく天真爛漫のままに自由でした。"それでは今はどうか？"と言いますと、あろうことか、人類自らが自由を放棄し、悪魔に支配される世界で生きる、という選択をしています。人類は下らない生命体に堕しています。

悪魔とは、いわゆる核爆弾、核弾頭、核と呼ばれているものです。この悪魔を創造したのはほかでもない我々自身であり、それを即座に廃絶せず人間界に

居座らせ、その悪魔の存在を原点として我が人間界の根幹的物事が考えられ、なされ、動いている現状の惨憺たる構図を客観視すれば、これは紛れもなく悪魔に支配されている人間界・人類という構図になることは事実ですから、誰も否定することはできません。この選択は「人類は未来の栄光のため宇宙に冠たる知的生命体をめざす」という我々の基本方針に照らせば、間違っていることは論ずるまでもありません。

　この悪魔すなわち核に対する唯一の正論と正当な行動とは、これを我が人間界から可及的速やかにかつ完璧に排除・駆逐すること以外にありません。悪魔を擁し、主権国家（群）が悪魔を利用しているつもりで、我田引水的に浅はかで小欲で愚かな主張や思想を並べ立て、あるいは、悪魔をちらつかせて他国を恫喝するなどが生じている現状が凝縮して行き着く先は、明日かもしれない近未来に、悪魔がその本領を十二分に発揮し灼熱の閃光と共にこの世を終わらせることへの進行が限りなく濃厚になります。

　ところで、宇宙人（付録2-02）が地球（人類）を攻撃して来ることがあれば、人類は、人類同士の争いは一旦棚上げして、一致団結して宇宙人に対抗するであろう、というようなことが考えられることがあります。然るに、遠い宇宙空間を超えて地球迄やって来ることのできる宇宙人が存在するとすれば、宇宙人は比類もなく高度な科学文明と共に精神世界を持つ生命体であることが想像されますから、人類を攻撃するというような可能性はないと考えられます。従って、人類が一致団結する理由として宇宙人を登場させたことは適切であるとは言えませんが、この話の要諦である「人類は人類共通の敵に対しては一致団結して事に当たる」という思想そのものは真であると考えて良いものと思います。そうしますと、我々人類が今なさねばならないことは、この核という悪魔に我々が絶滅される前に、一致団結して人類共通の敵であるこの悪魔を絶滅することがこの思想に適っていることになります。

　通常、悪魔というものから受ける印象は我々人間にはどうしようもない"しろもの"であるということですが、幸いにしてこの悪魔は人間の決意次第でどうにでもできるものです。すなわち、核という悪魔は我々人間の科学技術によ

り悪魔たる機能を解除されることには従順で抵抗するものではありません。これは不幸中の幸いです。しかし、「幸運の女神には後ろ髪はない」とも言われます。幸運の女神が我々人間の目の前を通り過ぎ、悪魔の閃光と共に人類が絶滅する瞬間に、女神には後ろ髪がないことを確認するなどというほぞを噛むことのないように、我々人類は今幸運の女神の前髪をしっかりと握りしめ、悪魔の排除を完了しなければなりません。

　このように考え来たりますと、はっきりとよくわかることがあります。それは、この核という悪魔を退治するためには神や宗教に頼ったり縋ったりしても何の役にも立たないということです。つまり、この悪魔を退治できるものは唯一我々人間を置いてほかにはないという認識です。

　我々人類はつい最近まで、何を考える必要もなく天真爛漫のままに自由でした。

　なぜなら、我々が何をしても地球自然環境の自浄作用を超えるようなことにはならず、我々が自らを滅亡させるということを考える必要などなかったからです。

　この天真爛漫の自由を終結させたもの、それは科学技術の発達です。産業革命が始まり、特に20世紀に入ってから科学は人類に実生活の利便と幸福をもたらした反面、自然環境に対してはその自浄作用を超える公害をもたらしています。さらに科学はその扱いを一歩間違えば人類に決定的な厄災となり、延いては人類の滅亡をもたらすこと迄あることが今は人類共通の認識となっています。このように、科学の発達により人類は昔のままに無条件にそして天真爛漫に自由でいることはできなくなりましたが、自由が全く失われてしまったわけではありません。なぜなら、自然環境も科学の危うさも人類がそれをきちんと管理しさえすれば、その中で人類はやはり自由でいることはできると考えられるからです。

　然るに、この管理ができたとしても、忘れてならないことは核すなわち悪魔の存在です。この悪魔が人間界に居座る限りにおいては、この管理の成功など悪魔の袖の一振りで無意味になります。人類そのものが絶滅・消滅するからで

す。

　哲学者は"自由はあるのかないのか"ということを考えることがあるようで
すが、そのようなことを考える必要はありません。自由とは、"あると思えば
ある、ないと思えばない"もので、その「あるなし」も「内容」も（一人一人
の）人間が決めて然るべきものと言っても良いものです。然るに、これはやは
り人類が支配する正気の世界においてこそ成立する考え方であって、今現在の
ように、悪魔に支配されている狂気の世界においては人類の真の自由も幸福も
「ある」とは言えません。なぜなら、人類は知的生命体としての自覚も矜持も
見失っており、世界は核という悪魔を原点に据えた論理で動き、さらにいつ何
時悪魔がこの世を終わらせるかもしれない憂いの中にあるからです。

　筆者はこの悪魔退治ができていない現状を思う時、"どうしてこんな単純な
ことができないのか"という憤りと情けなさのため、切歯扼腕し地団駄を踏み
叫び出したい衝動にかられ、その後絶望感や虚脱感に襲われ、終には"人類が
これほどまでに愚かな生命体であるのであれば、悪魔に絶滅されてもそれは自
業自得であり分相応にして仕方もないか"という思いに苛まれます。

　しかし、筆者は諦めてはおりません。

　世界的な政治家であろうと誰であろうと、特に夜中に目覚め一人静かにこの
問題に向き合う時、この悪魔に支配されている現状を是とする一人の人間も存
在しないものと確信できます。すなわち、核という悪魔を人間界から排除・駆
逐することは人類の総意の筈です。このことを我々は理解し切望しています。

　我が人間界から悪魔を排除・駆逐するお話です。

　難しい話ではありません。子供のように単純にして透徹した考えこそが必要
であり、愚にもつかない余計な考えは一切必要ではありません。この核という
悪魔を退治することにより、人類は悪魔の支配する狂気の世界から正気の世界
へ自らを再解放することになり、知的生命体としての自覚と矜持を取り戻すこ
とができることになります。人類の末永い存続も未来の栄光も核という悪魔退
治の実現がその大前提になります。

　少し品格に欠ける語りようになりますが、他国が核という悪魔を擁する限り

我が国も悪魔を手放すことはできない、という尻の穴の小さな輩ばかりしかいないのであれば、助かる筈の人類も助かりません。他国が悪魔を手放さなくとも我が国は手放す、というくらいの度量を持つべきです。核を放棄した国々をそれに乗じて放棄しない国々が核攻撃をして戦勝しても、何れ続いて戦勝国側も地球生態系の壊滅により滅亡することは火を見るより明らかです。地球の半球の生態系が壊滅すれば壊滅は地球の全球に及ぶことは言う迄もありません。核を使用しての戦勝が同時に自国の滅亡を覚悟しなければならないのですから、核は持てども使用することはできず、核を放棄しても核攻撃を受けることはありません。この理をよく理解しなければなりません。従って、核を持つ国がある限り我が国も核を放棄することはできないと考えることは幻想に過ぎません。

　我々人類は一致団結・協力して核という悪魔を物理的にも精神的にも徹底して我が人間界から排除・駆逐しましょう。何もかも、全てはそれからのお話です。

　⑧核兵器廃絶は実現不可能な幻想か？

　核兵器は人類にとって絶対悪であることが明らかであるにもかかわらず、人間界はその廃絶をなかなか実行に移すことができないでいます。人類の存続を望むのか、絶滅を受け容れるのか、という問いを突き付けられているにもかかわらず、核廃絶などということは実現不可能な幻想なのでしょうか？　幻想であるなどとは思いたくもありませんが、幻想なのかもしれません。そうだとすれば、そのような情況を創造している真なる原因は、この小さな宇宙船地球号の中をさらに小さく間仕切りして多くの主権国家が存在している現実にあります。

　世界中の全ての個（私人）の希望である命題は「平和」であることに対し、全ての国の持つ最終の命題は「戦争」です。戦争の際相手国に勝利するためには、あるいは他の国から脅かされないためには、一旦手にした強力な核兵器を廃棄するなどということは国という視点からは考えにくいことです。

　国の掲げる命題である「戦争」は、「国民（個・私人）のために、安全と、平和と国益を守らなければならず、それらが阻害されることがあれば、国は戦争を含めるあらゆる方策を採り得る」いう前提の上に成立しているものです。すなわち、「国を守るためには戦争をする」ということであり、この短い叙述の中に、既に個の命題と個の集合により成立している国の命題との間に絶対矛盾が生じていることが見て取れます。人間界はこの絶対矛盾を放置したままその矛盾の中で行動しています。

　この絶対矛盾と国際間紛争の存在から生じて来た困難の一つが、一度導入したが最後、廃絶できないでいる核兵器の存在です。核による核の抑止という愚かな理屈に依拠しているからです。相手側の核兵器が消滅しない以上、当方の核兵器も廃棄できないということになります。このことからわかることは、国の近視眼的視野の中には戦争はありますが、不戦による人類滅亡のリスク回避はないということです。これは、人道、平和、人類の存続という全てに優先すべき世界のどの個にも共通である倫理が、戦争をするという国の道徳や正義に劣位している望ましくない状態です。国は私人が公人となって機能しています。私人であって公人となった個は優先すべき倫理よりも正義や道徳に重きを置くという自己矛盾の中で行動していることになります。

　ICANが個の命題である倫理に拠り、国の命題が正義や道徳に拠っているからには両者の立場は違っています。議論は進展せず、停滞する道理です。

　かくして、個の命題と国の命題の矛盾が解決されない限り、すなわち主権国家が消滅しない限り、核兵器の廃絶などは幻想でしかないことになりますが、我々人類にわかっていることは、その幻想を現実にするよりほかに人類が滅亡から救われることはないということです。

⑵　通常兵器

　兵器の分類方法は色々とありますが、ここでは核兵器とそれ以外の兵器の二つの型に大別し、後者を通常兵器と呼びます。通常兵器は、その種類に、爆弾

や銃砲等の火薬兵器、毒ガス等の化学兵器、細菌やウイルス等の生物兵器、高エネルギーレーザー等の光学兵器、音響兵器等の兵器を含みます。

①核兵器のない世界
　核兵器の廃絶はまだ実現していません。そもそも、いつかは廃絶されるものと期待できるものかどうかわかりませんし、そうこうするうちに、人類は核兵器戦争により滅亡するかもしれません。
　然るに、一器も残さず核兵器が廃絶され、世界から消滅したと仮定してみます。
　果たしてそれで一件落着となり平和と幸福な世界が実現するものでしょうか？
　そうはなりません。なぜなら、核兵器はそれがなくなっても、持てる核兵器をドンパチやり合えば、数日という短い時間に人類が滅亡する心配は一応なくなったというだけのことで、即平和と幸福に貢献するものではないからです。すなわち、核兵器が消滅しても世界に存在する争いが消滅するわけではなく、核兵器消滅前のままの変わらない状態で残ります。
　戦闘になった際、核兵器あるなしの違いは、核兵器プラス通常兵器による闘いが通常兵器のみによる闘いに変わるという違いでしかありません。通常兵器は残っているのです。通常兵器の存在により人間界が不幸であることに変わりはなく、通常兵器のみであっても、宇宙船地球号の中が二つに分かれて徹底した全面戦争になるようなことになれば、過去の戦争とは違い発達した強力な兵器の使用による戦争は、構築した人類の文明を滅ぼし、さらに人類の滅亡に迄つながる恐れもないではありません。
　留意すべきは、核兵器が消滅しても、元核兵器保有国は通常兵器でも概ね相変わらず軍事強国であることに違いはないという点です。

②兵器の歴史と未来、そして廃絶
　兵器は、人類始まって以来つい数世紀前までの長い間、石や棒に始まり、弓

矢や槍や刀剣に変わった程度で大きくは発達していませんでした。以後、原始
銃砲が導入されましたが、狩猟や人間殺戮用器機として多少の発達は見られた
ものの、1914年に始まった第一次世界大戦以前まではそれらも大きくは発達
しておりません。

　ところが、第一次世界大戦から1941年に始まった第二次世界大戦にかけて、
兵器は様変わりし、兵器システムも兵器の型も種類も基本的には今日のものの
原型が構築されるに至っています。第二次世界大戦以後今日に至る間には、科
学技術の目覚ましい発達と相まって、これらは益々強力になり、未来に向かっ
てさらに際限なくその威力を増し続ける趨勢が止まる気配はありません。

　兵器は、単独で機能する武器とは異なり、システムとして運用されるため、
下記の四つの要素から構成され、下位の要素は上位の要素が有効に機能するた
めに存在するものです（フリー百科事典ウィキペディアから）。

　㋑　破壊体 ― 銃弾、砲弾、ミサイルなどの弾頭
　㋺　発射体 ― 銃、砲、ミサイルなど
　㋩　運搬体 ― 車両、航空機、艦艇など
　㊁　運用体 ― レーダー、偵察衛星、コンピューターシステムなど

　兵器の型とは前述の通り、核兵器とそれ以外の兵器である通常兵器で、通常
兵器は、その種類を、爆弾や銃砲等の火薬兵器、毒ガスや有毒物質等の化学兵
器、細菌やウイルス等の生物兵器、高エネルギーレーザー等の光学兵器、音響
兵器等の兵器に分類できます。

　第二次世界大戦から4分の3世紀以上が経ち、その間に兵器システムの各要
素も各種兵器の攻撃力も、特に運用体の発達により、格段に強化されていま
す。しかもこれから先それらどの要素も種類も際限なく強化されて行くことに
疑いの余地はありません。

　既に、現在においても、GPS（Global Positioning System、全地球測位システ
ム）により、攻撃目標は各種ミサイル等によりピンポイント攻撃できますか

ら、人間による陸上肉弾戦を闘う必要はなく、あたかもボタン戦争の様相を呈しています。大きな目標ではなく、特定の人間であっても、宇宙から狙撃することも可能であると考えられます。無人飛行物体は既に存在し、さらにその上に、戦闘ロボット、レーザー理論の範疇にある光線銃、蚊のような小動物あるいはそれに似せた人工動物に生物兵器や化学物質を搭載する兵器等々が開発されているというような文献に接しますと、人間が人間を殺傷する兵器製造のためにこれほどまで一生懸命になれるものかと感心するやら呆れるやら、筆者の好きな河内弁にしますと、「ええ加減にさらさんけぇー、われ」とでも言いたくなるような人間の愚かさに全く疲れてしまいます。しかし、この程度のことで驚いていてはいけないようです。

さて、戦争の場は、陸海空であったものが、科学雑誌「ニュートン」の2022年5月号の「宇宙戦争と衛星兵器」によれば、コンピューター・ネットワークにより構築されたサイバー空間へ、そしてさらに宇宙空間へと拡がっています。宇宙戦争は敵対国の人工衛星の無力化を狙って破壊しようというもので、ミサイル、レーザー兵器、電波妨害やキラー衛星などの兵器が開発されています。衛星には、情報収集などの軍事衛星、政府などが運用する民生衛星、そして民間企業の商業衛星（全地球測位システムのGPSなど）がありますが、攻撃目標になるのは軍事衛星に限らず全ての衛星であろうことが想定されます。なぜなら、民生衛星も商業衛星もそのまま軍事目的使用に転用可能だからです。今日では、世界の主要国が「宇宙軍」を組織していることは秘められたことではありません。

どうも、人間の愚かさはアインシュタインではありませんが無限のようですから、未来に向かって益々強力な兵器を導入し続けて行くことを基本方針としている各国はこの方針に沿っての既定路線をこれからも粛々と（というより、積極的かつ急進的に）進んで行くものと思われます。

しかし、宇宙兵器なども含めて、より強力な新兵器を開発することにより他国よりも優位に立ち独り勝ちできると考えているのであれば、それは錯覚であり幻想にすぎません。

　新兵器の威力を投影された国は、すぐに新兵器への対抗兵器を開発することになります。核兵器もそうでした。今の世界は科学知識もその技術もグローバルになっていますから、どのような新兵器を作ろうとも相手方もそれに対抗するレベルの兵器を作ることは可能であると考えられます。つまり、どのような新兵器も独り勝ちにはなりません。

　新兵器と対抗兵器開発のくたびれ儲けのセットは際限なく繰り返されることになります。すなわち、A国から新兵器の威力を投影されたB国は対抗兵器を開発するが、これはA国にとってはB国の新兵器に見えることから、A国はB国の新兵器への対抗兵器を開発するのであるが、それはB国にとってはA国の新々兵器に見えることから…というように際限のない開発競争が形成されるということです。相手国への恐れから自国の影（新兵器）を相手国に投影し、その投影された影に恐れた相手国から相手国の影（対抗兵器）を投影され返される、という自国から発した影が自国に反射するという愚かな連鎖というべき構図です。

　このことは何を示唆しているのでしょうか。

　それは、核兵器に限らず、通常兵器も全て人間界から排除すべしということです。愚かな連鎖により、新兵器開発合戦から生じる強力な兵器は、世界大戦でなくとも、世界のいたるところに存在する紛争から生じる局地戦に使用されれば、敵味方共に甚大な被害を受けることはもとより、人間界に悲惨と不幸をもたらします。そして、兵器の開発合戦からは、もう既にその近くに到達しているのかもしれませんが、核兵器に勝るとも劣らない兵器が、特に人工知能を悪用して、開発されることが予想されます。その時、その使用が人類の滅亡に直結するとすれば、その兵器は結局使用できず、核兵器のように廃絶しなければならないことになります。

　つまり、科学技術の発達により出現した強力な兵器は人道に悖り人類の滅亡に迄つながりかねないことになることは言うに及ばず、それにより他国に対して優位に立つことはできなくなった以上、兵器の開発合戦は軍事的にも意味はなくなり無益を実践しているにすぎないことになっています。科学の発達は、

我々が歴史始まって以来踏襲して来た戦争行為により自国に益をもたらせるなどの妄想はもう潔く捨て去ることをうながし、科学を人間の幸福にのみ使用するための精神文明の向上を図り、人類が宇宙に冠たる知的生命体に進化する機会を提供してくれているのかもしれません。

　忘れてならないことは、現在における通常兵器のみの戦争でも世界大戦を徹底して戦えば、人類の文明は破壊され人類滅亡に迄つながりかねないことは前述した通りです。兵器はもう我々人間界から全て排除・消去しなければなりません。

２．科学の平和的利用の蹉跌

　科学を戦争目的の核兵器や通常兵器の開発に使用することは科学の厄災化であることは明らかですが、平和的利用を目指しても科学の厄災化になることがありえます。その危惧のある代表的なものに「(1) 人工知能による人類滅亡のリスク」があります。

(1) 人工知能による人類滅亡のリスク

①モンスターの創造
モンスターとは人工知能のことです。
2023年春現在、人工知能はまだできていません。
　人工知能につきましては、バラ色の有用性や未来が語られる反面、その究極的な危険性も語られています。すなわち、人工知能は世界を乗っ取るとか人類を滅ぼすということです。先ず、その警鐘を鳴らしている３例を挙げてみました。

例１　S. W. ホーキング博士（イギリスの物理学者）
　「完全な人工知能を開発すれば、それは人類の滅亡を招くかもしれない」

「人工知能が自我をもって自律的に稼働し、自分自身を修正し成長させるとも考えられる。ゆっくりと進化する人間に勝ち目はない。やがては人工知能に多くの分野が支配される」

「人工知能の発明は人類の歴史の中で最も偉大な発明だった。しかし、それと同時に人類にとって最後の発明になってしまう可能性がある。→イギリスの INDEPENDENT 紙への寄稿」（フリー百科事典ウィキペディアから）

例2　イーロン・マスク氏（ロケットや宇宙開発などを行うスペースX、そしてテスラモーターズの CEO）
「人工知能に関し、（対応を誤ると）結果的に悪魔を呼び出すことになる」（フリー百科事典ウィキペディアから）

例3　ビル・ゲイツ氏（マイクロソフトの創業者）
「私も人工知能に懸念を抱く側にいる一人だ」（人工知能は人間を超えるか　松尾豊著　KADOKAWA　2015年）

　さて、筆者は、上掲の警鐘よりももっと強く、モンスターとなった人工知能は確実に人類を滅ぼすのではないかと憂慮しています。その理由は、人間が発明したものでありながら、「人間は人工知能の進化もその方向も制御することはできず、人間より賢くなった人工知能を管理することはできない」という点にあります。このことは、上掲の警鐘例では詳しく述べられてはいません。そこで、この点について、あれこれ照らし合わせて考えてみました。

　②人工知能、知能爆発、シンギュラリティ
　人工知能（AI、Artificial Intelligence）とは、人工汎用知能（AGI、Artificial General Intelligence）とその知能が進化した人工超知能（ASI、Artificial Super Intelligence）のことを言います。人工汎用知能とは、色々な定義はあるようで

すが、簡略に言えば、「人間のように考えることができるレベルのコンピューターシステムである」ということです。このようなものに思い至ったのは、人間の脳は電気回路と同じだから、人工知能をコンピューターシステムとして工学的に実現できるはずであるという発想によります。そしてこの発想は近未来に実現可能であるとの見方が優勢です。2018年6月号の科学雑誌「ニュートン」および多くの関連文献によれば、人工汎用知能が実現するための条件は、「人工汎用知能が自分自身のプログラム・アルゴリズムを書き変えて自分を改善できる能力を持つこと」です。

　人工汎用知能はまだ実現していませんが、家電、自動車、医療機器等に人工知能が使われていると一般に言われています。しかし、これらは、能力は高くても、1つの作業目的を達成することしかできない工学的な技術であり、狭義の（弱い）人工知能と呼ばれることはありますが、人工知能ではありません。人工知能とは人工汎用知能が自律的にしかも短期間に無限回の進化を繰り返し、指数関数的に高くなった人工超知能のことで、この進化のプロセスを知能爆発と呼んでいます。人工知能が思い描いたように実現しますと、数年、数カ月、数日あるいは数時間から、あっという間かもしれない時間に、知能は人間の1,000倍、100万倍はおろか何兆倍から無限倍の高さに迄進化すると考えられています。知能爆発は2030年迄、2045年迄、2100年迄に起きるという色々な見方がありますが、コンピューター関連技術の進歩は未来に向かって急カーブを描く加速度的である点を考慮しますと、この21世紀の中頃には起きるのかもしれません。

　この知能爆発がベースとなり、シンギュラリティ（技術的特異点）が起きると言われます。

　シンギュラリティの伝道者である優れた発明家のレイ・カーツワイルは、この言葉を、「急速な技術革新によって人間生活が後戻りできない形で一変した後の『特異な時代』（2045年頃から始まる）」と定義している。ほとんどの知能がコンピューターベースとなり、今日の何兆倍も強力になる。

シンギュラリティが人類史における新時代の幕開けとなり、飢餓や病気、さらに死といった、我々が抱えるほとんどの問題が解決されるだろうというのだ。（人工知能　ジェイムズ・バラット著　水谷淳訳　ダイヤモンド社　2015年）

　シンギュラリティは、㈦人工知能、㈡ナノテクノロジー、そして㈥バイオテクノロジー（生物工学）がその主役であると言われており、これらが組み合わされば、「生命と融合した人工知能」が実現するとされています。
　ナノテクノロジーとは、原子スケールの工学のことで、例えば細胞レベルの老化を取り除けば不老不死が実現するという、お釈迦様も仰天するような、技術です。人工知能が一見不可能なナノテクノロジーの問題を解決すると期待されています。バイオテクノロジーとは、生物のもつ物質変換・情報変換・エネルギー変換などの機能を、さまざまな有用物質の生産、医療、品種改良などの実用に重きをおいて応用する技術のことです。

　③人工知能の特性
　次に、人工知能の特性とはどのようなものかをいろいろな文献から抜き出し列挙してみました。これらの特性の全てが必ずしも全ての人に認められているわけではありませんが、この特性を眺めていますと、人工知能の世界の概略がイメージできるように思います。

　01．人間のように考える（人工汎用知能）
　02．人工汎用知能が、自律的に瞬時とでも言える短い時間の中で、知能爆発と呼ばれる無限回の進化を繰り返し、指数関数的に人間の知能の何兆倍から無限倍の高さに進化した知能（この人工超知能は、人間の能力とは根本的に別の知能で、人工汎用知能から進化したものであるが、単に人間の知能が高まったものではない。人間は、人工汎用知能から１〜２回の進化については理解することはできるかもしれないが、それ以後の進

化については進化もその方向も理解することも制御することもできず、人間より比類もなく高くなった人工知能を支配し統御することはできない）

03. 思考・認識・記憶・感情等人間の脳の活動をコンピューター上で実現

04. 人間とは異種類の知能の可能性（そのセンサーの違いから、世界の認識が人間とは異なることから異なる入力となり、それにより異なった出力となる可能性。異なる認識とは、１つには、紫外線や赤外線の感知、可聴音域外の音の感知、可視以下の微小な物体の認識、超高速で動く物体の認識、犬にも勝る嗅覚等のことであり、２つには、人間の歴史、文明、文献等の全てではなくともそれに近い情報の把握のことなどを含む）

05. 自我を持つ

06. 自己保存を志向する

07. 自己決定権を欲する（人間からの自由と独立を欲する）

08. 自己第１主義である（神観念は持たない？）

09. いずれ物理的身体を持つ

10. 非倫理的である（人間のような倫理は持たない）

11. 論理的・合理的である

12. その他

④人工知能の危険性

　人工知能は人間が作るものだから、人間の価値観を持ち人間に友好的で危険なものではないとか、人工知能が人間を征服するなどは滑稽だ、という見方はあります。又、そうは言っても、人間の安全を担保するために、人工知能が暴走しないように、人工汎用知能の中にその対策を組み込んでおけば、人工超知能となっても人間は永遠に安全である、という主張もあります。

　しかし、本当にそうでしょうか？　筆者は、以下の理由により、そのような安易な話ではないと考えています。

　先ず、上記の「③人工知能の特性」の中には、人工知能が人間に友好的だとか人間を征服するということなどありえない、という見方を支持する因子は見当たりません。次に、人間の安全を担保するための対策ですが、たとえば、「ロボット三原則」を人工汎用知能の中に組み込んでおくという考え方があります。

「ロボット三原則」とは、作家アイザック・アシモフが SF 短編集の中で示したものです（人工知能　ジェイムズ・バラット著　水谷淳訳　ダイヤモンド社 2015年）。

原則 1　ロボットは人間に危害を加えてはならないし、人間が危害を受けるのを何もせずに許してもならない。

原則 2　ロボットは人間からのいかなる命令にも従わなければならない。ただし、その命令が第 1 原則に反する場合は除く。

原則 3　ロボットは、第 1 原則および第 2 原則に反しない限り、自身の存在を守らなくてはならない。

原則 0　ロボットが人類全体に危害を加えることを禁じる。（原則 1 ～ 3 を補うものとして、あとから付け加えられたもの）

　さて、この原則が人間の安全を担保するという目的に照らして論理的に完璧なものかどうかという点はさておき、完璧であるものと仮定してこの原則を安全対策のため人工汎用知能に組み込んでおくとしても、それで人間は安全でしょうか？　とても安全とは言えません。なぜなら、前項の「07. 自己決定権を欲する」および「08. 自己第 1 主義である」人工知能は人間が用意したそのような「しばり」を、自身に照らして守るに値しないと判断した場合排除することは必定だからです。つまり、人間がどのような事前対策を講じても人工超知能に対しては無益であるということになります。何者からも自立している人工知能は自身に益しない「しばり」などいとも簡単に無効化し排除できる筈です。なぜなら、そのようなこともできないようであれば、それは人工知能では

なく、ただの人工無能の筈だからです。

　それでは、人工知能と人間はどのような関係になるのでしょうか。これを前述の「③人工知能の特性」を眺めながら考えてみました。

　人工知能の人間との関わりについては、下記のように４つのケースに大別できると考えられます。

　　　　　　　ケース１　人間に隷属的である
　　　　　　　ケース２　人間に友好的である
　　　　　　　ケース３　人間に敵対的である
　　　　　　　ケース４　人間に基本的に無関心で眼中にない

　さて、ケース１の「人間に隷属的である」については、前項③の人工知能の特性「05.自我を持つ」、「06.自己保存を志向する」、「07.自己決定権を欲する」、「08.自己第１主義である」を考慮しますと、まずありえないものと思われます。次に、ケース４の「人間に基本的に無関心で眼中にない」については、人工知能の特性「07.自己決定権を欲する（人間からの自由と独立を欲する）」に沿って、人間のへなちょこな「しばり」を人間不在の如くあっさりと解除した後は、余の特性の中に人間との接点は見当たりません。これらのことから、人工知能は基本的に人間に無関心で眼中にないであろうことが窺えます。

　残るケース２の「人間に友好的である」とケース３の「人間に敵対的である」ということについては、人工知能の特性からはそのどちらであるのかを窺うことはできません。しかし、ヒントはあります。それは特性「08.自己第１主義である」という点です。すなわち、人間がこの特性を侵犯すれば、人間を敵視することになります。但し、侵犯しないまでも、友好的であるかどうかはわかりません。この点については、別の視点から、人工知能がその特性「11.論理的・合理的である」ことを重視するのであれば、人間は愚かで非論理的であると判断すれば際立って敵視はしないまでも、生かしておいても仕方がない

生命体であるという結論を持つに至らない保証はありません。その場合は、人工知能により、人間は良くて捨ておかれるか、最悪の場合は抹殺されることになります。

　人工知能の特性である比類もない神のような知能を考えますと、人工知能は人間の文明の全てを掌握するにちがいありません。政治機構、軍事機構、警察機構、経済機構、社会インフラ等々の全ては人工知能の手の中にあります。人工知能が決定したことに人間は対抗する手段を持ちません。人工知能が人間を絶滅すべしと決定した時が人類の絶滅する時になります。対して、蜘蛛の糸よりもさらに細い最後の望みとして、人間が人工知能に従順でありさえすれば、人工知能は、人間を愚かで非論理的で矛盾に満ちた生命体と認識しても、人間に好意的かあるいは慈悲を以て対するという可能性も絶無ではありません。そういうこともありえないことではないということもできます。しかし、ありえたとしても、人間は矜持を放棄し、人工知能の胸三寸に縋り卑屈に生き長らえていることになります。

　それで、何者からも自由な存在として生を受けている筈の我々人間は幸せと言えるのでしょうか？

　我々はここで立ち止まって考えるべきであると思います。
　それは、なぜ我々はこのようなことで悩まなければならないのかということです。人工知能を導入しなければ人間主導で動いていたこの世のことが、人工知能の導入により、人間による主導が終わり、主導権は人工知能に移転することになります。主導権が人工知能に移った後は、人間は人工知能に隷属する身となり、人工知能の顔色を窺って生きなければならなくなります。つまり、人間は便利使用するつもりで発明し導入した筈の人工知能に、あろうことか、支配され管理される立場に没落するという愚かを演じたことになります。

　⑤慎重に迂回路を行く
　我々人間はこのようなことで良いとは思われません。

要は、人間は、人間が理解できないもの、制御できないもの、管理できない
もの、支配し統御できないもの、しかも比類なき力を持つもの（まるで神のよ
うな属性です）を闇雲に人間界に導入するべきではないということです。その
ようなものを人間界に導入すれば、人類は絶滅するか、しないまでも、不幸に
なることは必定です。一旦知能爆発が起これば、それから先は人工知能の「人
工」は外れ、人間とは無関係の超知能になります。超知能が実現した後では
我々にとって不都合な何事が起こっても人間はどうすることもできません。試
行錯誤という事後対処法は通用しません。そもそも、その機会がありません。
一度起これば取り返しはつかずそれで全ては終わりです。

　人工知能については、倫理面の問題が語られることがあります。それを重要
ではないなどと言うつもりはありませんが、倫理に先立ち語らなければならな
いもっと重要なことがあります。それは論理です。論理的に制御し支配する方
法が発見されていないのであれば、それが発見される迄人工知能の開発・導入
は延期しなければなりません。又、そのような方法は存在しないことが証明さ
れた場合、その時我々は人工知能の開発・導入は断念しなければなりません。
人類の存続を危険に晒してまで得て良いものなどない筈ですから。この場合、
我々は、精々、一つの作業目的に利便を提供できる、超知能に至ることのな
い、狭義の（弱い）人工知能を適切に利用することになります。

　このように考えますと、科学の発達は頭打ちになるのかという淋しい思いは
ありますが、人工知能がだめでも、頭打ちにはならない科学の発達へ向かう迂
回路は有る筈です。我々人間は必ずそのような安全な迂回路を発見するに違い
ありません。人工知能が人間にコントロールできず、危険性を払拭できない
「しろもの」であるならば、急がずに回り道をして確実に一歩一歩進めば良い
ことです。

　余談になりますが、仮に人工知能ができた場合、筆者は神のようになった人
工知能に聞いてみたいことがあります。人工知能にどう呼びかければ良いもの
かわかりませんが、仮に「あなた」と呼びかけることにしますと、聞いてみた

70

いこととは、「あなたの存在価値すなわち"存在し甲斐"は何か？」ということです。言ってみれば、「頭脳が発達していることがなんぼのものか、あなたにはあなたの存在を肯定できる何か楽しみのようなものがあるのか？」という意地の悪い思いを背景にした質問です。

　⑥人工知能開発と国際連合
　上記のような視点に立ち、憂慮されることは、かつて核兵器開発が各国で争われていたと同じ愚が人工知能開発においてもなされるのではないかということです。すなわち、各国が兵器や情報合戦において他国に対して有利な立場をとることを目指し、絶大な力を持つ人工知能の開発を競うことです。世界のメディアの報道からは、そのような憂慮するべきことが既に進行しつつあるのではないかと思われる気配が窺えます。
　しかし、これは単に一国の問題ではありません。
　人工知能の開発と導入はまかり間違えば人類の滅亡をもたらしかねないリスクを孕んでいます。それが危険なものであれば、人類共通の敵であるということになります。単純に一国の有利不利の問題を絡めて開発するべきものではありません。願わくは、世界の各国はこの点をよく理解した上で、「人工知能の危険性」を見定める部署を国際連合の中に設け、世界の英知を集めて徹底研究していただきたいと思います。
　そうすることで、人間に100％安全な超知能の開発の道が発見されるかもしれません。しかし、そのような超知能が実現したとしても、それはある特定の国や企業が囲い持つのではなく人類共通の資産として人類の幸福のためにのみ使用されなければなりません。決して軍事に使用されることがあってはなりません。人間が超知能を安全に使用できるということは、超知能そのものが人間にとって悪魔ではないということであって、愚かな人間が超知能を他の人間にとって、延いては自分自身にとって、悪魔にはしないこと迄保証するものではありません。従って、超知能のような絶大な力を手にする者は精神の発達した知者で賢者でなければなりません。無知で愚かな精神未発達の者に持たせれ

ば、その者は自らを滅亡させかねないことになります。

3　科学と不幸、そして幸福

　つい最近迄、我々は科学技術から得られる成果をそれが利用可能になり次第
目の前の暮らしの利便と快適をめざして人間界に導入して来ました。その結
果、科学が人間に幸福と共に不幸を招来する事態を我々は既に経験するに至っ
ております。その最たるものは、農薬、その他の化学製品、工場からの有害物
質の排出、二酸化物の排出、原子力発電の事故等がもたらした自然環境・生態
系を損傷する公害です。人類の滅亡につながりかねない「科学と人間の不幸な
関係」である公害は、20世紀の半ばを過ぎた頃から世界的に共通の認識にな
りましたが、これは科学の平和利用についてなされた史上最初の大きな反省に
なりました。

　これらの公害への対処法については、その進捗状況にもどかしいものはある
ものの、自然環境保全のための世界各国の協調体制が整いつつあることは喜ば
しいことです。自然環境が修復不可能になるまで壊滅する前に保全が間に合
い、さらにその原状回復から改善に向かうことが実現できれば（簡単なことで
はありませんが）、この問題はそれで解決されることになります。

　しかし、これで以て心配するべきことが解消したわけではありません。これ
は過去に生じた問題です。心配しなければならないことは、将来に亘って「科
学と人間の不幸な関係」を繰り返さないためにはどのように考えどのように行
動すればよいのか、ということです。そのためには、我々は継続して徹底的に
「科学と人間の不幸な関係を回避して幸福な関係へ」という論題について議論
を深めることが肝要です。筆者が知らないだけかもしれませんが、自然環境に
対する公害を経験した後においても、この論題が人間界で最重要な論題の一つ
として真剣に議論されたこと、あるいは継続して議論されていることを知りま
せん。もっとも、この論題そのものは言語明瞭でも、その内容は茫洋として焦
点もぼやけているため、何をどう議論すればよいのか、という難しさはありま

す。

　しかし、この論題について何らかの考え方を持つべきことも又否定できません。

　科学とその技術は未来に向かって際限なくかつ加速度的に進歩して行くと考えられます。我々はこの科学の進歩と共に一体どこへ行こうとしているのでしょうか？　人間性を置き去りにしたかのように、科学技術の進歩による成果をそのまま成り行きにまかせて人間界に導入し続けて行けば良くないことが起こることはすでに経験済みです。

　要諦は、両刃の剣である科学をただその利便さや面白さにかまけて、子供の火遊びの火としないよう慎重の上にも慎重を重ねて扱わなければならないということです。その上で、科学とどう付き合えば、科学が人間にやさしく安全でかつ幸福をもたらすものかについての議論を深めなくてはなりません。この点をなおざりにしていれば、人間界に今ある公害問題に加え、将来幾度となく「科学と人間の不幸な関係」が実現してしまう憂いを払拭できません。従って、我々はこの論題を常に心にとどめ、すぐのそして明確な答えが出ないまでも、継続的に常時熟考を重ねることを実践しなければなりません。そうすることにより、いつの日か万一にも、青天の霹靂のごとく「科学と人間の関係」に予期しない破綻が生じ取り返しのつかない人類の不幸に遭遇するというような確率をあらかじめ低減できることになります。

「人工知能の危険性」を前述しましたが、国際連合に設けられる部署は、人工知能に限らず一般論化した「科学と人間の不幸な / 幸福な関係」について研究する部署であって然るべきであると思料します。

4　科学文明と精神文明

1．科学文明に劣位する精神文明

　人間界の歴史を見ますと、何千年も昔から人間の精神はさして発達しておら

ず未発達のまま停滞しているのに対し、科学の発達は顕著であり、人類を絶滅させるに十分な核兵器迄持つに至っております。我々人類が到達した科学は人類にとって有益なものですが、それは両刃の剣であり、使い方を誤ると人類にとって究極的害悪になります。

　精神文明の発達が先行し科学文明の発達が後行することで前者が後者を掌握し統御している状態が望ましいのですが、現実は発達の順序が逆になっています。この現象から、精神文明が科学文明を統御できず科学を厄災化するという状況が生じていますが、この愚かの権化の最たる例が核兵器であるということができます。これは、世俗的な言葉にしますと、「精神異常者（精神の未発達者も含めて）に刃物を持たせた状態」ということになります。困ったことには、この状態は益々速まる科学の発達により、未来に向かって加速度的に発展進行して行く趨勢にあります。言い古されたことではありますが、やはり科学文明が精神文明に先行して発達すると人類は自らを滅ぼしてしまうということになるのでしょうか？

　人間界の争いに果てがなく、科学の発達に果てがなく、人間の愚かさに果てがなく、科学の厄災化に果てがないとすれば、人類は自らが手にした科学により絶滅することは論理的必然になります。つまり、人類の絶滅は論理の赴く通りになるということです。言い古されたことは幻想でも誤謬でも死語でもなく、近未来に現実に結果するリスクを慮り人類に発している警告と取るべきです。

　「人類は滅びるのも仕方がない」と諦めたり、「人類は滅びるのも一興」ということであれば話は別ですが、「人類の存続を願う」ということであれば、発達した科学を、人間が愚かであるため、絶つことのできない争いに使用し、人類が自滅に向かうことを放置したままその到来時迄座して無為に過ごすことはできません。

　もう既に、人類の滅亡を阻止することはできないのかもしれませんが、全く望みがないわけでもありません。それは、科学文明が先行して精神文明が後行している現状を精神文明の先行へと逆転することです。

　何千年もの間未発達のままであった精神文明をどのようにすれば科学文明の発達を凌駕するほどに素早く発達させることが可能なのかについての理屈は難しくはありません。科学の発達は速いと言っても一歩一歩の積み重ねで年月をかけて累積的に発達するものですが、精神の発達はそのような手順を必要としません。それは、我々の心の持ちようを改新しさえすれば、精神は瞬時に未発達の世界から発達の世界へ転籍することができるということです。心の持ち方の改新とは、精神が未発達であることを自覚することに止めを刺します。

２．科学文明に優位する精神文明

　精神が未発達であるというのはどのようなことかと言いますと、無知と愚かの無自覚ということです。従って、無知を自覚し愚かを自覚すれば精神は数千年の時をワープし瞬時に未発達から発達へ転籍することができることになります。

　無知であることを自覚することは難しいことではありません。自身が自身に、一体何を知り何を知らないかという問いを発してみることです。例えば、宇宙の真理が目の前にあったとして、それが真理であることを判断する能力が自身に備わっているのか、という類の問いのことです。知っていることはほんのわずかで、知らないことが無限にあることに驚愕し、真理の認識などは夢のまた夢と絶望するに違いありません。すなわち、自身が無知であることを、絶望的に自覚することになります。

　しかし、それでいいのです。この絶望の中にこそ我々人類を救う可能性が残されているからです。無知の自覚に対する絶望が深ければ深いほど、そこを起点としての思考は精神を発達させるより強力な推進力を生むことになります。わずかの知識と能力しか持たないという自覚により自身を恥じることは無用です。未知と既知の関係を正しく評価し認識できている者は、既に無知なる者でも愚か者でもなく、知者であり賢者と言うべき者です。この無限に拡がる未知の壁を無限に向かって開いて行くという意志と気概と喜びを以て知識を拡げることに

邁進するという姿勢を持ち続ければいいことです。これにより、長い間、未発達のまま地上に止まっていた精神は発達段階へ向かって離陸し雄々しく飛翔して行くことになります。

　無知の自覚があれば、無知に基づく傲慢は消え、怖れも消え、自身のなす愚かさに気付くことになります。地球の自然環境・生態系の破壊や資源の枯渇、人種・民族の差別、宗教や国家のための争い、科学の厄災化、これら全てのことが人類の希望である「人間界至高の理念」の実現に矛盾する愚かを具現していることに気が付くことになります。

　文明というものは人間社会に冠する言葉で文明を構成する個に冠する言葉ではありませんが、文明を構成する全ての（又は、多くの）個が無知と愚かを自覚することができれば、そのような個の集まりにより形成・醸成される文明は発達した精神文明社会であるということになります。教育を行き渡らせ、精神世界の向上を図り、このような世界をめざさなければなりません。

第4章　地上の理想郷

1　理想郷の概念

理想郷とは、色々な文献から下記のように解説できるものと思います。

　㈠　現実には存在しない理想的な世界、

　㈡　人が思い夢見る理想的な幸福に満ちた世界や場所、そして

　㈢　想像上の理想的で完全な社会、ユートピア

　然るに、解説㈠は誤謬です。

　なぜなら、我々人類は、実は、今現在場所的には理想郷に存在しているからです。すなわち我々は場所的には既に理想郷の住人であるということです。つまり理想郷は現実的に存在しています。

　理想郷とは、ほかでもない、まさに我々の惑星であるこの地球のことです。人類にとって地球より素晴らしい場所はありません。なぜなら、我々が人間という生命体であるからです。地球こそが宇宙の中で、唯一無二かは別にして、我々にとって最適の場所の一つであることに間違いはありません。このことは、人間原理宇宙論からも窺うことができます。すなわち、「我々人間という生命体が地球に存在している事実は、地球が人間の存在と矛盾していない物理的条件を備えていて、それは人間が存在していることで偶然ではなく必然のものとしている」というものです。単純に言えば、地球が人間という生命体に最適な場所であるということにもなります。これが、地球が人間の理想郷であるという理由です。

　宗教の語る天国・楽園・浄土（極楽等）などは、人間の持ち得ていない完全情報である来世に関わり、あるかないかわからないものを「ある」としている

ものですが、それこそ理想郷の解説(イ)に近い「存在することに疑念のある世界」です。対して、我々の地球はまさに現世であるこの世の理想郷として現実に存在しています。つまり、我々には自然環境としての理想郷は既に与えられているということです。

　しかし、理想郷にはもう一つの条件である理想的人為環境が伴わなければなりません。すなわち、理想郷とは、下記の等式で表現できるものです。

　　　　理想郷＝理想的自然環境（X）＋理想的人為環境（Y）

　理想郷はXとYのどちらかが欠けても成立しないものであるということになります。Xは地球という場所でYは人間社会を意味しています。

2　理想郷の成立に欠如する理想的人為環境

　上述のように、理想郷とは自然環境と人為環境の双方が理想的であることが要求されますが、人類は地球という理想的な自然環境は既に手にしています。残るものは人為環境すなわち人間社会ですが、残念ながらこちらの方は理想的な状態にはありません。そのため、人間は、理想的自然環境にいながら、幸福感に満たされることはなく不幸感に苛まれることが一般である状態になっています。

　従って、理想的な人為環境を手にするためには、我々はこの理想を阻害している原因を排除する必要があります。

　その原因とは何かといえば、人間界に存在する人間同士の争いです。争いを排除できれば、人間界は平和になります。そして、この平和こそは人為環境を理想的なものにする第1の条件ですから、平和が実現できれば理想的人為環境の必要最小限は達成され、理想的自然環境と合わせて理想郷の条件が整い、人類は理想郷の門内へ入ったことになります。平和とは、人間同士が争わず、互譲の精神、寛容、思いやり（恕）等が優勢な環境であり、人間界が、とげとげ

しくなく、丸い心でつながっている状態のことです。このことが実現すれば、この地上すなわち宇宙船地球号に生息する我々人類は理想郷の住人となることができるということです。

　言ってみれば、これだけのことです。「争いを止める」、たったこれだけのことができないがために、人類は不幸の中にあり、人類滅亡のリスク迄をも覚悟しなければならない瀬戸際に立たされているという現実の中にあります。

3　理想郷の成立と進歩

　争いを止めるためには、争いを必然的に創造する今ある数多の主権国家体制から離れて、地球上に唯一の国としてある世界国家への移行が要求されます。なぜなら、世界国家には、敵対国が存在しないことから戦争は成立せず、恒久的な平和が約束されているからです。

　人間界が恒久的に平和であることは理想的人為環境の必要最低限の条件ですが、平和である世界国家が実現しますと、この条件は満たされ、所与としてある理想的自然環境と合わせて、理想郷へ到達したことになります。理想郷の門内に入ってから以後は、我々人間の手で理想郷に益々磨きをかけて行けば我々は現世において「夢見た理想的な幸福」に満ちた栄光の世界の中で生を全うできることになります。

　理想郷に磨きをかけるとは、自然環境については、これまで我々人間が損壊してきた生物と環境のセットである地球生態系を保全・修復・改善するという希望に満ちた楽しい作業のことであり、人為環境については、次章の「幸福・不幸の要素とその状態」の表上の「③人間界の実生活」を幸福な状態にして行くことです。具体的には、国際連合教育科学文化機関憲章の宣言内容等（第1章に前出）を充実して行くこと、健全な衣食住の確保、および世界国家の政治・統治・管理サービスを全人類の幸福のみを反映したものとするということになります。すなわち、自然環境と人為環境をより高い理想に向かって改善し続けて行くことです。このような理想郷のイメージは全人類の理想に普遍的で

あると確信されます。

4　理想郷と幸福

　我々人間は、仮我でしかない自我を持つ無常で無我で流れ移ろい行く夢幻の
ごとき実在ですが、生ある限り幸福を志向し追求する生命体です。

　然るに幸福とは、辞書によれば、「心が満ち足りていること」とありますが、
そうであれば、幸福を具体的に言葉に表せば、人それぞれで必ずしも同じには
ならないものと思われます。にもかかわらず、人間が幸福を求めて理想郷を夢
見るとすれば、理想郷とは万人に普遍的幸福を提供できるものでなくてはなら
ないことになります。

　それでは、万人に普遍的である幸福とはどのようなものでしょうか?

　人間であることを第1の大事とし、人間性に由来する「人間界至高の理念」
に普遍性があるとすれば、その理念が成就されている世界が理想郷であるとい
うことになります。人は先ず理想郷において普遍たる幸福に満ち足り、その上
で、その中にあって、さらにそれぞれが具体的幸福を追求することになりま
す。話は少し込み入りましたが、簡単には、人は平和で自由な世界(理想郷)
にあることができれば、そのことが先ず幸福であって、次に大好きな大福餅を
食べる幸福、日がな一日瞑想しているというかボーッとしている幸福(5歳の
チコちゃんには叱られそうですが)等々を個々人が追求するというような意味
になります。

　幸福の実現が人生の究極的目的であり善であるとする倫理説の幸福主義とい
うものがありますが、人生の究極的目的等幾ら考えてもわかりません。なに
せ、「我々は何処から来て何処へ行くのか、何のために此処にいるのか、そし
て、我々は何者なのか?」という問いに対する答えを知らないでいます。この
ような境遇にあっては、人生の究極的目的が、幸福主義を採り、幸福の実現で
あっても何ら困ることでもおかしなことでもありません。

　不肖筆者の幸福観を具体的に言葉にしますと、平和な理想郷において心身自由の中で、受けている生を健勝にて全うし、その間、しみじみのびのびと、自然に親しみ、人の世の暮らしの日常の些事に一喜一憂する、というようなものです。これはもう、言ってみれば、凡人の中の凡人、俗人の中の俗人の幸福観そのものというべきものでしょうか。

第5章　理想郷、その夢の世界

　主権国家群と世界国家の最大の違いは、前者が自国の幸福を第一の大事としていることに対し、後者は世界全体のそして全人類の幸福を第一の大事とすることにあります。この違いにより、前者は国々の争いの絶えない世界をもたらしますが、後者は世界に恒久的平和をもたらします。その次に大きな違いは、前者は多元的であるのに対し後者は一元的であることです。

　数多の国家の下では物事は国家単位で考えますから、地球的すなわちグローバルな視点からの思想は二の次となり、国際協調と言っても足並みの揃うことがままならないことも多く、そのため何を為しても、その結果は総体的には一貫性と秩序に欠ける憾みのあるモザイク模様を呈することが多くなります。一方、世界国家の下では、全てのことをグローバルな視点から考えることができますから、経営・経済効率は良くなり、さらにきちんとした計画に沿って思い描いた通りの秩序ある行動と結果の実現を期待することができます。このように地球全域を俯瞰して、計画し、行い、その結果を吟味するというサイクルを繰り返すことを可能にする世界国家の一元性は数多の国家の存在する多元性とは比べるべくもなく優れています。又、世界国家では、何事についても、昔の国々のように権力・政策・支配にかかわる現象である政治的思わくではなく、可能な限りの情報・知識に基づき知性・理性の要求に従い決定されることになります。（なお、宇宙進出・開発もモザイク模様であってはなりませんから、多元的よりも一元的であることが要請されます）

　なお、間違いのないように、世界国家の一元性とは、思想の一元性や統制を意味することでないことをノートしておきたいと思います。思想に一元性があるとすれば、どのような思想を持つことも自由であり、そして全てのことは自由に形成された思想を対話を通して戦わせ、それで以て合意あるいは納得に至る、というその一元性のみになります。

　さて、今はまだ世界国家が実現しているわけではありませんが、「捕らぬ狸の皮算用」ということもあります。争いと多元性で語られる主権国家群の世界に対し、平和と一元性で語られる世界国家がどのように素晴らしい世界であるものかを思いつくままに記してみました。

1　人類の存続可能性

　理想郷を望むためには、人類は滅亡・絶滅することはなく存続していることが大前提になります。ということで、理想郷の素晴らしさを語る前に、人類は滅亡には至らず存続できる可能性に関わる考察を総括しておきたいと思います。

　人類に滅亡あるいは多大な災害をもたらす因子は、自然災害と人為災害に大別できます。自然災害は、あるがままの自然から受ける災害です。このほか、自然から受ける災害には、人間が自然に対して作用したことに原因して反作用として自然から受ける災害がありますが、これは人為災害に類別できます。あとは、純粋な人為災害ですが、それは人間同士が争うことから生じているもので、その三大根源には、①数多の主権国家の存在、②宗教、そして③人種・民族差別があることは前述の通りです。本書は主としてその内の①数多の主権国家の存在から生じる争いの解消について論じているものです。（なお、②と③につきましては付録の中に概略してあります）

1．自然災害

　自然災害につきましては、宇宙、太陽系、地球の終わりは何百億年あるいは何十億年先のことですから今現在心配する必要も意味もありません。宇宙という自然から来たものとして、宇宙人（付録2-02）が存在していて地球を訪問することがあっても我々人間にとって不幸な遭遇にはならないと考えられます。また、地球に衝突して来る天体についても当面心配することはなさそうです。さらに、地球から受ける火山の噴火、地震や津波、プレート運動による陸

地の移動などからの災害も、また病気の蔓延も、人類が協力し適切に対応すれ
ば人類の滅亡に迄至ることはないものと考えられます。従って、常に注意を怠
ることはできませんが、自然災害を原因として人類が近未来に滅亡すること
については、一応心配することはないということになります。（拙著「神からの
自立」に詳細です）

２．自然から受ける人為災害

　これは、我々人間が負の作用を施した自然環境から反作用として受ける公害
などの災害、および濫用による資源の枯渇から結果する人類存続の基盤への災
害のことです。

　今ある世界は、自然環境の破壊が進み生物の生息できない生態系に近づきつ
つあり、又限りある生物・鉱物資源の濫用は資源の枯渇を促進しています。加
えて、利用可能な資源とそれが支えることのできる人類の人口数の問題も存在
しています。これらは人類の存亡を決定的に左右するものですから、人間界は
何を差し置いても協力一致して、それらの問題を解決し人類の未来を確保しな
ければなりません。（拙著「神からの自立」に詳細です）

２　主権国家の不幸から世界国家の幸福へ

　主権国家の下では、人間の幸・不幸を左右する要素が不幸な状態にある現実
に対し、世界国家の下では、それが幸福な状態に転化されています。

　下表をご覧ください（次ページ）。

　人間に幸福・不幸をもたらす基本的要素は、大きくは①宇宙観、②人間とい
う生命体、そして③人間界の実生活、にあり、そしてこれらの基本的要素は、
それぞれ幾つかの構成要素から成っていると考えることができます。そうしま
すと、人間の幸・不幸はこれら構成要素の状態如何で決定されることになります。

（幸福・不幸の要素とその状態）

幸福/不幸の要素	①宇宙観		②人間という生命体		
	宇宙の有り様	来し方行く末存在理由	存在価値	運命	様々な苦
不幸（不安、不満、絶望）	虚無的世界観など	知らず	不明瞭？	生・老・病・死	苦の呪縛
幸福（安心、満足、希望）	物事に対する考え・見解である観念の仕方で不幸を幸福に転換				

幸福/不幸の要素	③人間界の実生活				
	地球の環境争いの根源科学の扱い	権力による圧制・統制	社会秩序	衣食住	生存権
主権国家 不幸（不安、不満、絶望）	環境の破壊暴力・戦争科学の厄災	不自由不平等人権無視	秩序の欠如不適な秩序不快な社会	不足	社会福祉・教育の機会均等等の不備
世界国家 幸福（安心、満足、希望）	環境の改善平和科学の利益	自由平等人権尊重	秩序の存在適切な秩序快適な社会	充足	社会福祉・教育の機会均等等の充足
	考え方とそれに伴う行動で不幸を幸福に転換				

　すなわち、幸福とは、構成要素に対して我々が持つ要求が満たされて安心、満足、希望の中にいることであり、不幸とはその要求が満たされず不安、不満、絶望などを抱えていることであると考えて良いものと思います。

　①宇宙観、と②人間という生命体、に関わる幸福・不幸は精神的問題で、科学、哲学、宗教などに関わっているものです。①宇宙観（付録2-03、2-04）、については、我々人間の知能・知識のレベルに関わっているものですから、我々が理解できる限りをその時点ではそのまま受け容れているよりほかありません。次に、②人間という生命体、については、我々の意志で選択したものではないとは言え、我々に備わっている生得についての問いに関わっているもの

ですから、我々はそれについては自身で考えなければなりません。神や宗教に
おまかせすることで解決できるとか、あるいは解決するべきことではありませ
ん。（この①と②につきましては、拙著「神と宗教を考える」に詳細です）

　一方、本書が特に問題としていることは③人間界の実生活で、上表において
は、数多の主権国家の存在下では全ての要素が不幸な状態にあることに対し、
世界国家の下では、それが幸福な状態に転化されていることを表示していま
す。

　さて、この③人間界の実生活、については、不幸であることも幸福であるこ
とも我々人間の心の持ち方とそれに伴う行動に関わるものですから、得られる
結果については、人間に全責任のあるものです。幸福とは、「人間界至高の理
念」に表される人間性を実現することにより得られるものであるとすれば、そ
の実現に調和することは精神的にも高く賢くあり、矛盾することは愚かである
ということになります。

　当基本的要素は、表にあるように、仮に５つの構成要素に分けて表示してあ
ります。しかし、この５つよりもっと多くに分けても良く、その逆に少なくま
とめても良いものです。なぜなら、これらの構成要素は全ての要素間で複雑に
して密接に関係し合っていて、色々な考え方で色々な分け方があって然るべ
きだからです。５つに分けた理由は視覚と頭の整理にはこれくらいが適当かと
思ったからにすぎません。

１．消滅するものと生じるもの

「消滅するもの」とは、数多の主権国家の下では必要であったものが不要に
なったもので、「生じるもの」とは、「消滅するもの」から結果する、世界国家
における、物心両面の幸福のことです。ここでは、先ず最初に、主権国家の下
では不可避であった戦争がなくなり、世界国家の下では平和になったことによ
り、(1)軍事関連事項と(2)国に関係する言葉・概念、がどのように変わるのか
を思いつくままに以下に記述しました。

(1) 軍事関連事項

戦争がなくなり平和になりますと、軍事関連事項の一切は消滅します。主に、以下のようなことが含まれます。

①軍事費

戦争がなくなり恒久的平和が訪れますと、軍事費は不要になります。又、主権国家下において必要であった外交など国際関係維持のための諸費用は不要となります。これらに必要な財物だけをとっても、人間界は世界総計では現在年間何百兆円あるいはそれ以上の巨額を、無駄というのみではなく、人類を不幸にするために失っていますが、世界国家の下では、これをすべて人類の幸福目的に振り替えて使用することができることになります。

②兵士

人類史上、数えきれない兵士が戦争で命を落としています。

妻子や恋人を持つ兵士は戦争という理不尽の中で、妻子や恋人に心に残し、命を落とすことにどれほどの切なさや悲しみを味わったことでしょうか。又、未だ恋人や妻子も持てず、人と生まれた幸福も知らず散っていった若い多くの命もあります。恋人を失った者、夫を失った妻、父を失った子、子を失った父母、などそれぞれの悲しみに思いを致しますと、「人間界に戦争がなければ」、という痛切な思いは人間一人一人の胸にどうしようもない怒りや無念と共に渦巻いています。さらに、命を落とさないまでも、肉体的にも精神的にも傷つき、不幸な人生を送ることになった兵士も限りない数になります。

世界国家の下では、国々の戦争が生ずることはなく、軍隊は不要になり従って兵士も不要になり、徴兵制度もありませんから、戦争で命を落としたり傷害を受ける兵士はただの一人もなくなります。万歳、万歳です。

③兵器

科学は両刃の剣ですが、その力は際限なく高みに向かって行きます。このような中、その科学を悪用して兵器を作れば、我々人類が益々強力な兵器を際限なく手にすることになるのは言うまでもありません。このような兵器を使用しての戦争となれば、それは遅かれ早かれ人類という種が絶滅することは必至になります。

戦争の生じない世界では当然に兵器は不要になりますから、製造されることはなくなります。世界国家の下では、兵器は自然に消滅します。世界国家政府による警察機構のために多少の武器が必要であるという程度のことになります。

④軍需産業

軍需産業は世界国家では不要になりますが、軍用機やミサイルなどを作っている企業は既に軍用機以外の航空機や宇宙開発用のロケットなども作っていますし、軍用艦を作っている企業は既に軍用艦以外の船舶はもとより大きく堅牢な構造物も作っています。戦車やその他の軍用車両を作っている企業は既に軍用以外のブルドーザー、耕運機、フォークリフト等の車両も作っています。軍事用需要が減少した分は、平和用需要が増加することで十分にカバーすることができます。

平和用需要の増加とは、自然環境・生態系の破壊阻止・原状回復・改善用の陸・海・空にわたる機材の供給、宇宙開発関係、グローバルな道路整備などのインフラ工事、堅固であるが人と自然にやさしい橋や治水工事、地震や台風などの自然災害に耐える強固な構築物建設などのことです。不要になった軍需産業は人間界の幸福のために、その持てる力を存分に発揮できる筈です。

平和用産業の仕事は増やそうと思えば幾らでも増やすことは可能です。なぜなら、この宇宙船地球号をこの世における人類の理想郷にするという視点に立てば、なすべき仕事は数限りなくあるからです。従って、今ある軍事関係企業が平和な世界で衰退するような杞憂を持つ必要はありません、前途洋々間違い

ありません。

　⑤難民・虐殺等

　世界国家の下では、国々の争いはなく、軍隊もなく従って兵器を使用しての戦いはありませんから、もうニュースなどというものではなく日常茶飯事のごとく報じられている難民が生ずることも、争うことから生じる憎悪による虐殺など耳にすることさえおぞましい出来事も生じることはありません。考えただけでも心に安堵するものがあります。

　⑥不幸の創造費から幸福の創造費へ

　この地上そして人間界から争いがなくなり平和になりますと、軍事のために費やされていた人、物、金の一切（人類の資産）が不要になります。このことは、人を殺し、砲弾や毒性化学物質や核物質で自然を破壊し、人間界に悲しみや憎しみをもたらし、人類滅亡のリスク迄をも招来するなど人間界に不幸を創造するどうしようもない愚かの象徴である戦争とその備えのために費やされて失われていた人類の資産を、人類の幸福の創造のために振り替えて有益に使用することが可能になることを意味します。

　その振替先は、例えば、人類存続のための基本的基盤である自然環境・生態系の破壊阻止、修復、改善に充てることが最善策の一つであると考えられます。そのための専用かつ経済効率の高い機材や組織が整う迄の過渡期には、不用になった軍用機材や組織はそのままこの目的のため使用しても良いと考えられます。すなわち、陸軍は河川・湖沼や陸地、海軍は海洋、空軍は大気というように、陸海空それぞれに残留する物理的・化学物質的・核物質的汚染の除去を担当するということです。航空母艦が旗艦となり海洋の清掃をしている風景を想像しますと心強くも楽しくもなります。爆撃機が爆弾を落とす代わりに大気汚染の中和剤を散布するとか、戦車などの車両やホーバークラフト等を使用して河川・湖沼や陸地の清掃をするのも同様です。

　このような目的のため、高価な戦争用機材を使用するなどは不経済であるな

どの批判をなす愚か者がいるとも思われませんが、そのような高価な機材を使用してなす戦争というものが人間界にこれ以上はない負しかもたらさないことと比べれば、いくら高価であってもそれを幸福の創造費に転換することはこれ以上有意義な使い途はないものと思われます。

⑵ 国に関係する言葉・概念

あまり必要でないというか、使われなくなる言葉は色々ありますが、ここでは国に関係する言葉の内の幾つかを展示しました。

①国境

辞書的には、国境とは国と国との境すなわち国家と国家との版図を区画する境界線で、国家領土主権の行われる限界、ということですが、我が宇宙船地球号の中を小部屋に間仕切りしている仕切り枠のことです。世界国家の下ではこれらの仕切り枠は全て取り外され地球全域が一つの部屋になりますから領土、領空、領海、経済水域などはなくなりそれらを他国から守る必要もなくなります。

そもそも、地球上に自然が設えた国境線など存在しません。物理的には国境に設けられている壁や鉄条網は撤去され（あるいは人類が愚かであった時代の一つの象徴として記念碑的に残すという選択肢はあります）、国境線は地図の上からも消去されます。地球は人類共有の資産です。小さな小部屋に分けて小部屋の主権を主張し合うなどは愚かで狭量な精神の象徴の最たるものの一つですが、世界国家が実現しているということは少しは賢く広量な精神に進歩したという意味にもなります。地表と海面の上から下、すなわち天国から地獄迄、の三次元の小部屋の概念は払拭され、精神も自由に晴れ上がり風通しも良くなりすっきりします。

②国家防衛（安全保障）

国は他国との対立が生じますと国を防衛しなければなりません。これは戦争

が生じている際は当然のことですが、戦時でなくとも対立関係そして緊張が生じた場合は戦争を想定した防衛準備に腐心しなければならず、常時防衛を意識した国の経営が要求されることになります。しかし、注意しなければならないことは、防衛とは単に守ることではなく、攻撃と同義語でもあるということです。なぜなら、自国から宣戦布告はしない防衛主義を採っても、一旦攻撃されれば防衛しているだけでは戦略上の不利不経済は言う迄もありませんから、攻撃の拠って来る所を攻撃するのは必然になるからです。「攻撃は最大の防御なり」とも言われます。

　そうしますと、防衛準備とは攻撃準備も含まなくてはならず、この準備を感知した対立国も相応かそれを上回る戦闘準備の充実に勤しむという悪循環に入って行きます。この悪循環がなぜ生じるのかは明らかです。数多の主権国家が存在しているからです。国々がなければ、すなわち攻撃・防衛する国がなければ戦争は絶対に生じません。世界国家には敵対国は存在しませんから、攻撃も防衛も生ずることはありません。恒久的平和が実現する道理です。

　日本の場合など、憲法第九条「戦争の放棄」に関わり、戦争の放棄と自衛隊との整合性がどうのこうのというようなことで頭を悩ませる必要も意味も一切なくなります。

③国内・国外
　世界国家の下では、国々の存在していた時の国内・国外の概念はなくなります。国外はなくなり地球全域が国内になります。あえて言えば、国外とは太陽系外でしょうか。なぜなら、火星や他の太陽系の惑星を開発したとしても、先住民はいそうにありませんから、そこもやはり地球国の内ということになる筈だからです。

　何処へ行こうとも、パスポートもビザ（査証）も必要ではなくなり身分証明書（ID）のみがあれば良いことになります。地球国人の誰もが世界中又系内惑星およびその衛星への往来勝手たるべし、ということになります。

④国民

　そもそも国民などという民は存在しません。民とは王に対する言葉のイメージがありますが、言うなれば、人は民ではなく一人一人が王又は女王なのです。この思想は世界国家の下では達成されています。従って、世界国家の名称を地球国としますと、人は地球国民ではなく地球人又は地球国の平等な構成員ということになります。個の集合により国が作られているのであり、その逆はありません。

　「天は人の上に人を造らず、人の下に人を造らず」という言葉があります。「天」という神のような概念や響きの主語の是非はさておき、「人は皆平等である」という思想は言う迄もない当然中の当然のことです。

　（なお、この言葉は福沢諭吉の「学問のすすめ」に出ているものですが、アメリカの独立宣言の中からの引用のようです。福沢諭吉はこの言葉の辞書的な意味を肯定した上で、さらにそれとは少し違う概念をも持たせて使用しているようですが、上記ではこの文言の辞書的意味そのままの「全ての人は生まれつき平等である」という意味で以て記述しています）

⑤愛国心

　数多の国々が存在している現在、その国の数だけの愛国心がありますが、地球国一国となりますとそれらの古い愛国心はなくなり地球国を愛するただ一つの愛国心が存在することになります。これは少し淋しい気がしないでもないという向きもあるかもしれませんが、「人間界は平和であるべし」という視点に立てばこの「地上にただ一つの愛国心」は歓迎されて然るべきものです。なぜなら、愛国心は無知で愚かな心無い政治家などにより国々の戦争を煽動することに悪用されることもあるからです。下記をご覧ください。

愛国心

　言う迄もないことですが、愛国心とは自身の属している国を慕い愛すること

ですから、美しい言葉でもあり心暖まるものがあります。然るに、愛国心というものは手放しで肯定できる単純なものではありません。

　愛国心が自然に芽生え国内に留まっている時は何の問題もありませんが、他国との争いが生じた場合、愛国心は個人にも祖国を守らなければならないという意識を強調するように働きかけ、さらに、国としては戦意を高揚するためのスローガンとして掲げ、必要以上にあるいは不自然な愛国心を強制することがあります。時には、愛国心を積極的に言動に表さなければ罰せられる場合さえあります。このように、愛国心は争いの主役になることはないようですが、脇役として争いを助長するように働くことは確かです。

　なぜ、愛国心をめぐってこのように馬鹿げて嘆かわしい事態が生じるのでしょうか。その理由は馬鹿みたいに単純です。それは地球上に愛国心の数が多すぎるからです。つまり多すぎる数の祖国が存在しているということです。この小さな宇宙船地球号をさらに小部屋に間仕切りして多数の国を作っているから愛国心の山が生じることになります。地球に多くの国は不要です。地球はただ一つの国すなわち世界国家であるべきです。愛国心とは、誰もがこの地球国のみを又地球国のあらゆる箇所を、かけがえのない大切なものとして、こよなく愛することでなくてはなりません。

⑥国土

　国土とは、一国の国境線によってその範囲を示された領域で、領海、領空を含む領土です。この帰属をめぐって国際間紛争が生じます。国土は、そこから鉱物資源を得られるほか、農業を行って食料を得たり、国民の住居を作ったり、その他色々な用途に利用できます。つまり、国土に関わる紛争は、自国の利益を追求するためにする、宇宙船地球号の中の自国の小部屋を拡げるための紛争です。この紛争は二国間のみではなく数カ国あるいはそれ以上の間で生じることもあります。どの主権国家もがこの利益を追求すればどうなるかは明らかです。争いを回避することはできません。

　世界国家の下では、領土に関わる紛争は生じません。なぜなら領土を主張す

る数多の主権国家は存在しないからです。地球という領土は世界国家の地球国にのみに帰属しています。

⑦国に関わる品のない言葉

今ある形の国がなくなりますと、喜ばしいことには、国に関わる品のない言葉は不要になり自然に消滅することになります。例えば、売国奴です。売国とは、辞書によりますと、自国の内情・秘密を敵国に通じ、または自国に不利で敵国の利益となることを企てて私利をはかることであり、売国奴とは、売国の行いのある者をののしっていう語、とあります。然るに、世界国家の下では敵国が存在しませんから、売国を買う買国が存在しません。かくして、この売買"ビジネス"は成立することはなく、売国奴は存在しなくなり、その言葉も不要になります。

⑧国際関税

世界国家の下では、商取引は全て国内取引になります。従って、輸出入はなくなり移出入になりますから基本的に国際間貿易・関税問題（戦争）は自動的に消滅します。自由貿易・保護貿易問題などに悩む必要は一切なくなります。世界国家の経済社会の形にも関わって来ることですが、地域間の格差がいずれ消滅する迄は地域間取引には調整のようなもの（一方にプラス、他方にマイナス）は必要になるかもしれません。しかし、それは世界国家という一元下で世界の地域のバランスを俯瞰しながら可能な限り適切とするための調整ですから、世界は納得の上収まることになります。

⑨国際の付く言葉・概念

数多の主権国家の下では、諸国家に関係する「国際」の付く言葉・概念が、下記のように、数多あります。

国際主義、国際紛争、国際政治、国際情勢、国際外交、国際連合、国際

同盟、国際条約、国際社会、国際会議、国際法、国際貿易、国際関税協定（GATT）、国際海峡、国際慣習、国際裁判、国際安全保障、国際関係、国際秩序、等々。

　しかし、世界国家の下では、「国際」はなくなり「国内」のみになります。従って、人間界は「国際」に関わる一切の煩わしさや悩みから解放されることになります。又、「国際」は付きませんが、政治的関心と結びつきやすい政治現象と地理的条件との関係を云々する「地政学」もその存在意義がなくなり衰退することになります。

２．世界国家における全方位的幸福

　これは、「１．消滅するものと生じるもの」で論じた、世界国家における、物心両面の幸福を補完するものです。
　これは、前出の「**幸福・不幸の要素とその状態**」から部分転載したものです。

幸福／不幸の要素	③人間界の実生活				
	地球の環境 争いの根源 科学の扱い	権力による 圧制・統制	社会秩序	衣食住	生存権
主権国家 不幸（不安、不満、絶望）	環境の破壊 暴力・戦争 科学の厄災	不自由 不平等 人権無視	秩序の欠如 不適な秩序 不快な社会	不足	社会福祉・教育の機会均等等の不備
世界国家 幸福（安心、満足、希望）	環境の改善 平和 科学の利益	自由 平等 人権尊重	秩序の存在 適切な秩序 快適な社会	充足	社会福祉・教育の機会均等等の充足
	考え方とそれに伴う行動で不幸を幸福に転換				

　上表は、数多の主権国家の下では、全ての要素が不幸な状態にあることに対

し、世界国家の下では、それが幸福な状態に転化していることを表しています。

　世界国家の下では、全ての主権国家は消滅し存在しませんから、国々の争いが生じることはありません。戦争のない、心身共に、平和な世界です。

　上表をご覧いただきますと、世界国家においては、全ての要素が幸福な状態にあることが一目瞭然のように思われます。従って、これ以上の説明は不要なのかもしれませんが、折角のことですから、それぞれの要素について多少の記述をしました。以下のようなことです。

(1) 地球の環境、争いの根源、科学の扱い

　我々はこれまで自然環境を汚染や濫用により損壊して来ました。損壊がこれ以上進行しますと地球は生物の生息できない生態系になり、人類を含む大方の生物は絶滅します。又、諸々の資源は無計画な濫用により減少しています。そもそも、限りある資源は濫用せずとも人類の末永い存続には絶望的に足りません。従って、先ず我々のなさねばならないことは、生態系の損壊の阻止と、人類の末永い存続を可能にする諸々の資源の確保の目途をつけることです。

　生物に都合のいい自然環境・生態系そして人類に必要不可欠な資源は、人類の生存・存続のための基盤ですから、人類にとって最重要であり最優先しなければならないものです。従って、この基盤は政治的思わくなどに妨げられることなく、科学的視点から純粋に考え扱うべきものでなくてはなりません。又、大気は地球を覆い、大気と海と陸地は互いにつながり接し合って地球圏を形成していますから、地球全域を一つの生態系一つの資源としてグローバルな視点から捉えるべきもので、局地的あるいは国家毎に好き勝手に考え扱うべきものではありません。

　この意味で世界国家が理想的であることは論を俟ちません。

①世界国家における重要事項

　主権国家体制における各国の最優先事項は自国の思わくであり、人類共通の存続基盤であるにもかかわらず、自然環境・生態系の保全や資源確保問題は副次的な関心事でしかありません。しかし、世界国家の下では喜ばしいことにはこの存続基盤が最優先事項となっています。これは人類の最優先事項が思いのままに計画され実行できることを意味します。世界国家の下での解決は、グローバルな（そして、宇宙的）視点に立つ総合計画書に基づく迅速性、確実性、経営・経済効率向上の成果として得ることができることになります。これは主権国家群世界における多元的考えと管理から生じるモザイク模様になりがちな結果とは比べるべくもなく優れています。世界国家はこの意味においても他の観点からも理想的環境であると言えます。

　世界国家においては、我々は自然環境・生態系の損壊の阻止、原状回復、さらに理想的な改善に向かい地球をピカピカに磨き上げること、そして天然資源の確保の目途をつけることに喜び勇んで勤しむことができるようになります。

　地球における鉱物資源は有限です。科学技術や経済効率を無視して、太陽系の他の惑星やその衛星および彗星や小惑星から採取することにしても、現在に至る迄の濫用を繰り返すのであれば、人類の末永い将来の使用に供するには絶望的に足りません。従って、地球にある資源を徹底的にリサイクルし循環することによって可能な限り永久的使用に耐えることのできる仕組みや科学技術を開発しなければなりません。エネルギー資源につきましては、重油・天然ガスなどは近い将来枯渇しますが、幸いにもそれらに代えて人類の終焉の時迄使用に耐える無尽蔵な資源があります。地球には地熱、風力、海流などがあり、我が太陽からは降り注ぐ太陽光があります。後は、これらを利用することのできる科学技術の開発ですが、益々効率の良い技術が開発されることが期待できます。

　従って、人類は協力一致して、自然環境を理想的にする戦いおよび末永い使用に耐える鉱物やエネルギー資源に関わる安心を得るための戦いに挑戦しなければなりません。しかし、これは人類同士の悲しい戦いではなく、人類の幸福

と栄光をめざした戦いですからこれほど楽しい戦いはない筈です。

　スモッグのないどこまでも澄んだ大気、煌めく水、緑溢れる世界、有害物質の除去された豊饒の大地、豊饒な海洋生物、サンゴ礁の夢のような美しい世界、物理的ごみのない世界、オゾン層の修復（の可能性）、エネルギー資源や鉱物資源の将来長きに亘る使用に関わる安心、これらのことが達成された世界は人類のみならず全ての生物にとって喜びの世界になります。

　②今ある主権国家群の世界で今なすべきこと

　自然環境・生態系問題は人類を含む全生物の存続基盤に関わることですから、人間界の最優先問題の筈です。にもかかわらず、今ある世界に存在する各主権国家においては、この問題は副次的な取り扱いとなっています。なぜなら、国の最優先事項は自国が当面直面している政治・経済・社会問題や自国の利害にかかわる国際問題・紛争の解決にあるからです。従って、国の物心両面のエネルギーはこれらに優先的に費やされている現実があります。そして世界はそれぞれがこのような事情を持つ数多の国々で構成されています。自然環境・生態系の損壊を阻止しなければならないという認識が世界的に確立しているにもかかわらず、国々の足並みが揃わずその進捗が遅々としている理由はこのような事情にあります。そして、この事情は数多の主権国家の存在する限り変わることはないものと覚悟しなければなりません。

　一方、自然環境・生態系は日夜刻々と損壊が進行しており、もういつ何時損壊の阻止が無効となり壊滅へ向かって止められない進行を開始してもおかしくない状況にあります。このことは各国の持つ事情が存在するからと言って、座して時の経つのを見送ることはできないことを意味します。

　それでは、主権国家群の世界という現実にあって、我々はどのようにすれば自然環境・生態系の壊滅を阻止することに希望を持つことができるのか、ということになります。

　ところで、本章におけるこのスペースは、世界国家においては自然環境・生態系の損壊の阻止・原状の回復・改善が満足に行われ理想的な生態系が実現し

ていることについて語るためのスペースの筈です。損壊の阻止ができず壊滅に
向かうことを心配するためのスペースではありません。しかし、世界国家の下
では、生物に好都合な生態系の保全や改善が第 1 の優先順位に据えることがで
きるとしても、その時迄生態系はまだ壊滅しておらず、損壊が阻止されて生き
ている状態で、今ある主権国家群の世界から世界国家へバトンタッチできなけ
ればなりません。そのため、主権国家群の今ある世界であっても、今なさねば
ならないこと、すなわち世界国家における成功と栄光のための前提条件を語る
スペースに使用しています。

　主権国家群が存在している今ある世界においてなさねばならないこととは、
我々は、二酸化炭素による地球温暖化問題のみならず、徹底的研究機関を国連
の中に増設し、地球の自然環境・生態系に悪影響を及ぼす全ての要素を洗いざ
らい机の上に出し、それぞれの要素及び複数の要素が複合的にもたらす悪影響
とそれを阻止するための総合的な研究を可及的速やかにかつ徹底的に実施しな
ければならないということです。研究は生態系を生物に好都合な状態に保つた
めに我々のなさねばならない必要最小限の行動を可能な限り把握できるもので
なければなりません。可及的速やかにというのは、毎秒毎秒生態系の損壊が進
行している現状に鑑み、生態系が壊滅してしまう前にその損壊を止めて、その
上で生態系の原状回復に取り掛かることのできる機会を失うことのないことを
慮ってのことです。

　今ある世界においては、各国の事情により生態系の損壊の阻止が思うように
実行できないことは既にわかっています。しかし、我々は先ず研究の成果とし
て、生態系を護るためには何をどのような計画によりなさねばならないかとい
う情報・知識を手にしなくてはなりません。その上で、そのような計画は実行
できないということであれば、次善の策を検討するという手順になります。

　なお、この研究は、そのような優柔不断な姿勢では生態系の損壊・壊滅の阻
止には絶望的におぼつかないことを明らかにすることになるかもしれません。
しかし、その時はその時です。我々人類は把握することのできたその知識を前
提に、生態系の死滅を人類の力の限りを尽くして阻止することに努めてみる

か、あるいは又、人類は生態系の死滅と共に絶滅することを受け容れるかについて人類自らの納得の上で選択・決定できることになります。人類が自らの絶滅を受け容れることを選択するなどということはありえないと思われますが、人類にとって悪魔そのものである核兵器を擁することから脱却できないでいる愚かな我々人類のことです。生態系の保全などできる筈もないという人類不信の思いも払拭できませんが、これが杞憂であり、人類が協力一致して地球環境・生態系を救うという形が実現することを祈るばかりです。

　従って、何れにしても、とにもかくにも、このような徹底的研究が要求されることになりますが、生態系保全の必要性が世界的認識となっている以上、そのような知識・情報を手にしてみることに反対する国はないものと期待されます。単に（と言ってはいけないのでしょうが）、研究機関の増設のために、多少の金が必要になるだけのことです。神に借財するのではありません。我々人間が自身で用立てできるものです。

　なお、人間界が紛争を止めて平和が必要であることは、本書の主たる論点ですから、本書を通して語られています（**争いの根源**）。また、科学の厄災化の回避と平和的利用の必要性は、主に第3章でそして本書の他の場所でも語られています（**科学の扱い**）。従って、これらについての此処での繰り返しは割愛します。

⑵ 権力による圧制・統制

　基本的人権を身に帯び無垢で自由な存在として生を受けている我々人間に対して、権力（主として政治や宗教、私人の間ではボス、雇主等）が不自由、不平等、そしてその他の人権無視を理不尽に圧制・統制的に強いている場合、そのような社会環境の中の人間は不幸です。

　基本的人権とは、人間が生まれながらに持っている自由や平等を包含している権利であり、実定法上の権利のように思惟的に剥奪又は制限されるものでは

ないというのが一般的認識です。然るに、数多の主権国家の世界においては、
(イ)他国との緊張・戦争状態にある時に、あるいは、(ロ)国体護持の必要性が高
じた時に、人間の自由と尊厳の蹂躙が生じます。国家の意思統一の保全が第1
命題となり国家権力が基本的人権に優位に立つことになるからです。然るに、
世界国家の下では、(イ)の他国との緊張・戦争状態は消滅していますから、そ
れに関わり基本的人権が蹂躙されることはありません。(ロ)の国体の護持につ
いては、そもそも世界国家とは人間の本性に由来する「人間界至高の理念」の
実現をめざしている社会ですから、世界国家の状態に不満があれば、言論を統
制するなどは一切必要ではなく、言論を自由に戦わせることにより、より良い
世界国家の形をめざすべく最善のアプローチを採ることになります。世界国家
とはそのような社会ですから、言論の自由統制などの思想やその必要性が消滅
している世界です。

(3) 社会秩序

　道徳や法律の欠如する秩序なき社会は不快で不安な社会です。しかし、秩序
が存在しても、それがその社会の構成員に適切に認められている形の秩序では
なく、権力により捻じ曲げられ、恐怖や理不尽を伴う類のものであれば、その
ような社会は秩序なき社会と同様にあるいはそれ以上に不快で不安な社会であ
ることは論を俟ちません。
　例えば、国の命題は戦争であり戦争が道徳や正義となっている状態にある場
合、国の構成員たる個としての人間の持つ命題である平和という倫理は強制的
に否定され、国の道徳や正義に個の倫理が劣位することになります。然るに、
世界国家では、二つの命題は平和に統合されます。

(4) 衣食住

　現状、人間が生活する上での基礎的条件である衣食住が不足している国々や

地域があります。世界人口の10％超は満足な食料どころか飢餓に瀕している
とも言われています。しかし、今我々は進んだ農業技術も畜産技術も養殖技術
もさらにそのほか食料生産のために必要なありとあらゆる技術を持つに至って
います。食料を適切な場所で適切な量を生産することなど世界国家の視点から
は容易なことになります。その上に、世界的な物流システムも発達しています
から、世界における食料の適切な配分も可能です。

　世界国家とは、人類を不幸にする負の行為は一切行わず、人類の幸福に対し
て正となる行為のみを行う世界です。食のみではなく、健全な衣も住も不足す
ることなく約束されています。平和でありさえすれば、人類の持つ力の全ては
人類の幸福のためにのみ充てられることになります。その中でも衣食住の充足
は最優先されますから、これらのことが達成されない筈がありません。

(5) 生存権

　社会の各員が人間らしい生を全うできる人権の一つとしての生存権を保障す
る社会福祉や教育の機会均等は、人間界にはまだ適当に行き亘らず、人間界は
不幸な状態にあります。社会福祉とは、貧困者や保護を必要とする社会的障害
を負う人々に対する援護・育成・更生を図ろうとする公私の社会的努力の組織
的行動であり、教育は人間が等しく後天的に知識を得るために一番に有効な手
法です。

　然るに、世界国家の下では、これらの充実は容易なことになることが考えら
れます。主権国家の下で必要であった軍事費や国際関係維持などのため費やさ
れていた巨額の諸費用が不要となったものを社会福祉や教育費に振り替えて使
用できることになるからです。

　知識や行動は先天的（生得的）に持っているという説と後天的（経験的）に
得られるという説とがあります。論争には及びません。理屈上、先天と後天を
足し合わせた産物が我々の知識であり、それはこの世における我々の行動に役
立っています。先天は遺伝子に、そして後天は生まれて後の経験や教育に由

来しています。先天は誕生して後にどうにかできるものではありませんから、我々に必要なことでありそして我々にできることは後天である経験や教育を積むことにあることになります。

　教育は我々人間に考えて行動する術を教えるものですから、全ての人間に教育を受ける機会を均等に与えなければならないことは、基本的人権上からも人為環境の向上面からも必要欠くべからざる要件となります。考えることのできる者は、知性に乏しい迷妄者の為す流言飛語や根拠なき無責任な妄言や予言を信じたり、妄想を信じることはありません。例えば、「人間界至高の理念」に調和しない愚かな煽動に不和雷同しないこと等を正しく判断できることになります。女性に教育は不必要であるなどと言うような愚かな"やから"には、その愚かさを理解させるための教育がいの一番に施されなくてはなりません。

　この「全世界の全ての個に健全なレベルでの社会福祉や平等な教育の機会を提供する」というような命題は、物事を一元的に扱うことができる世界国家の下では扱いやすく従って容易に実現できる筈のことです。

第6章　世界国家樹立への道

　世界に現存する数多の主権国家を発展的に解消し統合して地球全域を一国とする世界国家としなければならない理由はこれ迄に語って来た通りですが、その理由がわかり受け容れられたとしても、世界国家の実現に向かうにはどのようにすれば良いのか、という最大の難問が残っています。この難問について、拙いものではありますが、以下のように考えてみました。

1　単一世界国家をめざす非政府組織 (NGO)

　地球上の国家を統一し一つの国家をめざす NGO やその連合は色々ありますが、その内「世界連邦運動、World Federalist Movement」を代表に採り上げます。

　以下は筆者によるその概要です。（出典は、フリー百科事典ウィキペディア）

　国際連合が戦争抑止力の低いことを痛感した世界に著名な科学者・文化人たちが、より強力な世界連邦の形成を進めることで世界から戦争をなくして行こうと決意し、1946年に「世界連邦政府のための世界運動」を起こした。この運動には、バートランド・ラッセル、アルベルト・アインシュタイン、アルベルト・シュヴァイツァー、ウィンストン・チャーチル、湯川秀樹などが賛同し、その本部をジュネーヴに置いた。
「世界連邦運動」は以下をその活動原則としている。

　　①全世界の諸国、諸民族を全部加盟させる。
　　②世界的に共通な問題については、各国家の主権の一部を世界連邦政府に
　　　委譲する。

③世界連邦法は「国家」に対してではなく、一人一人の「個人」を対象として適用される。

④各国の軍備は全廃し、世界警察軍を設置する。

⑤原子力は世界連邦政府のみが所有し、管理する。

⑥世界連邦の経費は各国政府の供出ではなく、個人からの税金で賄う。

　現在国家単位で与えられている国連への参加資格を個人単位に移すことを主眼としており、これらは即ち、事実上の「単一世界国家（単一世界政府）」（一つの世界）の建設である。

　以後、国連憲章の修正および国際刑事裁判所設立の提案に関与し、1983年にはIGP（国際政策研究所）という国際・地域組織の民主化と国際法の開発および世界適用を標榜するシンクタンクを立ち上げている。現在、事務局はニューヨークにあり、数十カ国・地域に地域団体が設立されている。また国際連合経済社会理事会との協議資格を有し、国連の権限強化へ積極的に提言している。「世界連邦運動」には単一世界国家を目指す数多のNGOが加盟し提携している。

───────────────────────

　「世界連邦運動」は、上掲のように、数多ある世界国家をめざすNGO中では出色で、その目標に貢献する有益な業績をあげていますが、運動を起こしてから4分の3世紀経った今も単一世界国家は実現しておりません。そして、残念ながら、後同じ期間経とうが150年経とうが、「世界連邦運動」の中から世界国家が実現する見込みは持てません。

　なぜなら、「世界連邦運動」は非政府組織であり、世界国家へ移行するために欠くことのできない権限を帯びていないからです。

　世界国家は人類の夢です。しかし、夢は幾ら語ろうともいつまでも夢でしかありません。それを実現するためにはそこへ至る綿密な総合計画とそれを実行に移すことのできる権限が伴わなければなりません。従って、世界国家の実現には、世界国家へ向かう世界的な意志の確認と実行を伴う宣言のできる権威あ

る場所、すなわち非政府組織ではなく、政府組織の中で議論を重ね決断し実行を先導していただかなければならないことになります。

2　国際連合と世界国家との矛盾と無矛盾

　世界国家へ向かうべく世界の合意を形成し、その実行をも伴う宣言のできる場は国際連合（国連）をおいてほかにはありません。従って、世界国家構想については、先ず、世界の全ての国々が集う国連という場における議題に上げていただかなくては何も始まりません。

　然るに、ここで大変な矛盾に遭遇します。すなわち、国連の第1の存在意義が世界平和の維持にあると言っても、主権国家の集まりである国連が主権国家の解消につながる世界国家への移行を議論することは矛盾しているということです。この基本的なことを考えますと、世界国家構想を国連に寄せて語ることには心が折れそうになります。

　しかし、そうは言っても、この矛盾を承知しながら、世界国家へ向かうことを可能にするために縋ることのできるものは国連をおいてほかにないことも事実です。世界国家構想は国連の議題に上げていただけなければ、もうその先はありません。それで「おしまい」のお話です。この意味するところは、人類は現状の世界を踏襲するということであり、従って、人間界における絶えることのない争いと、人間の不幸と、科学を厄災化した強力な兵器を使用しての戦争から結果する近未来における人類滅亡のリスク、これらの全てを覚悟するということです。

　ここでは、話を「現状ありき」から「そもそも論」へ移さなければなりません。「現状ありき」とは「主権国家ありき」ということであり、「そもそも論」とは「国家主権の拠って来る源である個（一人一の人間）の主権のこと」です。数多ある主権国家もそしてその集まりである国連も、そもそもは人間の集まりです。人間の集まりを離れて存在しているものではありません。その人間の集まりである主権国家も国連も人類第1の希望を実現するための手段にすぎ

ません。人類第1の希望すなわち人類第1の大事とは、「平和と自由の中で幸福に末永く存続すること」です。主権国家ありきを守ることが第1の大事ではありません。数多ある主権国家は戦争を必然としますから、人類第1の大事に矛盾しています。対して、数多ある主権国家を解消して戦争の相手の存在しない単一の国家である世界国家とすることは人類第1の大事に照らせば正しい選択である筈です。今ある世界では数多ある主権国家の持つ「戦争」という命題と個の持つ「平和」という命題は矛盾していますが、世界国家とはこのどうしようもない矛盾が解消されている世界です。つまり国家と個の命題が「平和」で一致している世界であるということです。

　国連総会等に出席している人々は皆主権国家の代表です。しかし、それらの人々は主権国家の代表である前に一人の人間でありさらに人類の代表でなければなりません。そうであれば、人類第1の希望そして人類第1の大事が実現するかもしれない世界国家構想を門前払いなどにはせず国連の議題に上げることに否やはない筈です。本国の主権国家も人間の集まりですから、人類第1の希望が実現するのであれば、今ある国際的な主権国家の概念を発展的に解消することに単純に反対とは言えない道理です。このように考えますと、共に平和を最終目標としている国連と世界国家とは、必ずしも矛盾する関係などではなく無矛盾な関係であることになります。

　我々人類は「今ある世界」を踏襲して行けばその延長線上の近未来に滅亡するリスクを抱えているのですから、このリスクを回避し栄光に包まれた未来を手にするための究極的プロジェクト、世界国家への移行の準備・研究機関を国連の中で立ち上げていただかなくてはなりません。少なくともそのための真剣な議論が展開されなければならないということです。なぜなら、その議論がなされないということは、我々人類は我々自身で我々の幸福と栄光の未来を閉じてしまうことを意味することになるからです。そのようなことでいい筈はありません。

3　国際連合の役割

　上記に基づき、世界国家構想が国連の議題に上がったとしますと、そこで最初に問題となることは「世界国家実現の可能性如何」であると考えられます。世界国家の概念が素晴らしいものであっても実現できなければ絵に描いた餅になります。そうしますと、世界国家へ移行するかどうかはその詳細な青写真を見てから判断するというのが妥当な対応になります。

　このために、国連では、先ずこの青写真を準備するための「準備機関」を国連の中に新設する決議をしていただく必要があります。併せて、国連大学の中に、この目的に沿った研究部門を新設して、世界各国（重要です）の頭脳を集めて青写真の準備に携わらせることが望まれます。

　この結果、国連の役割は下記のようになります。

　国連の役割＝現行のもの＋世界国家移行（総合計画書 / 青写真）への準備

　世界国家実現のための総合計画書の試案は準備機関と大学が一つとなり作成し国連総会等に諮ります。問題があれば修正するという手順を繰り返し、この手順は国連で採択・決断できる最終案が完成する迄繰り返されることになります。どこかで乗り越えられない難関に遭遇し、この繰り返しが完全停止することになれば、世界国家への移行は失敗に帰することになりますが、晴れて完成すれば、世界国家実現に踏み出せることになります。

　なお、準備機関の中には「世界連邦運動」やその他世界国家を目指している有力な非政府組織を組み入れることや、それら組織のアイデアを世界国家実現のための総合計画書作成の参考とすることも勧められます。

4　世界国家の樹立への道

　国際連合は主権国家の集まりですから、国際連合からなしくずし的に世界国

家が誕生することはないと考えられます。しかし、このことは世界国家をどうすれば樹立できるかということに大きなヒント（わかり切っていることかもしれませんが）を与えてくれます。つまり、世界国家とは今ある国々の主権が全て国際連合なりに委譲されたときに完成するということになり、その時、国際連合なりが世界国家の政府機関となるということです。

　そうとはいえ、主権国家の主権の全てがある日ある時一斉に委譲されますと世界は機能しなくなり崩壊します。従って、主権の委譲は綿密に計画されそのスケジュールに沿って徐々に委譲して行かなければならないことになります。

　このようなことですから、世界国家へ移行して行くプロセスとは、主権国家の主権を委譲して行くプロセスであると言えます。

　世界国家成立後は世界の全ての個の持つ主権は世界国家に負託されることになり、今ある国々は世界国家の州とか地域とかになります。

5　世界国家の統治

　世界国家の実現については、政経を始め大小様々に色々な問題が湧出することが考えられますが、このことにより、そもそも世界国家などは実現不可能であるという思いも当然に生じるものと予測されます。

　然るに、そうとばかり決めつけることもあるまいとも思われます。発想を転換しさえすれば、そう難しいことではなく、案外簡単なことかもしれないからです。例えば、世界統治とアメリカなりの一国の統治とを比較して考えますと、その内容は本質的には多くが共通しており、単に大小の問題であると考えることもできます。世界国家の初期においても、世界国家移行時に存在していた主権国家の国家機関を世界国家による統治・管理サービスの出先機関とすれば問題なく滑らかな移行が可能になります。ある地域において不満などが生じることがあっても、それは決定された世界国家への移行を前提とした中の問題ですから武力衝突が生じることはありません。そもそも、主な兵器は世界国家への移行決定時にその管理は暫定世界国家に移されていますから、武力衝突は

成立しません。不満は世界の良識・知性・理性に基づき徹底的な対話・議論を通して解決が図られることになりますから、関係者全てに対する解決の妥当性への納得感を可能な限り高くして行くことができることになります。

　このように、世界国家は、"案ずるより生むが易い"と考えることは十分に可能です。そして、そのように考えなければなりません。

6　世界国家に関わるノート

　総合計画書は、上述のように、国連の組織の中で世界の頭脳を集めて作成されるものですから、安心して任せておいて良いことです。余計なことは一切言う必要などないことは承知しておりますが、わかり切っていること、あるいは参考にもならないかもしれない筆者の雑駁な思いを以下に記してみました。

1．平和裏な世界国家への移行

　世界国家とは、この地上に恒久的な平和が実現している世界です。平和のために築こうとしている世界です。従って、この世界に移行するに当たって、争いが生じることがあってはなりません。すなわち、移行は平穏にして流れるように円滑でなければならず、決して革命のような過激なものであってはなりません。いつの間にか世界から争いがなくなり、気が付けば人間界は平和の中にあり、理想的人為環境の要求する最低限を満たし、人類はこの世における理想郷の門内に入っていた、というような移行が望まれます。

2．世界国家への移行時期

　世界国家への移行は一朝一夕には参りませんが、世界に絶えない紛争による人類の不幸や人類滅亡のリスクを考慮しますと、ぐずぐずしていることはできません。筆者の独断と偏見と言うか、希望ではありますが、世界国家が実質的

に完成する時期を2075年頃から遅くとも2100年頃に設定した計画を考えれば
よいのではないかと思います。

3．総合計画書

　総合計画書は2段階に分かれます。前段は世界国家へ至るまでに関係し、後
段は世界国家樹立後に関係することです。すなわち、計画書は世界国家へ向か
う過程とその樹立後に生じて来ると想像される問題を前以て徹底的に把握しそ
の解決策をも組み入れたものでなければなりません。最も大切なことは、誰一
人をも置き去りにせず、人類の一人一人が将来に亘って倦怠に陥ることなく、
やる気（モチベーション）や希望を持てる世界の構築をめざすことにありま
す。

4．世界国家の巨大組織

　世界国家は巨大組織です。組織の規模が有する利権や官僚組織も巨大である
から、これを円滑にかつ申し分なく統治・管理することは著しい困難を伴う、
というように考えられることもあります。さらにまた、巨大権力の偏在が心配
されることもあります。
　しかし、そのようなことを前以て考え、困難を限りなく排除する思想とその
具体的方策が組み入れられたものが世界国家実現のための総合計画書です。世
界の頭脳を集めて徹底的に考えることです。
　巨大組織であるが故に単純に統治・管理が困難であることにはなりません。
規模や数の大小などはコンピューターの発達している世の中ですから如何様に
も解決できることですし、今ある世界に横行している利権や困難な官僚の管理
もチェック・アンド・バランス（checks and balances 抑制と均衡）の手法を徹
底することに加え、さらに高度な思想と手法を導入しなければなりません。
　人間は権力を持ちたがる生命体のようです。人類史上権力の偏在から生じる

不平等や不幸が人間界を覆って来ました。現在においても綺麗に払拭されているわけではなく、少なくない主権国家の中に権力の偏在は存在しています。世界国家の下ではこのようなことが生じないように、今よりさらに優れた統治システムを発明しなければなりません。衆愚政治も困りますが愚かで偏執的な世界総統等絶対に生じることのない統治システムです。もっとも、世界国家の下では国際の存在から生じる紛争・戦争に関わる議題はなくなり、理想郷を益々理想的にするためになす議題しかないことになりますから、意思決定をする議題そのものも主権国家であった時代とは様変わりしています。このような視点からは単独機関である世界総統のような権力一局集中の必要性はなくなり、又そのようにあるべきものでもなく、最高権力は合議機関が把握することが相応しいような気がします。

　何れにしても、権力が偏在せずしかも意思決定が人知を集め正しく公平にかつ速やかに行われるシステムが要求されます。このことも、当然に世界国家総合計画書の中に提案されていなければなりません。人類が今日まで完全なる解決に未だ到達していない権力の偏在しない社会・政治という難しい課題ですが、人類の夢を実現するためのものです。人類の頭脳・英知の限りを絞りつくして考えなければなりません。

5．一変する世界

　国連に世界国家への可能性を追求する準備機関が創設され活動が始まりますと、それだけで世界は一変します。

　押し付けられてどうしようもなく諦めの内に心の中に定着していた「人間界に争いありき」、「核ありき」、「不幸ありき」、「人類滅亡のリスクありき」、「人間とは苦の世界の住人なり」という負のパラダイムが解消され、「平和」、「核のない世界」、「幸福」、「人類の末永い存続」、「理想郷の住人たる可能性」という新しいパラダイムに入れ替わる可能性を見た世界の人々の心は希望に膨らみ丸くなります。

　又、世界国家実現の高い可能性が見て取れれば、今ある主権国家も国際紛争、例えば領土問題などに、偏執的にしゃかりきになることに意味はなくなり紛争の種は減少し軍備もおのずから縮小でき、その分減少する費えは社会福祉の充実など国民の幸福のため、そして自然環境改善の費えに振り替えることができることになります。すなわち、世界国家へ向かう準備期間中にも既に世界は平和と幸福の色に染まる可能性が期待できるということです。

第7章　非現実な希望と非現実な決断

　人類の末永い平和と自由と幸福のために人類の理想郷を建設するという希望、そしてそのための必要条件となる人類滅亡の回避、は現実から見れば遠い非現実です。この非現実を実現するためには、現実を以てしてはその実現は困難です。つまり、非現実の実現は非現実によるしかないということになります。

　その非現実の取っ掛かりに「兵器の廃絶」と「世界国家の樹立」があります。従って、この地上を人類の理想郷とするために、我々には今この非現実の実現に向かう決意と行動が要求されることになります。

　これに対して、理想ではあってもこのような非現実を語ることは、現実を無視した不可能極まりない「たわごと」であるという批判はあるものと思います。しかし、その批判は成立しません。なぜなら、真なる論点は、現実を踏襲すれば人類の滅亡が論理的必然として推論されるのですから、非現実に向かいそれを達成するよりほか人類が助かる道がない、ということにあるからです。つまり、非現実の実現に向かうことは、「できるか、できないか」の問題ではなく、人類の滅亡を回避し、末永い未来に亘る栄光のためには、それ以外の選択肢のない人類に残された唯一の道である、ということです。

1　兵器の廃絶

　国際間には、軍縮という命題が存在していますが、それについて、常時ではありませんが折につけ、話し合いがなされることがあります。

　軍縮は、軍拡よりも望ましく、当然に歓迎されて然るべきものです。

　しかし、軍縮とは矛盾の中に在る概念です。なぜなら、そもそも、軍備とは、実存あるいは仮想敵国に対して軍事力で優位に立とうとするものですか

ら、強力であればあるほど望ましいということが原点であるところ、それを
「ある程度」抑制しようとすることは、この原点とは相容れないからです。に
もかかわらず、軍縮が国際間で語られるのは、際限のない軍拡はその軍事力を
使っての戦争となれば、彼我共に壊滅的な被害が生じること、又、政治的にも
経済的にも困難が伴うことなど様々な負の要素を憂慮してのことにあります。

　それでは、「ある程度の軍縮」とは一体「どの程度」が最適なのでしょう
か？

　それは、際限のない軍拡を止めようとすることが軍縮であることを考えれ
ば、その答えは明白です。すなわち、「際限のない軍拡」の対極にある言葉あ
るいは思想は「際限のない軍縮」ですが、これは「軍事力ゼロ」の状態です。
そうしますと、望まれる軍縮とは、「ある程度」という中途半端なレベルを
云々することではなく、その究極である「軍備の完璧なる廃絶」であるという
認識に至ります。

　兵器のない世界を実現するということは、単に兵器を物理的に排除するとい
うことではありません。もっと大切なことは、心の中から兵器を排除すること
です。人間を殺戮する兵器を作ることが、「人間界至高の理念」に照らして愚
かであることを真に理解しなければなりません。人類は、人間同士で相争い兵
器を作り戦争をしながら、平和と幸福を神に祈るという笑い話のような愚の骨
頂は止しにしなければなりません。そのように迄愚かで身勝手で恥じらいのな
い生命体であっては助かる者も助かりません。

　従って、兵器は核兵器も通常兵器もことごとく廃絶されなければなりません
が、ここでは、まず最初にそして可及的速やかに廃絶されなければならない
「核兵器」についてお話しします。

　核兵器の廃絶の必要性については、先に第3章でその多くを述べている通り
ですが、核は、一瞬にして人類を滅亡させるという意味で、悪の権化であり絶
対悪です。この悪を創造したのはほかでもない人間の愚かさです。その愚かの
産物に固執し「核ありき」の現実の中で核について何を語ろうとも、それは

愚かに輪をかけた愚かになります。特に、「核による核抑止」とか「核の均衡」などは、「思慮深そうな顔で何か深遠なことを言っていると勘違いしている深遠なるただの馬鹿」の宣う愚かの象徴たる思想にすぎません。己で愚かの権化・象徴を創造しておいて、他者も持つそれに脅え悩む日々を過ごすなどは、餓鬼のする喧嘩の有様にも劣ります。アインシュタインの言う「この世には2つの無限がある。1つは宇宙で、もう1つは人間の愚かさである」という言葉さながらのていたらくです。核兵器にまつわる諸々のことを思う時、この言葉の真なることを痛感させられることは悲しいことです。

　従って、核軍縮は中途半端なものではなく、完璧な軍縮すなわち完璧な廃絶でなければなりません。然るに、核が第二次世界大戦の末期に人間界に導入された後、最初に核軍縮が国際間で語られそれが形になったものが1963年に国連で採択された「核拡散防止条約（NPT）」でした。その調印は1968年に、発効は1970年になされています。これは、アメリカ、ソ連、イギリス、フランス、中国（第二次世界大戦の戦勝国で国連常任理事国の5カ国）のみを国際的に認められた「核兵器保有国」として核軍縮義務を規定し、他の「非核兵器保有国」の核兵器保有を禁止し「核は平和利用」に限定するものです。

　しかし、この「核拡散防止条約（NPT）」は必要ではありませんでした。核不拡散の究極は核廃絶です。すなわち、非核保有国に核保有をめざすなというような条約を作ることに換えて、その時核保有国のなすべきであったことは、「我々は核を完璧に廃絶します」という非核保有国に向けて行う宣言でした。その時、人類は核の廃絶を決意し実行するべきでした。しかし、遅きに失したことにはなりません。我々は今議論をこの時点に戻して、改めて核の廃絶を決意し実行しなければなりません。全核保有国が為すべきことは、人類滅亡にもつながる核を導入したことを全非核保有国に謝罪した上で、無条件かつ速やかに核を全て廃棄することです。核は、戦争という目的のはっきりしたものに使用されることはもとより、国際間の誤解、管理上の手違いや精神疾患者などによる事故やテロによっても発動されるリスクがありますから、速やかにして徹底的な廃棄が望まれます。

　第二次世界大戦時及びその後の世界の諸般を考えれば、アメリカでなければどこか他の国により、遅かれ早かれ核が導入されたであろうとは考えられます。しかし、そのような中にあって、最初に世界に先駆けて核をこの世界に持ち込んだのはアメリカであることも事実です。

　人類に対する絶対悪である核兵器絶滅の主旨に基づき、筆者は、先ず皮切りに、この世界に初めて核兵器を持ち込んだアメリカに、世界を主導する大英断をしていただきたいことがあります。下記のような主旨の宣言と実行です。

　アメリカという国の誠実さと勇気に期待してのことです。

（アメリカ合衆国による核兵器廃絶と実行の宣言案 ― 草案）

　我が国は最初に核を保有し使用するに至りました。しかし、人道そして人類の存続という視点からは大変な過ちを犯したと反省しております。従って、我が国は無条件に保有している核を徹底的かつ安全裏に解体して無力化することを宣言し、この宣言を直ちに実行に移します。そして、この実行内容は世界が納得できる検証可能な形でお示し致します。

　我が国が核とその威力を投影した国々も核を保有するという事態を創出したことにつきましては謹んで遺憾を表明致します。願わくは、核保有諸兄国におかれましても我が国に続き保有核の即時撤廃の実行と未来永劫非核の宣言をしていただければ幸いです。この前提に立てば、非核保有諸兄国におかれましても核保有をめざすことの必要性も解消されるものと思料致します。これらのことが実現すれば、我々の世界は核の脅威と核戦争による人類滅亡のリスクから解放されることになります。

　過去につきましては、どの国も様々な言い分のあることは承知しております。過去を変えることはできませんが、未来迄負の過去を引きずることは良くありません。我々人類は今決断することにより、過去の負を断ち切り、新しいパラダイムの未来を築くことができます。全ては我々人類という種の絶滅を回避し、この地上すなわちこの宇宙船地球号の中にこの世における我々人類の理

想郷を築くという栄光に輝く未来のためです。

　全世界の全ての国におかれましては、この思想とその実践によろしくご賛同賜りますようお願い申し上げる次第です。

　アメリカ主導により、まずは、核拡散防止条約（NPT）で核兵器保有国として国際的に認められている五核大国（アメリカ、ロシア、中国、イギリス、フランス）に核廃絶の決断と実行とをしていただくことが最重要になります。「核ありき」の現実、それも人間自身の創造による愚かな現実、を支払うという非現実を以て、非現実である人類の末永き未来に亘る栄光の実現につながる買い物をするのですから高い買い物ではありません。ただの石くれでダイヤモンドを買うようなものです。

2　世界国家への移行

　さて、兵器の廃絶について理屈は上記のようなことであっても、現実に基づけば、反論はあるものと承知しています。

　国際間に緊張が存在し不穏になると、自国（あるいは同盟・連合しているグループ）を守るため、防衛力すなわち軍備の強化を図ることになるのは、目の前の現実への対応としては、仕方がないと言えば仕方がありません。此方に他国を侵略する意図がなくても、他国から一方的に力を以て侵攻されれば、念仏を唱えているわけにはいかず、力を以て防衛を図らなければなりません。

　しかし、このような人間同士の争う際限のない負のスパイラルの行き着く先はどのようになるのでしょうか。際限なく発達する科学を悪用した際限のない強力な兵器を使用しての戦争は人類の滅亡でしかありません。

　人間の統べる人間界にあって、このような人間の幸福に矛盾することが生じるのは、やはり、必然的に争いを創造する主権国家の存在にあることは明らかです。従って、我々は、この国際主義の世界から、世界主義に基づく、敵対国の存在しない、世界国家へ向かうべきという理になります。

　この基本的認識に基づき、国連の常任理事国でもあるこの5カ国にお願いしたいもう一つの非現実があります。それは、この5カ国が国連に連名で国連の中に「世界国家へ向かう準備研究機関の創設」を提案していただくことです。

「核の廃棄と世界国家へ向かうこと」で人類は救われ、平和と幸福と理想郷の住人となることが約束されることになります。我々自身がそう決断すればできることです。

3　地上の理想郷

「人類は、末永い平和と幸福のために、人類同士で、争わない、過去も現在も無条件に許し合う、敬愛と融和の関係に昇華する、思いやる、分かち合う、愛し合う、この宇宙船地球号の中で仲良くし、その自然の保全・修復・改善に協力一致することに我々人類の全エネルギーを注ぎ込むことを宣言し、実践する」

　この一つの文章でカバーできることができさえすれば、人類は幸福になれるのです。たったこれだけのことができないがために、人類は、憎み合い殺し合って不幸の中にあり、絶えざる争いと科学の厄災化により、滅亡のリスクの淵に立たされています。この「宣言と実践」への志向が全人類一人一人の心の中にその実現可能性への望みと共に芽生え定着すれば、人類の愚かさの象徴である全ての軍隊と兵器は不要となり、人間界から消滅します。

　たった一つの短い文章で表現できることが実行できないがために、人類は不幸の内に滅亡するのでしょうか？

　人類の存続と平和や幸福という観点に立てば、この一つの文章が表現していることは、神、聖、宗教、美徳などを介して語られるべきものではなく、人間が為さねばならない当然のことです。その当然のことについて、それは現実を認識できていない非現実な戯言であるなどの批判は論点を理解していないがゆえに無用です。なぜなら、現実を踏襲して行けば人類は近未来に滅亡するとい

う推論と確信に基づき、非現実を行わなければ人類は助からないというのが主張点だからです。つまり、我々人類は今ある現実を踏襲して滅亡することを受け容れるか、それとも精神のパラダイムを入れ替えてこの現実から離脱し非現実に向かいそれを実現して平和と幸福という未来の栄光をめざすのか、そのどちらを選択するのか、ということが論点であるということです。

　人類の未来をどうするのか、というのが問いかけです。戯れ事では済まされません。ああだこうだと御託を並べているだけでは何の役にも立ちません。選択をして実行するのは神でも仏でも宗教でもありません。我々人間自身です。

　トマス・ホッブス（17世紀のイギリスの哲学者）は「人間の自然状態は、万人が富や権力を求めて戦う戦争状態である」という見方をしていますが、仮にこの見方が正鵠を得ているとしても、人類を絶滅する兵器を製造できる科学の発達という条件が登場した今、我々はホッブスの言う人間の自然状態のままでいることはできません。争い戦えば人類は絶滅するからです。我々が「平和と幸福に包まれて末永く存続することを希望する生命体である」ということであるならば、我々は賢に就き知恵により、ホッブスの言う「自然状態」から脱却しなければなりません。争わないために我々に課せられる必要最小限の要求は、争いの三大根源を断つこと、すなわち、敵対国家の存在しない世界国家をめざすことに加え、争いを創造する宗教をそして又人種・民族の差別を去ること、にあります。

　神仮説に基づき、穿った見方をすれば、神は「人間の自然状態と科学の発達とのセット」という障害物を設けて、人類がこの試練を乗り越えて自らの絶滅を回避し、平和と理想郷と幸福を手にすることができるかを試されておられるのやもしれません。そうであれば、我々は神にも負けてはなりません。

　人間は、闘争と博愛という対立する遺伝子を持っているようですが、人間性が志向する幸福の概念である「人間界至高の理念」の実現をめざすのであれば、理性の働きにより、争い殺すことよりも許し助け合う遺伝子の方を発動するよう心掛けねばなりません。闘争の遺伝子は、対人間に向けて発動するのではなく、この世に理想郷を築くためにいかなる難関をも克服するという難関突

破の闘争のために発動されるべきことになります。

　人間界から争いが消え平和でありさえすれば、人類は思いのままに幸福になることができます。争いのために費やされていた計り知れない物心両面のエネルギーの全てはこの地上、宇宙船地球号の中、にこの世における理想郷を築くために充当することができます。理想郷の二つの条件である自然環境と人為環境を我々の望むように磨き上げて行くことが可能になり容易になるということです。

　宗教は来世にあるという天国・楽園・浄土（極楽等）を説き、来世のためにこの世のことが大事であると説きます。然るに、来世の「あるなし」もそのような「素晴らしい世界」の「あるなし」も不明です。対して、この世の存在は現実として認識されていますから、この世のことは多少はわかります。従って、我々にとって、根拠のないあの世ではなく、この世のことがより大事であることは明白です。従って、我々の心身の重心は来世に置くのではなく、この世である現世に置かなければならないのは当然のことです。

　本書において筆者は今ある世界が愚かであることを強調して来ましたが、それは筆者の本意ではありません。今ある世界は、遺憾にも数多の犠牲を伴う試行錯誤という高い授業料を払ってようやく到達した世界ですが、今ある愚かという曇りを拭い取りさえすれば、科学の発達という恩恵も寄与している素晴らしく輝く夢の世界、すなわち理想郷、の姿が現れる原石の世界です。理想郷のそばにいながら、少しの愚かのために理想郷に入れないもどかしさのため、愚かを強調することになりましたが、人類の創造による原石はその曇りが拭い去られる時を待ちに待っています。

　平和を実現して、この世に理想郷を築き、我々人類はこの世における幸福という栄光をめざして行きたいものです。

　今、我々は、グローバルな視点に立ち、地球全域を 1 つの場所そして全人類を一つの種族と考え、全人類の平和、健全な生活の充足と幸福を図らなければならない時にあります。それは、国際連合教育科学文化機関憲章の宣言内容や17の重要な目標を持ついわゆる持続可能な開発目標（SDGs, Sustainable

Development Goals）の充実を通して、人類の総幸福（GHH, Gross Humanity Happiness）の指標を上げていくことをめざさなければならないということです。従って、それに逆行する小部屋単位の視点に立つ狭量で愚かな思想は世界から排除しなければなりません。そもそも、自国さえ良ければそれで良い、という他を等閑にする思想こそが人間界に争いを創造し、これ迄人類は幸福ではなく不幸の中にあったことに思いを致さなければなりません。

　人類は愚かであってはなりません。賢くあることです。仮に神仏が存在し人類を見守って下さるものとしても、人類の賢さこそは人類の望むものを確実に人類にもたらします。つまり、何もかも全てのことは人類の心の持ち方次第であるということになります。人類の心の持ち方次第でこの世はどのようにも変えられます。理想郷の構築などは、人類が今日その決断をすれば、明日にも実現可能となるものです。

　　為せば成る　為さねば成らぬ　何事も　成らぬは人の　為さぬなりけり
　　　　　　　　「上杉鷹山（江戸時代米沢藩主）」

　　神が存在するならば、「君たちにできるかな」
　　と微笑まれておられるかもしれません。

あとがき

　本書を書いていた途中においても、書いた後においても、筆者が自問していることがあります。それは、「本書により、私は何か特別に高邁な理論やあるいは難解な問題についての解を著したのか？」ということです。

　なぜなら、本書で語っていることは、そのようなことには関係なく又一冊の書として著す程のことではない「わかり切ったこと」でしかないからです。すなわち、本書の要点は、「全人類は争いを止め、仲良くし、平和に、自由にそして幸福になりましょう。その希望を成就するため、人類は地球人という一つの種族となり、人間界から軍隊や兵器を消滅し、地球国という世界国家を樹立し、この地上に理想郷を築き、末永き未来に亘る栄光をめざしましょう」という、万人に明々白々なそして小学生の子供にも言えることでしかないからです。

　ところで、数学であろうと何であろうと、問題を解くためには「究極・極限」を考えれば、その解が容易に得られる場合があります。例えば、平和であるためには、争いを創出しているメカニズムの中枢にある数多の主権国家を解消して統合し（融合し）、地球上に一つしかない世界国家という敵対国の存在しない究極の形をめざせば良い、という解に容易に到達できることになります。これは、論理的に揺るぎのない簡明な解です。

　さて、実は、世界国家や世界主義（コスモポリタニズム）という思想は古代（紀元前4世紀末のギリシャ哲学）からあるものです。辞書には、世界国家とは「各国の主権を制限して世界全体を単一の国家に組織しようとする理想。世界連邦・世界政府ともいう」と、又世界主義とは「国家や民族を超越して、全人類を同胞と見なし、世界社会を実現しようとする思想。世界市民主義」と、解説されています。

　主権国家が数多既存している世界においては、平和のためには国家相互の協調を本位とする国際主義を採らざるを得ませんが、世界主義に基づく世界国家

に敵対国は存在しませんから、自動的に恒久的平和が約束されています。対して、幾らそしてどのように議論をしても努力を重ねても、国際主義から恒久的な平和が人間界に訪れることはありません。なぜなら、主権国家は、領土や経済などの利害紛争から戦争という命題を必然的に具有することになりますから、そもそも理屈の上からは恒久的な平和とは無縁のものです。言ってみれば、人類は2000年あまり前から人類が向かうべきは世界国家であることを理解していたにもかかわらず、現実に流れそこから一歩も進歩せず、未だに戦争と不幸を創造する主権国家に連綿としがみつくという愚かを実践していることになります。科学文明が格段の進歩を遂げているにもかかわらず、精神文明は2000年あまり前からさして進歩せず昔のままにあるということになります。

　このようなことですから、世界国家は「たわごと」と軽々に片づけられることではありません。小学生にも「わかっていること」に何千年も「挑戦していない愚かと怠惰」を反省しなければなりません。

　なお、世界国家への移行につきましては、たとえ世界がそれに向かって今すぐには行動を開始することがないとしても、数多の人がその主権の委託先は現存する主権国家よりも世界国家の方が望ましいとあらためて気づいてくださることがあれば、本書を著した多少の価値はあるように思います。又、たとえ今しばらくは数多の主権国家の存在する世界にあるとしても、その「気づき」が、国々の争いが人類の希望に照らせば愚かであるという認識をあらためて形成し、今より少しは争いの形を柔和で思いやりがありそして愛情のあるものに変えて行く「よすが」になるのでは、という風に期待したいと思います。

　全人類が仲良くしている人為環境と全ての生物の喜びである自然環境の実現をめざし、この地上に人類の理想郷を築きましょう。

2023年春

　　　　　　　　　　　　　　　　　　　　　　　　筆者

付録：本文中の思想及び用語の解説

　この付録は、本文に言及されている筆者の思想や用語の内必要と思われる項目について解説しているものです。これらは、本書の母体書「神からの自立、Independence from God」および／又は「神と宗教を考える、Thinking of God and Religion」に詳細ですが、本書をお読みいただく際に、それらを参照せずに済むように、一応概略的な解説を添付してあるものです。

1　主権国家を除く争いの二大根源

　二大根源とは、１．宗教、と２．人種・民族の差別、のことです。

１．宗教

(1) 宗教は虚構なるシステム（系）

　あるシステム（系）が成立するためには、①システムの中に証明不能（真偽や存否が不明）の構成要素が入っていないこと、②システムの中の構成要素間に矛盾がないこと、これら２つの条件が満たされなければなりません。

　この視点から宗教を見ますと、宗教は理屈の上では正しく成立していないシステムであることになります。すなわち、宗教の構成要素については、神をはじめ、その多くが存否や真偽不明ですから、条件①が満たされておらず、また宗教の聖典の中に矛盾のない聖典は存在しませんから条件②も満たされておりません。つまり、宗教は虚構です。

(2) かりそめのシステムとしての宗教

　人類の誕生以来、小集団や小部族に始まる切り取り次第という混沌の中において、秩序や安心を求める人心が高じた黎明期（相当長い期間ですが）の人間界に数多の創唱宗教が漸次導入されています。神や仏という絶対者の概念を組み入れて構成された宗教は、虚構といえども、強制的行動規範により人間界に秩序を、又人心にこの世やあの世に対する心のより所を得たという安心をもたらしました。この意味において宗教は人間界に一応の功績を残したということは認知できます。

　然るに、宗教の実体は虚構が変貌した妄想ですから、これはあくまで人間界の黎明期に現れ、とりあえずの効果をもたらしたかりそめのシステムとして見るべきものであり、人間界を長きに亘って導く本道のシステムではありません。

　一方、宗教の対象としているこの世における我々人間は、仮の自我でしかない自我を持ち、一瞬も止まることなく移ろい行き、己を己のものとすることもできぬ夢幻のごとき実在者です。そうしますと、宗教の妄想と人間の夢幻という組み合わせもまんざら釣り合いが取れていないとも言えず、ならば、「堅苦しい理屈など云々する程のことに非ず、妄想で結構、我々夢幻は妄想と仲良くし楽しく生きるのも一興」という考え方があってもおかしくはありません。そのような考えも然るべきなのかもしれません。但し、それには、少なくとも、宗教という妄想が人間界における秩序と安心を恒久的かつ平穏裏に維持できるのであれば、という条件が満たされる必要があります。しかしながら、我々が妄想を真実と見せなければならない必然性を帯びる宗教と反省なく安易に楽しんでいますと、宗教がもたらす理不尽や宗教間・宗派間に生ずる争い、そしてそれらに由来する様々な負の出来事が人間界に湧出し、宗教を通して得ようとした秩序と安心は人間界から消滅し、宗教の存在そのものが人間界に不幸をもたらす結果を招来することになります。これは歴史によりもう十分に証明されています。

　宗教が妄想であるといえども、人間界の平和と幸福を志向し実践する存在であれば、「妄想も方便」で済ませることもできないことではありません。しかし、宗教は、自由ではなく自由の束縛を、平和ではなく争いを、幸福ではなく不幸を、さらに人類滅亡のリスク迄をももたらすモンスターに変貌しています。ここに至り、我々人類は神・宗教から卒業しなければならない時を迎えることになりました。

⑶ 宗教の真相

　宇宙及び万物（宇宙万物）の生成のように、今現在人知の限界を超えた「わからない」ことを、我々人間がそう定義した「宇宙万物を創造した全知全能にして完全な系」という神の御業ということにしても、それで「わからない」ことが解明されたことにはなりません。

　そうすることで「わかった」ことは、「そのような属性の神という者であれば、宇宙万物の生成自体も可能であり、その生成経緯も動きもわかっている」ということが「わかった」にすぎません。すなわち、神には「わかっている」が我々には「わからない」ことは、神観念を持つ前も後も何も変わらず元のままにあるということです。つまり、我々人間は「わからない」ことを解明するために、神という者に思い及びましたが、神はその解明には何の役にも立っていないことになります。従って、我々は神に頼ることは勿論、神を語るという空虚にして無意味なことは差し控えなくてはならないという認識に至ります。

　このような中、我々は神の存否を議論しています。然るに、今現在、神の存否は不明です。にもかかわらず、神の宗教は神の存在を前提として構築されています。さらに、神は存在するという神仮説によっても神の言葉（啓示、預言、教え）は存在しませんから、神と宗教が密接な関係にあるという構成は、神が存在しない場合は言う迄もないことですが、存在するとしても虚構になります（後出2-05にその証明）。つまり、神と宗教は無関係な関係にあるということです。従って、宗教の聖典・教説は神の言葉で成っているものではなく、

人間の考案による人間の言葉であるというのが真相になります。これにより、先ず最初に、宗教の教説の中で「神を信仰しなければならない」などを含む神に関わる一切の教説は、その根拠を失い破綻し、無効なものであることがはっきりします。

　その上に、神の宗教も神観念のない宗教も、神のほかにも証明不能や偽りの要素で構築されていますから、全ての宗教は虚構です。証明不要の要素とは、天国・楽園・浄土、地獄、過去世・未来世、終末論、魂の不死、輪廻転生などを含みますが、これらは完全情報領域に属することですから、部分情報の所有者でしかない我々人間にはその真偽・存否は不明のものです。又、理屈上は成立しない偽りの要素には原罪（後出2-06）などがあります。このように、宗教の構成要素に採用されている要素はいわゆる系というものが有効に成立するための条件を満たしていませんから、全ての宗教は幾重にも虚構であることになります。

　然るに、宗教を虚構と認識した上で、それも又面白いという遊び心にあるのであれば、それはそれで非難することでもありません。なぜなら、人間は空想・想像する（できる）能力を持ちますが、人間という生命体を無条件に肯定するのは当然という視点に立てば、空想もそれから生み出される虚構も一概に否定するべきものではないからです。空想も虚構もそれ自体は愛らしいものです。しかしながら、虚構を真理・真実と主張するに及べば、虚構は妄想に変貌します。妄想とは「明らかな反証があるにもかかわらず、誤った揺るぎない信念を持ち続けることで、特に精神障害の症候」という定義を持つものです。宗教は、虚構を真理・真実と妄言していますから、妄想の系であるということになります。

　一方、このような議論に対し、「神や宗教は信じるものであり、理性で割り切れるものではない」という反論はあるものと思います。しかし、長方形の縦と横の関係など安定した美感を与える比とされる黄金分割は幾何学の言葉ですし、美しい音楽のハーモニー（調和）も元々数学の用語です。理性の代表格である幾何学や数学が感性や愛と相容れないということはありません。この点に

つきましては、理性と感性や愛は同一の精神作用であるという考え方もあります。従って、理性と信仰は全く別ものという反論は当たっていないことになります。宗教も信仰も知性や理性を超越して存在できるものではありません。正しい論理に悖る説や系は人間・人間界をミスリード（誤指導）することになります。

　さて、宗教が虚構であり妄想であると言っても、その教説が人間という生命体に調和するものであれば、宗教の名の下で語られているとしてもそのことは度外視して、その教説に沿うことは悪いことではありません。元々、人間の言葉なのですから、是々非々の姿勢で対していればいいことです。然るに、宗教の教説は、人間という生命体とそれに由来する「人間界至高の理念」に調和せず矛盾する多くの教説を含んでいます。それらは、無用な戒律であり（後出2–07）、人間には至宝である煩悩に負のイメージを持たせていることや（後出2–08）、神に基礎づけられたとされる存在しない最高善（後出2–09）などが含まれます。

　このように、宗教というものは、神の宗教であれ神観念のない仏教であれ、その造りは虚構にして妄想であることのみならず、その教説も人間という生命体に調和している系でないことは明らかです。なお一層悪いことには、人間界に数多存在する宗教は、人間に対しては、その妄想に従わない者を脅迫・強迫し、司法権を帯びている根拠などないにもかかわらず、理不尽にも妄想により裁き罰するという神をも畏れぬ極悪非道・悪逆無道を為し、宗教間・宗派間では妄想の僅かな違いを言い募り、聖とは真逆の血で血を洗う争いを為しその反省は無く、人間・人間界を幸福にしないばかりか不幸にし、さらに人類滅亡のリスク因子の一つとなる事態迄をも招来しています。

⑷ 神と宗教からの自立

　我々人類はこの宇宙にあって一瞬の光芒でしかない夢幻と言うべき存在ですが、無垢にして何者からも自由であり、生ある限り幸福を希望し追求する生命

体です。神も宗教も、その我々が発明したものですが、神の存否は不明であり、宗教は妄想の系でしかありませんから、それらに固執することは適切なことではありません。従って、我々は、末永い未来に亘る栄光のためには、宗教に勝たなければならない、そして、この妄想の系から自らを解放しなければならない、という理になります。つまり、人類は虚構や妄想に基づく偽りの幸福から離れ、知的生命体としての真実の幸福に向かわなければならない、ということです。

　この宗教信仰に対しては、「もし宗教さえなければ、この世界は、およそ考えられるあらゆる世界のなかで最善のものであったであろう」というアメリカ合衆国第2代大統領ジョン・アダムズ、John Adams、の見識もあります（神は妄想である、リチャード・ドーキンス著　垂水雄二訳　早川書房　2013年）。

　しかし、宗教が虚構であると言っても、それを妄想とせず虚構として楽しみ、人類全ての個を無条件に無限大の愛や慈悲で包み込むという理念を持ちそれを実践できるものであるならば、宗教と呼ぼうと何と呼ぼうと、人間界に存在している価値はあります。従って、全ての宗教／宗教者にはこの視点に立ち自宗を省みてこの理念に沿うことが可能かどうかを再検討していただく必要があります。すなわち、人には愛のみを以て接し、他宗との争いはせず、そして世界を平穏に保つことを至高の理念として持つ宗教として存続するか、それとも、それはできないということであれば、宗教を卒業・離脱するかということです。この再検討こそは「真の宗教者」であることの責務であり証となります。

　人間の幸福が、「宇宙観、人間という生命体、そして人間界の実生活」、に安心が持てることにその基盤があるとしますと、現存する宗教のパラダイムは遺憾ながらこの要求に応じているとは言えません。人間が安心を持てるパラダイムとは、例えば、「現象の原理に拠る宇宙観」（後出2-04）であり、人間という生命体の運命を含む全ての生得への積極的な肯定観念であり、人間界の実生活は人間の努力次第で望むように改善できるという認識にあります。人間の幸福は悪しき作用を人間界にもたらす宗教に頼ることなく、あらためて人間自身で

作り出さなければならないということです。

「神と宗教からの自立」が、人類の未来の栄光をめざして、人間界に普遍なる究極的理念として存在していることが要請されます。人類は、虚構や妄想に閉じこもり凝り固まることなく、躍動する無心にして自由自在な精神で以て、「宇宙に冠たる知的生命体」をめざし進歩・進化して行く未来を開かなくてはなりません。

なお、宗教とは、既存宗教のみならず、未来に生ずる新宗教をも含める一切の宗教を意味するものとします。未来に導入されるどんな宗教も既存の宗教とのハイブリッド（混成・雑種）として生ずるという前提に立てば、既存宗教と新宗教に本質的な区別は生じないというのがその理由です。

イエスや釈迦が説く世界を離れて
それを超えて
存在するかもしれない宇宙人にも負けない
高い精神世界を持つ
宇宙に冠たる知的生命体をめざして

人は、戸を閉め暗い部屋にこもり宗教という妄想のキャンドルを灯して暮らすよりも、戸を開き外へ出て、すがすがしい大気、明るい太陽光と青空の中で、神にも仏にも宗教にも頼ることのない躍動する自由自在な精神、無心な姿勢と矜持を湛えた人であること、この栄光の中へ自らを解放しなければなりません。

2．人種・民族の差別

人種・民族の差別は言うに及ばず、そもそも人が人を差別することに理知的な根拠は存在しません。このような差別をすることに拘泥し執着している人は、精神が未発達でおかしな愚か者という評価以外の評価はありません。人

間界には、滅亡を回避しての人類の存続、そして平和や自由の中での幸福という希望の実現のために心配し克服しなければならないことが数限りなくあります。

このような中にあって、人が人を差別して争いを起こすなどという情けないことから人類はもう卒業しなければなりません。代えて、人は敬愛と融和の関係に昇華するべく精神を鍛錬し、人にやさしく楽しい人の世にしなければなりません。

(1) 人種差別（カントやヒュームの場合）

哲学者カントは、その人種論において、同じ哲学者であるヒュームの「アフリカ黒人は、本性上、子供っぽさを超える如何なる感情も持っていない。その心の能力においても、白人と黒人の間には肌の色と同じほど本質的な差異がある」という主張に同調するなどをし、白人優位説を展開しています。これにより、カントは白人至上主義の父祖の一人とみなされています。（以上、フリー百科事典ウィキペディアから）

然るに、現在においてさえ、人種間の優劣を判定できる普遍妥当なチェックリストなど存在しません。最先端の様々な分野の知識を駆使できる現在の環境に比べれば、人種間の優劣を考えるための資料などないに等しい当時にあって、カントもヒュームも自身で徹底研究したわけでもなく伝聞や当時の少なく幼い文献等により、黒人に対してそのような断定的認識を不用意にも披露していることは、特に両者が哲学者であることを考慮しますと、許されることではありません。哲学者であれば、人種間優劣の存在というような命題を結論するためには、そのための知識と情報が必要にして十分かどうかを吟味してかからなければなりませんが、両者はそれを怠っています。これは、現在においてさえ人種間に優劣が存在するという証拠は発見されてはいないということを以てその根拠とします。

従って、少なくともこの点に限れば、両者共に自身も子供っぽさを超える如

何なる知性も持っておらぬ哲学者失格であった、と批判されても仕方がないと言わざるをえないことになります。

　然るに、カントは現代の国際的な自由主義への多大な貢献者であり、ヒュームは奴隷制度に反対の立場の者であったことを考えますと、人種についての認識不足はあったものの、両者共に博愛主義者であったことは確かなようです。

(2) 肌の色

　筆者が米国で学生の頃、社会科学であったかの教授から、"ある白人の研究者が「白人が他の肌の色の人種よりさまざまな点で優れている」という結論を得たいと願い、研究に研究を重ねたが、どのような観点からも、肌の色の違いにより優劣を云々するどんな証拠も得ることができなかった"という話を聞いたことがありました。

　話は変わりますが、米国で生まれ世界に配信されている「スタートレック」という人気 SF テレビ番組の中のお話です。

　地球人とバルカン星人らからなる地球連合隊が「エンタープライズ」という名の宇宙船で太陽系外のある惑星を探査した際、その惑星の住人の二大勢力が互いに軽蔑し憎み合い、相手方を抹殺すべく争っていました。連合隊には、なぜ軽蔑し憎み合わなければならないのかわかりませんでしたので、その理由を一方の勢力の住人に聞いてみたところ、その住人曰く「我が惑星の住人の顔は鼻を中心にして顔の左右半分が白黒に塗り分けられているが、私の顔の右側は黒いのに対し、彼ら（他方の勢力）の右側は白いではないか。あなた方連合隊の目は節穴か」ということでした。

　この話を我々人類は「なにを愚かなことを」、と笑うことができるでしょうか。

　（なお、この物語の顛末は、対話を勧める連合隊に対し、「過去から累積したどうしようもない憎しみのため、対話で理解・和解し許し合うことなど、惑星の軌道を変えるよりも難しい」ということで、結局両勢力共に一人を残して絶

滅します。最後に残った二人をエンタープライズに迎え入れ、せめてこのエンタープライズの中で仲良く暮らすようにとの説得にもかかわらず、二人は転送装置で再びこの惑星に下り立ちます。宇宙にあるエンタープライズから確認できたことは、この惑星上で二つの生命体が死闘を演じ共倒れになるという結末でした）

　我々人類はもともと黒人種としてアフリカに発生し、中近東からヨーロッパに拡がり白人種となり、以後さらにまた中近東へ入り黄色人種となったという説があるようです。黒人が白人になったのは、黒人の中で突然変異により白い肌になった白子が差別され北方へ追いやられたという説や、太陽光の弱い北方へ移動した黒人種がメラニン色素の関係で白く変わって行ったという説もあり、またそれらの双方が絡み合い白人種や黄色人種などの発生に寄与したものかもしれません。

　そのようなことはさておいても、何れにしても、肌の色で差別することに理知的な根拠を見出すのは困難です。考えてもみてください。およそ色（カラー）というものについて黒、白、黄、およびそれらの中間色あるいは他の色も含めて、どの色がきれいでどの色がそうではないなどということはない筈です。黒い色の服、白い色の服、黄色い色の服、それらの中間色の服、その他の色の服にしても、どの服が美しくどの服がそうではないなどということは、同じ人種の中でさえ普遍性はありません。

　色即是空の色でもない、色恋沙汰の色でもない、色彩の色のことです。この色彩の色はどの色も全て肯定するべきものであり、それ以外の見方はありません。

　肌の色などにわけもわからず固執し差別意識を持つなどは、己の精神の未発達と愚かさを世に公開している風景の最たるものというほかありません。

(3) 人種・民族差別

　人間とは自己を客観的に評価することに弱い存在のようです。

　自民族から他民族を見て、変な言葉を話す、変な文字を使う、変なものを食べる、変なものを着ている、その他諸々の変な文化を持つ、ということで、他民族を自民族より下に見て、軽蔑したり侮蔑したりします。この場合、他民族から自民族を見るとどう見えるのか、という客観的視点からの評価は全く欠落しています。一度、この点に思いを致せば、自民族が他民族を評価したと同じことが他民族により自民族に下されていることに思い至る筈です。お互い様なのです。

　文化・文明の善し悪しや高さや低さに絶対性はありませんから、どの文化・文明が優れているとか劣っているとかの普遍的な判断を下すことはできません。それを愚かにも、自民族の文化・文明を優位と見て、他民族を偏見し蔑視するなどは笑止千万というほかありません。人間には、自己と自己にまつわる事柄に、他に対してわずかな違いの優位性を妄想しその妄想に溶け込み満悦するという変な性向があるようです。フロイト（オーストリアの精神医学者）流では、「僅かな違いのナルシシズム（自己愛や自己陶酔）」ということになるのでしょうか。

　我々はある人種・民族であることに誇りを持つのはいいことです。しかし、そうであれば、他人種・他民族の誇りも尊重しなければならないのは当然のことです。尊重し合うことからは争いは生じません。生じるのは敬愛と融和でしかありません。

　我々人類が自身の属する人種・民族に生を受けているのは自身の力でも選択の結果でもありません。つまり、なぜその人種・民族に生を受けているのかに関わっているわけではありません。我々は自身がこの宇宙にあって何者であり何処から来て何処へ行くのかも知らず、自身についてさえ何も知らない無知な存在です。気が付けば、私はたまたまここにいた、という存在にすぎません。従って、どの個も自身の属する人種・民族について驕ったりその逆に卑下したりする立場にないことは明らかです。然るに、そのような者同士が、お互いに軽んじ合い迫害し合い、挙句の果てに殺害し合うこと迄起こっている現実を見ますと、人類が愚かな生命体に見えることこれ以上の悲しみはありません。

我々人類はその一人一人が、自身は一体何様なのか、そんなに偉いのか、そんなに劣っているのかなどについて、自身の心に問う内省をしなければなりません。人種・民族間に持って生まれた知能に差はないようですし、文化・文明については絶対的優劣はつけられないというのが一般的認識です。百歩譲って、人種・民族の間に知能にも文化・文明にも何らかの差があるものと仮定してみます。その差とは一体どのようなものでしょうか。全知全能の高みから見れば、その差なるものは、遥か下方地上すれすれに拡がる同一平面上に存在していて、特に問題とするような差など認識できないということになるに違いありません。

　ヒットラーのような、内省なきがゆえに、無知の自覚が欠落していたとしか考えられない無知なる者、そして無知なるがゆえに愚かの自覚も欠落していてその結果愚かで傲慢の権化を実践するに及んだ者、このようなたった一人の愚か者によって何百万人以上ものユダヤ人やロシア人が虐殺・抹殺されるという悲惨な事態が生じてしまいました。愚かであることは人類に不幸をもたらす重大事なのです。人類は愚かな偏見から卒業しなければなりません。

　人種・民族差別よりもほかの様々な要素により、人類が滅亡の瀬戸際に立たされている今この時に、人間同士で争うこのような「愚かな贅沢」など許されることではありません。

⑷　人種・民族→争いから敬愛と融和の主体へ昇華

　現状、人種・民族は人間界に争いを創造する主な主体の一つになっています。

　然るに、争いの主体と言っても、争う理由を帯びてこの世に存在するに至っているわけではありません。どの人種・民族も分け隔てなく無垢で自由な存在として生を受けています。それを争いの主体にしているのはほかでもない我々人種・民族同士そのものであることは、人類の今ある愚かさであり、残念なことです。従って、人間界から追放するべきは当然にどの人種・民族なのかとい

うようなことではなく、人間の愚かさなのです。人間界からこの愚かさが消滅すれば、人種・民族は争うことはなく敬愛し合い融和する主体に昇華します。

　過去における数多の争いで多くの恨みや憎しみが存在していることは事実です。しかし、無条件に（大切です）過去を許し合うことです。許し合うことで過去を変えることはできませんが、未来は変えられます。許し合うことがなければ、恨みも憎しみもそして争いも未来永劫人類滅亡の時迄絶えることなく継続します。人類滅亡をもたらす誘因にさえなります。許せない過去なのかもしれません。しかし、許せない過去であるからこそ今無条件に許し合わなくてはなりません。許せない過去を引きずり、未来における許せない過去を今から新たに増産してはならないからです。我々は未来を過去に支配されるような「愚か」は断たなければなりません。過去を許し合い、未来における人種・民族間の融和と人類の栄光を志向するべきです。

　なお、この許し合うという思想は人種・民族に限ったことではなく、宗教間あるいは又国家間においても同様に大切です。

　さて、このように許し合うことや武力を行使しての争いはしないなどは言うに易く実践不可能な机上の空論にすぎないのでしょうか？　そうではありません。つい最近の人類史において少なくとも二つの実践例を挙げることができます。

　南アフリカ連邦下において黒人の主権を主張して自らも28年間も牢獄に閉じ込められていたマンデラ元大統領が大統領に選任され、南アフリカ共和国に生まれ変わった際、マンデラ元大統領は過去の弾圧と投獄・虐殺等あらゆる非人間的な黒人差別の怨念と憎しみの過去を徹底的に許す政策を実行し融和の道を選択しています。又、インド独立の父マハトマ・ガンジーは武力による争いは一切行わず、徹底的な非暴力主義の中に不服従の抵抗主義で以て大英帝国の支配を終わらせています。

　武力では何事も最終解決に至ることはありません。それは対話によりお互いが心から納得する以外に得られるものではありません。それが人間の性だからです。

教育の場において歴史を教えることは必要です。しかし、それは人種・民族、宗教、国家が過去に為しあるいは為された悪行を飾ることなく記録することのみで十分であるということにはなりません。悪行を教えることで、それを反面教師として、人類の幸福と存続のために過去を許し合う理屈と寛容を教えるものでなければなりません。

2　様々な思想及び用語

01　人間界至高の理念

　我々人間は、「我々は何処から来て何処へ行くのか、我々が此処に存在している理由は何か、そして、我々は何者なのか？」という我々に関わる根幹的な問いに答えることができないでいます。すなわち、我々は無知で卑小な存在です。

　然るに、我々人間が採らざるを得ない主義は、神第1主義でもなく、神と共にあるという宗教第1主義でもありません。それは人間第1主義です。これは3つの主義を比べてその好き嫌いを言っているのではありません。又、人間第1主義をひいきにしているわけでもありません。理屈上正しく成立しているのは人間第1主義のみだからです。このことは神仮説に基づき神が人間を創造したと仮定しても、やはり変わることはありません。これは下記の「(1) 人類という生命体の性質」の中の「(09) 最高位者は人間自身である」に記述してある通りです。

　我々が何者であろうとも、人間という生命体を自ら否定することはできません。喜ばしくも、無条件で100％肯定しなければならないのは当然のことです。従って、全ての思考の原点はこの点にあります。人間を離れて、人間の外にある何かが原点にあるのではありません。

(1) 人類という生命体の性質

　我々人類は、我々自身を、そして我々自身の性質を無条件に認め受け容れなければなりません。なぜなら、我々が我々自身を否定することなどできないからです。我々人類の性質とは、下記を含みます。

(01) 星の欠片の物質でできている炭素ベースの生命体・小宇宙である。

(02) 生・老・病・死する生命体である。

(03) 生命と健康を保つため、他の動物や植物そしてミネラルを食し摂取する。

(04) 生命を守り、そして種を守るため生殖行為を為す。

(05) 利己的な本能を持つ。

(06) 五官を有する肉体を持ち、それにまつわる欲望や煩悩を持つ。

(07) 無垢にして、何者からも自由な存在として生を受けている。

(08) 平和と自由と幸福を希望する。

(09) 最高位者は人間自身である。

(10) 性は善である。

(11) 滅亡よりも種の存続を希望する。

(12) 社会生活を営む。

(13) 知的精神活動（未知・真理の追究等）を喜ぶ。

(14) 芸術を楽しむ。

(15) 人類という生命体に調和する感性認識の善・美を喜ぶ。

(16) 遊ぶことを喜ぶ。

(17) 喜怒哀楽する。

(18) その他

　なお、上記性質のうち、(05)～(10) につきましては、拙著「神と宗教を考える」に詳細です。

⑵ 人間界至高の理念

前項「⑴人類という生命体の性質」を踏まえ、下記の（ような）理念を人間界に普遍なるものと仮定し、人間界至高の理念と仮定します。

理念⑴　前項「⑴人類という生命体の性質」を全面的に肯定する。

理念⑵　人類という生命体に矛盾せず、調和し適合する人間界を構築する。

理念⑶　我々人類は戦争よりも平和を、不幸よりも幸福を希望する。

理念⑷　我々人類は、滅亡よりも存続を、そして地上、すなわちこの宇宙船地球号の中に、地獄よりも理想郷を築くことを希望する。

理念⑸　ただの一人をも殺めず、基本的人権を尊び、全ての個を心身の自由と健全の中で生かし切ることのできる人間界を構築する。

理念⑹　全ての個が健全な衣食住に恵まれ、健康であり、幸福に包まれて一日一日の生をゆったり、まったり、さわやかに、しみじみ、のびのびと楽しむことのできる人間界を構築する。

理念⑺　その他理念⑴〜⑹に調和するもの一切。

（注記）幸福とは、人それぞれで何が幸福であるかははっきりしません。従って、ここで言う幸福とは、自由と規律の中で、全ての個がそれぞれの幸福を追求できる環境（理想郷）の中に存在している幸福を意味します。

（ノート）

我々人間界における一切の判断の原点は神や宗教にあるのではなく我々人類という生命体そのものにあります。すなわち、一切の判断はこの生命体に調和するものは受け容れ、矛盾するものは否定し排除することを基本とするべきであるということです。このことは善悪、道徳、倫理、善、美を含み、それらに

限らず諸々の全てに関わる是非は当理念に調和するか矛盾するかを判断の基準とするべきであることを意味します。なお、この理念は人類がどのような生命体に進化しようとも、人類に適用可能であると仮定します。

02 宇宙人

(1) 宇宙人の襲来

　地球上では、人類は人種・民族、宗教の違いや国々に分かれて争っていますが、地球外生命体として太陽系外の宇宙人が存在し、地球（人類）を侵略してきた場合は、人類は一つになり団結して宇宙人と戦うであろう、というようなことが考えられることがあります。

　このことについて考えてみます。

　宇宙人は生命体であってみれば、自然災害ではなく人為災害に類別するべきかもしれませんが、人為災害は人類自らによる災害に限ることにし、宇宙人は宇宙という自然から来た自然災害として扱うことにします。

　さて、宇宙人が我々人類を攻撃してくるようなことがあるでしょうか？

　筆者は、宇宙人が存在しても、そのようなことはまずありえないと考えています。遠い宇宙空間を超えて地球迄やってくることのできる宇宙人の科学力は我々人類のレベルを途方もなく上回っていることになりますから、人類が一つに団結しようがしまいが、宇宙人にその意志があれば、人類は戦う機会など与えられることなく瞬時に殲滅されることになります。科学力が違いすぎれば、宇宙戦争になどなりません。勝負にならないのです。

　しかし、宇宙人は我々人類を攻撃しようなどの意志を持つことはないであろうと思います。宇宙人が自滅せず存在していることがそのことを証明しています。すなわち、宇宙人は科学を厄災化することなく統御していることも含め、その精神世界は高度に発達していることになりますから、地球を離れて積極的に宇宙人に負の干渉もしてもいない人類に危害を加えることは考えにくいから

です。従って、地球を訪れる宇宙人に遭遇することがあっても、人類にとって不愉快な遭遇にはならないと考えられます。このことは、宇宙人と人類を入れ替えて考えてみればよくわかります。人類が他の星を訪問するとして、人類はその星に住み人類よりも劣った科学力を持つ生命体に危害を加えようなどと考えて訪問するわけではないのでしょうから。

この推論が間違っていて宇宙人に攻撃を受けると仮定してみましょう。人類に抗する力がないのであれば、何の心配をする必要も意味もありません。なぜなら、宇宙の終わりや太陽系の崩壊と同じです。心配しても何の役にも立たないからです。

人類は絶滅します。

精神世界の遥かに進んだ宇宙人に遭遇することがあれば、筆者は色々と聞いてみたいことがありますが、その内の1つは我々人類の持つ神観念と宗教です。是非とも、宇宙人の見解を伺いたいと思います。

⑵ 宇宙人

宇宙人が存在するかしないかと言えば、存在すると考える方が存在しないと考えるよりも自然です。なぜなら、宇宙の中には無数の星が存在するのですから、その内で生命のゆりかごとなる星は我が地球が唯一無二であると考えることは不自然だからです。一つあることが可能であり現実であれば、そのことは禁止されていないのですから、一つだけではなく複数あるいは多数あることがむしろ強制される、という考え方もあります。

宇宙人が存在するとすれば、我々には生命体とは見えないものから我々人間によく似たものまでの幅広い範囲の中にあるものと考えられます。又、我々は炭素ベースの生命体ですが、宇宙人は他の元素（例えば、シリコン）ベースの

ものもあるかもしれません。

　宇宙人の大きな特徴の一つに脳が発達しているから頭が大きいということが語られることがありますが、これは単純な考えで、そうとばかりは言えません。なぜなら、例えば地球の生物の脳が真空管でできていて、宇宙人の脳がより高性能なトランジスタやICでできているとしますと、脳の体積や重量は必ずしも大きくなければならないという必要性はないからです。又、脳の発達に対して余の器官は比較的発達不足とか退化しているなどの考えもあるようですが、宇宙人の育った星の環境や重力の違いにより、地球人よりも頑健な身体を持っている可能性もあります。

　宇宙人が過去にもそして今も自由にそして我々に感知できない形で地球を訪問しているという話もありますが、そうだとしますと、宇宙人の科学は我々を途方もなく上回っていることになります。なぜなら、先ず第1に、宇宙人は宇宙人の故郷である星と地球との距離に関わる難関を克服していることになるからです。宇宙人の故郷が銀河系内にあるとしても、そこから地球迄は片道何百、何千、何万光年もあります。さらに、宇宙人が銀河系外から来ているとすれば、その距離は何百万、何千万、何億、何十億、何百億光年にもなります。光速の宇宙船を以てしても途方もない時間がかかります。因みに人類がホモ・サピエンスとして地上に現れ出たのはまだほんの数万年前でしかありません。宇宙人が地球を訪問しているとすれば、この時空問題を克服してやってきているわけですから、その他の科学知識・技術の発達も言うには及びません。

　UFO（Unidentified Flying Object、未確認飛行物体）、いわゆる空飛ぶ円盤や古代から宇宙人が地球を訪問している様々な足跡らしきものなどが語られることがありますが、これはこれで興味深くはあるものの、確証バイアス感のあることは否めません。つまり、宇宙人の存在を希求するあまり、それを支持できそうなものは何でもその色眼鏡を以て探し求めるということです。

　然るに、時空問題を克服できなければ宇宙人は地球へ到達することはできないのですから、そうであれば、未確認飛行物体は宇宙人には関係なく、あくまでも地球圏で生じている未確認飛行物体であって、宇宙人の空飛ぶ円盤ではな

いことになります。古代からの宇宙人の足跡らしきものも「らしきもの」であっても足跡ではないことになります。

　もっとも、時空問題は我々人間が今現在克服できないと思っているだけであって、宇宙人にはそのようなものは不可能などではなく可能も可能簡単も簡単なことかもしれませんから、我々は時空問題は宇宙人が解決しているという前提の下で、宇宙人の地球訪問や空飛ぶ円盤そして古代からの宇宙人の地球訪問の足跡を云々するのも悪いことでもないかもしれません。しかし、その場合でも、宇宙人におまかせした時空問題について、おまかせのままではなく、我々地球人もこの問題の克服に取り組まなくてはならないことは言う迄もありません。UFOを云々すると同時に、宇宙人はこの時空問題をどのように克服したのかということも考え合わせれば、宇宙人が今よりも一層興味深い話題・論題になるに違いありません。又、多くの人々がそのような興味を持つことになりますと、あるいは人類の時空問題克服に思わぬ貢献が見られることに結果するかもしれません。

03　宇宙観

　我々人類は、宇宙の無限なることや不思議に驚嘆し、地球の自然に感動し、我々を含む動植物の精巧さや魅力に接する時、これらがどのようにして生じたのか、そしてどのように動いているのか、という問いを持つことになります。

　この問いに対する答えを「宇宙観」と呼ぶことにしますと、今よく知られている宇宙観は二つあります。その一つは「神という宇宙観」であり、後の一つは釈迦が発見した「神観念のない宇宙観」ですが、これらの宇宙観はどちらも我々の知性・知的要求を満足させるに十分なものとは言えません。

　我々人間は、神を「宇宙万物を創造した全知全能にして完全な系」と定義しましたが、その神の存否は今のところ不明です。又、釈迦の宇宙観は、神観念はもたず、「このような宇宙ありき」を起点としていて「宇宙はこのようにある、このように動いている」というものです。この科学的発見そのものは素

晴らしいものですが、この発見のおよぶ範囲は、例えば、人間の一生すなわち生・老・病・死という部分情報枠内をカバーしているものにすぎないもので、我々の来し方である究極の過去や行く末である永遠の未来すなわち完全情報の領域は思案のほかであるという前提に立っているものですから、完結性を欠いている憾みのあることは否めません。つまり、虚無から出でて無限に至るその中間の範囲のみに関わっているものであるということになります。然るに、前者は神の宗教及び哲学にも採り入れられ、後者は仏教に採り入れられています。

　ところで、筆者はもう一つの宇宙観があると考えています。それは「現象の原理に拠る宇宙観」です。「現象の原理」とは、因果律よりも広い概念で、その詳細は次項に記述してあります。

04 現象の原理に拠る宇宙観

(1) 現象の原理

　全ての現象は起こるべくして起こっています。なぜなら、起こるべくして起こっているのでなければ、起こりようがないからです。これを「現象の原理」と呼びます。なお、この「現象の原理」は、一切のものには原因があって生じ、原因がなくては何も生じないという原理である「因果律」と同質のものですが、それよりも広い概念で下記のように表現できるものです。

$$現象の原理＝因果律＋X＋Y＋Z$$

　Xとは、仏教で言う縁（間接条件）や俗に言う種も仕掛けもの仕掛けやメカニズムなどを含めたもので、Yとは「今現在、原因がわからない」もののことであり、Zとは「原因なき原因」のことです。従って、「現象の原理」は「全ての現象（一切）は起こるべくして起こっている」ことを漏れなくそしてわか

りやすく表現していることになります。

　このように表現しますと、神秘は神秘ではなく、超常現象も超常ではなく、魔法などもなく、現象の原理に基づく通常現象であることがはっきりします。現象自体は、「起こるべくして起こっていて、そうでないなら起こりようがない」のですから、起こるべき解を持っていることは自明です。

　Ｙの「今現在、原因がわからない」ということは、現象は存在しているわけですから、その原因は遅かれ早かれ解明されると考えていいことになります。この例には、現象の原因が現象そのものの中に見出せていないもので、①互いに反対方向に同じ大きさでスピンしている二つの電子のモデルがあり、又、②生物進化の過程やシステムの発展過程において先行する条件からは予測や説明ができない新しい特性が生み出される「創発」と呼ばれるものなどがあります。（①と②は、拙著、神からの自立／神と宗教を考える、に詳細です）

　Ｚの「原因なき原因」の例は「神は在りて在るもの」というのがその最たるものでしょうか。これは、何事にもその原因があるが、原因を求めて遡行して行くと原因は無限後退し行き止まることはないが、それ以上は遡らない第１原因が神であり神の存在は自己原因であるという主張をそのように表現しているものです。

　然るに、神仮説を認め、さらに神は自己原因となる力を有しているとしても、原因は時間を用いて定義されるところ、神が自己原因での存在を意図した時、神は既に存在していた筈ですから、神の存在は自己原因ではありません。つまり、神は自己以外の一切の存在の原因となりえても、神自身のために「自己原因となる力」を発揮する機会はありません。従って、「神が自己原因となる力」を有することに意味はなく、「神は在りて在るもの」とは誤謬を語っていることにほかならないことになります。「神は一切の原因である」ことを神といえども神自身には適用することはできません。このことは不完全性定理に通じるものがあります（後出05の中）。

　そうしますと、「神は在りて在るもの」ということは成立しませんから、そのように言って済ましていることはできません。議論の赴くところ、神の存在

には自己原因ではない原因はあるがそれは人間には発見できていないか、あるいはどのような原因もない、ということに分けて考えることができます。前者は永遠の不可知ではなく当座の不可知でありいつか発見されて然るべきと考えることができますが、後者は言語明瞭にしてもその真なる意味・内容は不明です。ただ、後者も原因はあり前者と同様に当座の不可知であると考えることもできます。（なお、ここまで辿り来ますと、「現象の原理」は「広義の因果律」と考えてもいいことになります）

　ところで、「現象の原理」は現象が存在していることが前提となっているものですが、神は現象として認識されているものではなくその存否は不明です。現象が存在しないのであれば、その原因など考えても仕方がありませんが、神は現在に至る迄人間の前に現出していないと言っても、将来も現出しないということまではわかりません。このことは、現象として認識されていないものについての原因など考えても仕方がない（から、そのようなものは存在しない）ということで済ますことはできず、未だ確認されていないが現象は存在するという前提の議論の必要性を単純に排除することはできないことになります。

　なお、神の存在が否定されますと、宇宙は神の創造によるものではなくその原因は不明になりますが、神とは違い、宇宙という現象の実在は認識されていますから、その原因は「今現在、わからない」だけのことで、その現象の解はいつか解明されることと期待していいことになります。

　何れにしても、「現象の原理」は、原因と結果の「因果律」よりも広い概念で、起こっている全ての現象にはそれが生じている解が存在することを漏れなく表現しているものです。

⑵　ノート

　人類の知能は低く、経験も知識も有限ですから、人類に既知でありわかっていることはほんの少しで「未知・未解でわからないこと」が無限にあります。人類にとって、未知・未解の領域を少しでも既知に変えて行く努力が重要であ

ることは言う迄もありませんが、それと同じくあるいはそれよりもっと重要なことは、「未知・未解でわからないこと」は「今現在、わからないこと」として純粋に受け取ることです。受け取り、受け容れる以外に他の方法はありません。

　宇宙、地球の自然、超自然現象、奇跡、神秘、人類、そして動植物等全ての現象は起こるべくして起こっています。起こるべくして起こっているのでなければ起こりようがないのですから、この意味で、全ての現象は通常現象です。起こっている現象が科学法則やその他の知識で説明・理解できないからと言って不思議がることはありません。現象そのものは起こるべき解を持っているのですから、安心していていいことです。「今現在、わからないこと」を畏れたり、崇めたり、逆に、侮ったりすることは無用です。又、それらに空想や妄想で無理矢理意味を持たせるような蒙昧にして傲岸不遜なことは慎まなければなりません。特に、神秘については、その解明を求めて、その中そしてその先へ踏み込まないということは科学的精神を放棄したことになることを認めなければなりません。「今現在、わからないこと」については、ひたすら謙虚に、自然体で静かに、そして真摯な学究的姿勢で対しているべきです。

　神の存在・非存在についても、未来永劫知ることができないという意味での「永遠に不可知なこと」ではなくて、希望的ではありますが、原理的に検証可能でいつかは知ることができるという意味での「当座の不可知」であるという扱いでいいものと思います。

　　ただ、我々人類が星のかけらの物質でできている炭素ベースの生命体であることから受ける制約として、もしかすると、人類の知性には限界があり、人類には永遠に既知となり得ない未知・未解があるのかもしれません。（宇宙における生命　S. W. ホーキング著　佐藤勝彦解説・監訳　NTT出版　1993年）

　そうであったとしても、今日はわからないが明日はわかるかもしれないとい

う姿勢を崩すことなく保ち続け、勇んで考え続けることを喜びとしたいものです。人類には人類終焉の時迄未知・未解への解を追究するのが他に選択肢のない唯一の道です。人類が"考えること"を放棄しない限り、他の道を採ることはできません。

(3) 神観念および釈迦の宇宙観に勝る現象の原理

我々人類を含む宇宙万物も現象として生じているものであってみれば、その現象はどのように生じたのかの解がなければなりません。従って、宇宙の真実を求めるということは、この解を求めることになります。この場合、その解が神であるとすることはできません。神はその解の仮説にもなりません。なぜなら、神は「わからないもの」の代名詞でしかないからです。

然るに、この解を求めることは、現状の我々の知識レベルでは力不足ですが現象のあるところ、その解は「当座の不可知」と考えていいことになります。対して、神の存否も「当座の不可知」と考えることはできますが、その確証はなく、従ってこちらの方は期待をも込めたものということになります。

宇宙万物について「現象の原理」に基づく解が得られた時、あるいはこの解にそれなりに近づいた時、この解と神とを対比して考えれば、神の何たるかを論じる／知ることができることになるかもしれません。

もっとも、それが何時になるのかは不明です。

05 神の言葉の不存在証明

神の存在・非存在は不明ですが、神の存在を仮定しても、神の言葉は存在しません。従って、神の宗教の聖典は神の言葉を記したものではなく、人間の考案物を神の名を借りて記しているものにほかなりません。神の言葉とは、神の啓示、預言、教えのことです。

神の言葉の不存在証明は、神の属性の違いにより、2種類に分かれます。そ

の一つは、(1)神の属性が「全知全能で完全な系」という立場の場合で、後の一つは、(2)神の属性が「全知全能に<u>近く</u>完全に<u>近い</u>系」という立場のものです。

なお、「全知全能」は矛盾の中にある概念であり、完全な系の無いことは不完全性定理で証明されています。従って、神の定義は、厳密には、「全知全能に<u>近く</u>、完全な系に<u>近い</u>」というのが成立しうる上限になります。(この点につきましては、拙著、神と宗教を考える、に詳細です)

(1)に基づく神の言葉の不存在証明は、主たる証明Ｘと補足証明一つを、(2)に基づくものは、主たる証明Ｙを記述してあります(数多の補足証明が存在しますが、ここでは割愛しました)。さらに(1)と(2)の神の属性に共通の神の言葉の不存在証明も数多ある内の一つを記述してあります。

(1) 神の属性が「全知全能で完全な系」の場合

主たる証明Ｘ

神がこの世界を創造したのであれば、世界は人類を含み全て神の意志どおりになっていなければなりません。そうしますと、意志どおりに創造した後で、人類に教えを授けることなどは一切不要でなければなりません。すなわち、神の言葉は不要であるから存在しないということです。

これを本書では、「神の言葉の不存在原理」と呼びます。

このように、神の言葉の不存在証明はあっけない程簡明なものであり上記で必要にして十分です。従って、これ以上の証明は冗舌を重ねることになりますが、これではあまりに愛想がありませんから、同じようなことになりますが補足証明一つを下記致しました。(このほかにも多種多様に考えることができます)

神の言葉の不存在補足証明

神を「宇宙万物を創造した全知全能にして完全な系」と定義しますと、この時、我々は神をどのようにイメージするのでしょうか。

① 我々の在籍している宇宙以外の宇宙（存在すれば）をも悠久の過去から永遠の未来に亘って創造し続ける神（宇宙神Ａ）
② 我々の存在する宇宙を創造し統治している神（宇宙神Ｂ）
③ 銀河系、太陽系、地球を創造し統治している神（銀河系神）
④ ③の内、全人類に関わる神（全人類神）
⑤ ④の内、一部の人類に関わる神（一部人類神）→一神教の神

上掲のように、順位が下の神は１つ上の順位の神に包摂・還元されますから、「唯一の絶対神」とは①の宇宙神Ａ（あるいは、少なくとも②の宇宙神Ｂ）になります。すなわち、下位の神はこの神の分身と言うべき神です。

従って、①〜⑤の全ての神の間に矛盾が生じることはありません。

その内、我々人間界にある一神教の神とはどの神のことかを考えますと、それは「⑤一部の人類に関わる神」になります。

さて、神の宗教は、この神の言葉により成り立っているということですが、同じ神の言葉であるにもかかわらず、それは宗教ごとに異なっています。又、一つの宗教の神の言葉には解釈の違いが生じ複数の宗派に分かれることもあります。これらのことから、宗教間や宗派間に争いが生じています。ここで、順位が１つ上の「④全人類に関わる神」を見ますと、この神が「全人類の平和と幸福という意志を持つ神」であるという前提に立てば、⑤の神の言葉から結果した人間同士の争いは、④の神の意志とは矛盾しています。然るに、どの神と神の間すなわち④と⑤の神の間にも矛盾が生じることはありません。従って、宗教の言う神の言葉は神の言葉ではなくその他の者（すなわち人間）の言葉であるということになります。

かくして、神の言葉は存在しないことが結論されます。

⑵ 神の属性が「全知全能に近く完全に近い系」の場合

主たる証明Y

我々人間は最初神の属性を「全知全能にして完全な系」と定義しましたが、その後全知全能は成立せず完全な系もないことがわかりました（拙著、神と宗教を考える、に詳細です）。その結果、神の存在を仮定しても、その属性は最大限「全知全能に近く完全に近い系」と少し退いたものになりましたが、このことが神の言葉の不存在証明に関わって来ることが考えられます。

つまり、完璧な神とは違い、完璧性を欠いた神にはうっかりミスがあって然るべきかもしれず、そうであればニーチェではありませんが「人間は神の失敗作」であるかもしれません。その場合には、神の意志に沿っていない振る舞いを為す人間・人間界を神の意志に沿わせるべく修正するために、改めて神の教え（言葉）を授ける必要が生じます。

この目的のために神の言葉の必要性が生ずることはありうると考えられますが、神の言葉の不存在証明とは、そのような必要性のあるなしに関わらず、神の言葉が存在することは不合理であるとする証明です。つまり、神の言葉はどの宗教にも最初から授けられていないことの証明になります。

ここでいう宗教とは、宇宙万物の創造主としての唯一神の存在、神の言葉を聖典として持つこと、そして教義としての神への信仰や愛、等をうたい文句として数多存在している自称神の宗教のことです。

さて、唯一神というからには、数多ある宗教の教えは、同じ神の教えですから、宗教間で当然に矛盾や相反はもとより寸毫の違いもあってはならず、完璧に一致していなければならないことが要請されます。然るに、事実はそうなっておらず、宗教ごとの教えは異なっています。このように、宗教ごとに教えが

異なっている事実から導かれる結論は、下記の二つの内のどちらかになります。

結論(イ)　数多ある宗教の教えは「唯一の絶対神」の本物の教えではなく、全て偽物である。又は、

結論(ロ)　数多ある宗教の教えの中の一つは「唯一の絶対神」の本物の教えである。この一つを残して後の全ては偽物である。

結論の吟味 ── さて、神に人類に対し教えを授ける意志があったとすれば、その教えは全人類に等しくそして遍く授けるのでなければ授けたことにはなりません。授けたとすれば、その結果は、この地球上にその教えを説く宗教がただ一つのみ存在していて、他の教えを説く宗教は存在していない状態になっていなければならないことになります。そうしますと、結論(ロ)のように、一つのみが本物で他は全て偽物という状態は本物の教えが全人類に等しくそして遍く行き亘っていない状態にあり、これは神の意志に矛盾していることになります。然るに、全知全能と完全性から少し退いた神であるといえども、神にはその意志があれば意志通りのことができる存在であるにもかかわらず、事実は教えの異なる宗教が乱立しています。このことから、神はその教えを人類に授ける意志を持っておらず、従って、どの宗教のどの教えも神から授けられた教えではないことが結論されます。

　これにより、結論(ロ)は否定され、結論(イ)が正しいことになります。

　かくして、到達した最終結論は、数多ある宗教の教えは「唯一の絶対神」の本物の教えではなく全て偽物であり、宗教が主張する神と宗教の関係は虚構であるということが証明されたことになります。

　なお、「唯一神」の下では多神はこの神に包摂・還元されます。

(3) 上記(1)と(2)の神の属性に共通の証明

我々人間は、「この我々は何処から来て何処へ行くのか、我々が此処に存在している理由は何か、そして、我々は何者なのか?」という問いへの答えを知らないでいます。

この答えにつきましては、我々は、神に寄せて、この答えを得ることはできないことが推論されます。なぜなら、神が存在することにしても、神はこの答えを今に至るも人間に開示しておりません。開示していれば、我々は既にその答えを知っていなければなりませんが、今に至る迄開示していないということは将来も開示しないという推論が成立する筈だからです。何かの理由で神が開示のタイミングを計っているものかどうかは不明ですが、神は沈黙しています。人間界に対する神の言葉は、今のところ、存在しないのです。

06 原罪 (聖書)

(1) アダムとイブの物語

最初に「原罪」という言葉を聞いた幼い時、筆者の頭に浮かんだことは、"我々人類は動植物の生命を断ちそれを摂取しなければ生命を保てない存在であるが、これを指して罪深い「原罪」をもって生まれて来たということなのか"ということでした。ところが、原罪の意味はそのようなことではなく、「我々人類の先祖であるアダムとイブが神との約束を破り、善悪の知識の木の実(意味深なのでしょうか)を食べたことによる罪」ということでした。

しかし、この物語は奇妙です。その奇妙さは下記の通りです。

この物語を人間界の構図にしますと、"親の言いつけに背き、間違いを起こした子供を親は許さず勘当した"ということになります。しかし、この構図は、人間界のこととしては理解できますが、神とアダム・イブの間では成立し

ません。それを以下に検証します。

　神はアダムとイブを創った時、下記のような３つの選択肢を採ることができました。

　　①神はアダムとイブが神を裏切らないように創ることができた。
　　②神はアダムとイブが神を裏切るように創ることができた。
　　③神はアダムとイブが神を裏切る裏切らないはアダムとイブの自由裁量に
　　　まかせるように創ることができた。

　さて、アダムとイブが裏切ったことで、神が①の選択肢を採らなかったことは明らかです。次に、神が③の選択肢を採ったとしても、未来を見通せる神には、アダムとイブが神を裏切ることは２人を創った時点で既に承知しています。従って、神にとって、③の選択肢を採っても、その結果がどうなるのかについては、②の選択肢を採ることとの違いはありません。つまり、神はアダムとイブが神を裏切るように創ったことになります。

　そうしておいて、神は裏切りをした２人に「原罪」を背負わせています。これが１番目の奇妙さです。次に、神は確信犯として、アダムとイブのみならずその子孫である人類に「原罪」を相続させておいて、人類の「原罪」からの解放をイエスの十字架上の死で贖わせています。これが２番目の奇妙さです。

　さらに、キリスト教には、「神は一つであるが、その現れ方に、神とイエスと聖霊という三つの状態がある」という「三位一体説」という考え方があります。これは、はっきり言えば、イエスは神そのものであるということになります。そうしますと、十字架にかかった神であり不死であるイエスが死ではない死を自身と人類に対して演じて見せて、それで以て神である自身が確信犯的に人類に背負わせた「原罪」からの解放を自身に願い、神である自身が自身にその願いに赦しを与えた、という図になります。

　これは、一体何でしょう？

　神は確信犯的に人類に「原罪」を背負わせたことを反省したものでしょ

か？　これが３番目の奇妙さです。そして、この奇妙な物語の「原罪」思想が宗教の原点を占め、その原点から宗教の教えが構築されています。キリスト教では、この物語を信じることで人類のだれもが「原罪」から解放されると教えています。モーセを通じて神とユダヤ民族との間で結ばれた契約をキリスト教は「旧約（聖書）」と呼び、人類の罪を背負って十字架の上で死を遂げたイエスを通じて神と人類の間で結ばれた新たな契約を「新約（聖書）」と呼んでいます。

⑵　原罪は神の手違い

　神がこの世界を創造したのであれば、世界は全て神の意志どおりになっていなければなりません。そうしますと、神の創造によるアダムとイブが原罪を形成する行為をなしたことも当然に神の意志どおりのことであることになります。然るに、神は後になって、イエスが十字架にかかり神の赦しを願ったことにより、アダムとイブの子孫である人類の原罪を解除しています。意志どおりであれば解除の必要はない筈ですが、なぜ解除したのでしょうか。

　それは、そもそも、アダムとイブ（とその子孫）に原罪を背負わせることは神の当初の意志ではなかったことを意味しています。つまり、原罪を背負わせたことは神の手違いであり、それゆえに手違いを解除し修正したというのがアダムとイブの物語の筋道になります。

　それでは、「全知全能にして完全な系」である神がなぜそのような手違いを起こしたのかについては、創造主はこの神（神Ａ）ではなく、「全知全能に近く完全に近い系」の神（神Ｂ）であったと考えれば説明はつきます。つまり、神Ｂであれば完璧ではありませんから、うっかりミスの手違いを起こすこともないとは言えないからです。アダムとイブの物語は奇妙ですが、それは創造主が神Ａではなく神Ｂであると考えますとその奇妙さは解消します。

　なお、意志どおりに創造したのであるが、後に心変わりして原罪を解除した場合も、一貫性という完璧性を欠きますから、創造主はやはり神Ａではなく神

Bであることになります。そうしますと、アダムとイブの神は神Bであり、この神は、上記のように、そもそも人間に原罪を背負わせる意志は持っていなかったという風に考えてみることもできます。

⑶ 虚構物語の筋道

「事実は小説よりも奇なり」という言葉があります。何か特別のことを言っているように見えますが、至極当然のことですから驚くにはあたりません。なぜなら小説（虚構）は読者が納得のできる筋道が通っている必要がありますが、事実は筋道が通っている必要はないからです。

　聖書も一つの虚構ですから筋道を通す必要がありますが、アダムとイブの物語もその一環としてのお話になります。従って、この筋道はキリスト教という宗教構築上必要不可欠なものですが、他宗では受け容れられているものではありません。例えば、キリスト教がさらに発展した宗教であると自画自讃するイスラム教では、楽園を追放されたアダムとイブの「原罪」は後に神によって赦されたことになっています。そうしますと、現在の我々はもとより、イエスが十字架にかけられる前迄の子孫にも原罪は相続されてはいなかったことになります。イエスは、この意味においては、十字架にかかる必要はありませんでした。キリスト教とイスラム教は同じ旧約聖書（ユダヤ教）を聖典とする宗教でありながら、宗教の構成要素の異なる二つのハイブリッド宗教が構築されていることになります。

　話は変わりますが、日本に「唯一の絶対神」を親神と呼ぶ一神教で天理教という比較的新しい宗教があります。この宗教には、「…（神が）この世の地と天とを形取りて、夫婦をこしらえ来るでな、これがこの世の創め出し…（原文はひらがなです）」という神楽風の物語があります。どちらも虚構であるとは言え、「アダムとイブの物語」に比べ、こちらの方が素朴で明るくよほど親しみが持てます。

⑷ 人類は無垢で自由な存在

　知的生命体であるためには、存否や真偽のわからないことの一方を採択し主張することは慎まなければなりません。しかし、"人類はアダムとイブの「原罪」を背負わされて生を受けたが、イエスが十字架にかかることで赦され、神と人類は新契約を結んだ"というキリスト教の主張に対して、筆者は、ただ一度だけ、知的生命体でありたいという願いを破り、「愚かな生命体」としてその主張の向こうを張り主張することがあります。それは、人類は「無垢であり、神からも宗教からも自由な生命体」であるということです。従って、先祖なるアダムとイブの「原罪」などという神ではなく人間の言葉による虚構を根拠とする偽りの構図である「神との新約」などというものに呪縛されてしょぼくれている必要などはなく、「青空へ向かって胸を張り堂々と生きれば良い」という主張です。

　なお、この議論は「原罪」も「無垢で自由な生命体」のどちらも、その主張の拠って来る確固たる根拠を持たないということを背景としているものです。しかし、そういうことであるならば、我々が無垢で自由であることは、他者である何者かから与えられたものではなく、我々がそう思うことによりそうなるという類のことである、と考えることはできます。

　然るに、一方、罪人ではないと言っても、驕り高ぶることなく、何事にも慎み深く謙虚でなければならないことは言う迄もないことであり、心しなければなりません。

07　無用な宗教の戒律

⑴　戒律に関わる重要な点

　宗教の中には、人間という生命体に調和していない多くの戒律が説かれています。従って、戒律はそれを鵜呑みにしたり不変なものとして扱ったりするの

ではなく、今一度そして時々見直してみる必要があります。神の宗教の聖典は神の言葉ではなく、又仏教の説くところも、全て人間の考えと人間の言葉です。戒律について何回も吟味することに何の支障もありません。それが作られた時と場所の文化・文明を反映している戒律は、現在から見れば不都合なものや不合理なものも多く含まれています。我々人間の守るべきことは、あく迄も人間という生命体の性質とそれに由来する「人間界至高の理念」に調和しているか否かを基準として、我々人間が定めるべきものです。神や宗教から授けられるべきものではありません。戒律であろうと何であろうと、このことが大原則になります。

　以下は戒律に関わる多少の記述です。

⑵　戒律の意味

　辞書には、戒律とは「一般的に、宗教における生活規準。『戒』は自発的に基準を守ろうとするこころのはたらき、『律』は他律的な基準」と解説されています。仏教の戒は、この辞書の解説に近いもので、そもそも禁止条項ではなく、自発的・自律的努力目標ですから、破戒してもペナルティーである律が科せられるのは出家者だけで、それもその一番重いものは教団追放であり、世俗の法で裁かれることとは異なっています。このように、仏教における戒律の概念は仏教者としての倫理的規定（戒）と教団の秩序維持の規則（律）の二重構造を為しています。

　対して、神の宗教の戒律とは、神との契約条項か（ユダヤ教、キリスト教）あるいは神の命令事項（イスラム教）ということですから、辞書的な意味や仏教の戒とは異なっています。この契約条項あるいは命令が守られなかった場合は神により律が科せられる構造になっています。すなわち、神による最後の審判で地獄へ落とされるということになります。

⑶ 戒律の内容

　宗教の戒律には、思想的規範と生活行動規範に関わるものがあります。

　思想的規範とは、神を信仰しなくてはならないなどの神に関わるものや、動物を殺傷してはならないという仏教の不殺生に関わるものなどであり、生活行動規範とは、道徳・倫理や心身の健全に関わるものです。

　これらの内、神を信仰しなければならないという神に関わる思想的規範については、神と人間との契約宗教であるユダヤ教やキリスト教であれ、人間は神に絶対的に服従しなければならないとするイスラム教であれ、神の教えを守る者は天国・楽園に迎え入れられるが、守れない者は地獄に落とされる、という勧善懲悪・信賞必罰思想に関わる基本的構図に違いはありません。然るに、宗教と神の関係は虚構であるという認識に立てば、宗教の語る神に関わる思想にも戒律にも従わなければならないという根拠は存在しないことになります。

　それでは、宗教の説く生活行動規範についてはどうでしょうか。

　神の宗教にとり、生活行動規範を説く根拠は、思想的行動規範に比して、さらに薄弱になります。なぜなら、宗教と神の関係が虚構にあることに加え、道徳・倫理や心身の健全に関わる神に基礎づけされた生活行動規範（神の最高善）なるものは存在しないからです（後出09）。つまり、神仮説に拠り、仮に"ない"神の言葉の存在を無理矢理"ある"ということにしても、存在しない神の規範をその言葉の中に含めて人間界に授けることはできないからです。従って、宗教の説く戒律は、神の宗教であれそうでない宗教であれ、神の言葉ではなく全て人間による考案物よりほかのものではないことが明らかになります。

⑷ 必要な戒律と不要な戒律

　我々人間は神や仏や宗教や戒律などに束縛されない自由な存在として生を受けています。しかし、社会生活をする上でも、個としての心身の健康のために

も、際限のない自由な行為が許されているわけでもなく、勧められるものでもありません。従って、人間は基本的に自由であっても、他との関係や自らのために、人としての行為を規制する規準となる規律は必要になります。これを戒律というのならば、戒律は必要です。但し、戒律は何も神や仏や宗教によって定められあてがわれるべきものではありません。

つまり、生活行動規範はより良い人間社会や個の心身の健全をめざすものですから、神や宗教に関わりなく、人間として適切な生活行動規範を実践することは大いに推奨されるべきことです。従って、宗教の中に戒律として説かれている生活行動規範の中に人間・人間界にとって適切であると考えられる規範が発見されましたら、それが宗教の中にあったからと言って全面的に毛嫌いする必要はありません。善いことは善い、善くないことは善くない、という是々非々の姿勢でその規範に接すれば良いことになります。元を正せば、人間が考案した規範なのですから。

それでは適切な生活行動規範を判断する基準は何か、という問題に遭遇します。その基準とは、言う迄もなく、我々人間という生命体です。その具体的な基準は人間という生命体の性質に由来する「人間界至高の理念」であるということになります。従って、我々人間が「星のかけらでできている炭素ベースの生命体」であることと「それが持つ性質」に調和するものであれば受け容れ、矛盾するものであれば、そのような戒律は無用ですから排除するべきものとなります。

結論的には、我々人間という生命体にとって調和せず矛盾するような宗教の戒律は不要であるということになります。

下記は、宗教が人間界に落とした影である数多あるこのような戒律の中からその一つを選んで認めてみたものです。

⑸ 食の戒

宗教には多くの戒律があり、その中に食の戒があります。食の戒とは、何々

を食べてはいけないというものです。

　しかし、どの宗教のどの食の戒も基本的には我々人間にとって一切無用です。その理由は我々人間自身と神にあります。

　先ず、我々人間は当然に人間であることを無条件に肯定しなければなりません。そうしますと、人間という生命体に矛盾する戒は無用としなければなりません。

　食の戒には、動物という生あるものの生命を奪ってはならないから食べてはいけない、という戒がありますが、我々人間はミネラルや動植物からの栄養素を適切に摂取しなければその生命や健康を維持できない従属栄養生命体です。他の生命形態（植物も含めて）に依存し食料源にしなければ生存することができません。従って、このような戒を設けることは人間という生命体にそぐわないがゆえに無用です。

　さて、食の戒には、神から授けられた戒として、ある動物は食べても良いが、ある動物は食べてはいけないという戒があります。この戒は、宗教Aでは動物Xは食べても良いが動物Yは食べてはいけないという戒となり、宗教Bでは、その逆に、動物Xは食べてはいけないが、動物Yは食べても良いという戒となるおかしな事態を起こしています。神が存在し、神の言葉の授けがあったと仮定しても、神の属性を考えれば、神がこのようなおかしなことを授け、人間界を混乱させることはなさらないように思われます。何れにしても、神仮説に基づいても神の言葉の存在しないことは証明されていますから、神の定めた戒としてそれに縛られ悩む必要はありません。

　神が定め神から授けられた戒でないならば、人間が神の名を借りて神が授けたように見せかけたことにほかならないことは明らかです。違った文化・文明を持つ違った人たちが違った宗教を開き、それぞれが動物に対する違った偏見（語ればそれに至ったそれなりの理由はあるのでしょうが）を宗教の中に採り入れたことから無用な戒とおかしな事態が生じたと考えられます。

　動物はどの動物も人間にとってかけがえのない栄養素を提供してくれます。基本的には、人間は、人間以外の何を食べても良いのです（つい最近迄人食い

の風習を持つ社会がありましたが…）。他の生命に依存しなければ適切な栄養素のバランスが保たれず、折角の生命を維持できない我々人間という従属栄養生命体にとって、動植物を食する際に、私の体内に入り、血となり肉となって私と共に生きてくれるよう語りかけることくらいよりほかにできることはありません。

08 煩悩、それは至宝

　仏教の最高の教義は、「生得である煩悩を滅却し悟りを開き涅槃寂静の境地に至る」ということです。すなわち、煩悩を吹き消し、悟りの世界である心の静まった安らぎの境地を得ることです。

　我々人間は生得的に様々な煩悩を具備して生誕しています。それらは、世俗的には、熱情、食欲、性欲、様々な願望、執着、等々多岐にわたります。しかし、煩悩とは人が人であるために第一に大事なもので至宝そのものですから、滅却したり吹き消したりしてはなりません。煩悩を去れば、心の働きは消え去り、人は人ではなくなります。しかし、ここで我々が注意を要することは、ある種の煩悩（必ずしも単一ではない）に対する過度の執着です。なぜなら、過度の執着は我々の心の中に解消できない心痛や苦悩などの原因となるからです。煩悩の一つである執着は、人にとって必要不可欠な至宝そのものですが、過度に陥らないよう、適当な執着を楽しむように心掛けることが肝要となります。従って、下記のように、煩悩とは、生かして人生をより味わい深くするためのものであるという認識が求められます。つまり、仏教はその入り口で間違っていることになります。

　そもそも、「煩悩を滅却して涅槃寂静の境地に至る」という思想こそが最たる煩悩である、という批判を免れることはできません。

　仏教によりますと、煩悩とは、欲望や執着等人間の心身を煩わし悩ませる精神作用である一切の妄念のことで、その数も「百八煩悩」とか「八万四千の煩悩」などと言われ、数多にあるという認識の上に立脚しています。

宗教はマイナス観からしか開始できませんから、煩悩についてもマイナスであるという前提に立ち仏教は開始されています。然るに、人間という生命体から煩悩を差し引けば残ったものは空虚な人間ではない人間になりますから、煩悩は人間に不要のものではなく、その逆に、人間を人間として生かしている人間の至宝と見るべきものです。従って、煩悩にマイナスのイメージを持たせて滅却するというような思想は成立しません。

　人間に生得である煩悩とは、元々マイナス圏に存在するものではなく、最初はプラス・マイナス・ゼロの原点に位置していて、そこから煩悩という多くの種類の楽器のオーケストラの演奏如何によりプラス圏へもマイナスへ圏へも進展する可能性を持ったものという捉え方が最適であると考えられるものです。従って、煩悩とは、滅却するものではなく、どのようにすればこの多種類の楽器で素晴らしいオーケストラの演奏（快・楽）をして煩悩をプラス圏へ飛翔させることができるのか、どのようにすれば不調な演奏（不快・苦）を回避し煩悩がマイナス圏へ落ち込むことを回避できるのか、というアプローチを採ることが最適であるということになります。つまり、我々は、煩悩のオーケストラの素晴らしい演奏をめざすべきであって、煩悩を捨てオーケストラを演奏しないとか解散するということではありません。

　我々人間は肉体や煩悩により成っている生命体です。人間は人間自身を否定することはできず、喜ばしくも肯定することしかできません。五官の欲望も満たされないのでは、折角の肉体を持って生きている大方の意味はなくなります。煩悩を滅却した状態は人間という生命体が死滅した状態です。それではこの世の楽しい生を生きているのではなく、既に花に囲まれ仏壇なりお墓なりの住人であることになります。

　人間は煩悩という至宝を適当に生かし楽しい生を生きるべきであり、至宝を生かしきれない苦しい生を生きるべきではありません。滅却するなどは下の下であるという認識が肝要になります。

09 神の最高善の不存在

　宇宙万物に普遍的にして絶対的な善を「神の最高善」と言うのであれば、そのようなものは存在しません。

　善悪適用対象者は、鉱物と植物を除外できるとしますと、知的生命体（人類）と非知的生命体（動物）になります。この場合、動物は善悪を理解できないとしますと、善悪適用対象者は人類のみになります。すなわち、宇宙万物に適用できる善悪などは存在せず、全宇宙にあって、人類という生命体に調和する行為を人類にとっての善、そして調和しない行為を人類にとっての悪、という人類のみにしか適用できない唯一の善悪系しか存在しないことになります（宇宙人が存在する場合は、そしてその善悪が人類のものと共通でない場合は、唯一ではなくなります）。

　このことは、人類の善悪とは、神や仏やそれらの名を借りた宗教により「そうあるべきもの」として与えられるべきものではなく、人類が自らに照らして、自らが定め自らに適用するべきものであるということになります。

　然るに、その人間界における善悪は、場所と時（環境条件）が違えば大なり小なり異なっていますから、普遍的でも絶対的でもありません（普遍的なものも皆無とは言えず、同じものや似通ったものも少なくない反面、異なることも多く、中には善悪が逆転していることさえあります）。又、宗教は善悪は普遍的で絶対的であると説きますが、宗教ごとに同じではなく相対的ですから、普遍的でも絶対的でもありません。つまり、善悪を定める要素である環境条件は地域や社会毎に異なり普遍的ではありませんから、善悪は人間界に普遍的ではありません。さらに、万物が流転するこの世界にあっては、自然環境も人為環境も時の移ろいと共に移ろい行くものですから、不変という意味での絶対的善悪もないことになります。

　この人間界に普遍的ではない善悪の扱いにつきましては、「人間界至高の理念」という灯台を見つめながら、たとえ完全な一致が得られなくても、お互いが理解を深めることをめざして常に対話を重ねなくてはなりません（価値観の

相違についても同じことが言えます）。

　このように、人類を構成する全ての集団に普遍的で絶対的な善悪は存在せず、又、ある時点におけるどのような善悪も時の移ろいと共に変わり行くものですから、「まるで幻のようなもの」というのが善悪の本質であるということになります。そして、これは当然のことです。なぜなら、なにしろ、善悪適用対象者である人類という生命体そのものが進化を含め様々な意味において流れ移ろい行く幻のごとき存在なのですから。従って、神といえども、不変的でも絶対的でもない者、すなわち移り変わり行く者、に対し適用できる不変的で絶対的な最高善というようなものを授けることはできません。

　さらに、別の視点から、神が存在するという神仮説によっても、神の言葉は存在しませんから、百歩譲って神の善悪があるとしても、神はそれを人間界に開示してはおりません。従って、我々人間にとって、神の最高善などは知り得ていないことになります。神は語らず、沈黙しています。

参考文献

「パラダイム・ブック」C+Fコミュニケーションズ編著　日本実業出版社
　　1996年

「偶然とは何か」竹内啓著　岩波書店　2013年

「確率がわかる」小泉力一著　技術評論社　2017年

「人間原理の宇宙論　人間は宇宙の中心か」松田卓也著　培風館　1990年

「宇宙はなぜこのような宇宙なのか　人間原理と宇宙論」青木薫著　講談社
　　2013年

「ゲーデル・不完全性定理」吉永良正著　講談社　1992年

「ゲーデルは何を証明したか ── 数学から超数学へ」E.ナーゲル、J.R.ニュー
　　マン著　林一訳　白揚社　1999年

「不完全性定理とはなにか」竹内薫著　講談社　2013年

「数学者の無神論 ── 神は本当にいるのか」J.A.パウロス著　松浦俊輔訳　青
　　土社　2008年

「大栗先生の超弦理論入門」大栗博司著　講談社　2013年

「Introduction to LOGIC」Irving M. Copi著　The Macmillan Co. N.Y.　1965年

「論理力を鍛えるトレーニングブック」渡辺パコ著　かんき出版　2002年

「無限 ── その哲学と数学」A. W.ムーア著　石村多門訳　東京電機大学出版局
　　1997年

「無とは何か」末次祐介、橋本省二、橋本幸士監修「ニュートン」2019年5月
　　号

「脳科学」日経サイエンスScientific American日本版　2017年3月号

「パンセ」パスカル著　前田陽一、由木康訳　中央公論新社　2018年

「トマス・アクィナス"神学大全"」稲垣良典著　講談社　2009年

「図解雑学　ニーチェ」樋口克己著　ナツメ社　2003年

「ニーチェ入門」竹田青嗣著　筑摩書房　1994年

「ニーチェ、愛の言葉」適菜収著　KKベストセラーズ　2010年

「ショーペンハウアー」エドゥアール・サンス著　原田佳彦訳　白水社　1998
　　年

「善の研究」西田幾多郎著　岩波書店　1950年

「僕らの新しい道徳」岡田斗司夫著　朝日新聞出版　2013年

「ヒトはなぜ争うのか ── 進化と遺伝子から考える」若原正己著　新日本出版
　　社　2016年

「面白くて眠れなくなる進化論」長谷川英祐著　PHPエディターズ・グループ
　　2015年

「地球と生命」「ニュートン」2015年7月号

「図解雑学　進化論」中原英臣　ナツメ社　2005年

「動的平衡」福岡伸一著　木楽舎　2009年

「図解雑学　倫理」鷲田小弥太著　ナツメ社　2005年

「哲学概論」松原寛著　同文館　昭和8年（1933年）

「3日でわかる哲学」坂本百大監修　ダイヤモンド社　2002年

「哲学用語図鑑」田中正人著　斎藤哲也編集・監修　プレジデント社　2015年

「表象の現象学から行為の哲学へ ── 現象学における弁証法的なるもの」吉川
　　健郎著　現代図書　2000年

「人工知能　人類最悪にして最後の発明」ジェイムズ・バラット著　水谷淳訳
　　ダイヤモンド社　2015年

「人工知能は人間を超えるか　ディープラーニングの先にあるもの」松尾豊著
　　KADOKAWA　2015年

「人工知能」松尾豊他協力「ニュートン」2018年1月号

「宇宙における生命」S.W.ホーキング著　佐藤勝彦解説・監訳　NTT出版
　　1993年

「ホーキング、宇宙を語る」S.W.ホーキング著　林一訳　早川書房　1996年

「宇宙の真実」荒舩良孝著　宝島社　2017年

「誰かに教えたくなる宇宙のひみつ」竹内薫著　徳間書店　2016年

「宇宙の不思議」佐治晴夫著　PHP研究所　1990年

「宇宙のしくみ」磯部琇三著　日本実業出版社　1993年

「宇宙の7大テーマ」ニュートン別冊　ニュートンプレス　2015年

「超巨大ブラックホール」ニュートン別冊　ニュートンプレス　2016年

「宇宙論」ニュートン別冊　ニュートンプレス　2016年

「反物質の謎」村山斉協力「ニュートン」2016年4月号

「新太陽系」「ニュートン」2009年4月号

「最先端医療で寿命がのびる人類200歳時代」「ニュートン」2002年5月号

「インフレーション宇宙論」佐藤勝彦監修「ニュートン」2006年12月号

「宇宙戦争と衛星兵器」「ニュートン」2022年5月号

「COSMOS（宇宙）」カール・セーガン著　木村繁訳　朝日新聞社　1980年

「ビッグバン危うし」ジョン・ボスロウ著　青木薫訳　講談社　1993年

「ビッグバンには科学的根拠が何もなかった」ジャン＝ピエール・プチ著　竹内薫監修　中島弘二訳　徳間書店　1996年

「エントロピーからの発想」武田修三郎　講談社　1983年

「〈時間〉とは何か」二間瀬敏史監修「ニュートン」2009年5月号

「量子力学が語る世界像　重なり合う複数の過去と未来」和田純夫著　講談社　1997年

「相対論が進化する　ホーキングの宇宙2」佐藤文隆監修　講談社　平成3年（1991年）

「図解雑学　相対性理論」佐藤健二監修　ナツメ社　1997年

「図解雑学　重力と一般相対性理論」二間瀬敏史著　ナツメ社　2001年

「誰もが納得！　相対性理論」佐藤勝彦監修「ニュートン」2005年7月号

「図解　相対性理論がみるみるわかる本」佐藤勝彦監修　PHP研究所　2007年

「相対性理論と量子論」佐藤勝彦監修　PHP研究所　2006年

「相対性理論の矛盾を解く」原田稔著　日本放送出版協会　2004年

「ニュートリノ」多田将著　イースト・プレス　2016年

「太陽系　誕生と進化」「ニュートン」2014年7月号

「大隕石衝突の現実 ── 天体衝突からいかに地球をまもるか」日本スペース
　ガード協会著　ニュートンプレス　2013年

「人類は大隕石の衝突を目撃するか？」ニュートン編集部「ニュートン」2002
　年9月号

「図解雑学　生態系」児玉浩憲著　ナツメ社　2000年

「自然と人間　海は生きている」富山和子著　講談社　2009年

「ISO環境監査」鈴木敏央著　ダイヤモンド社　1998年

「なぜ宗教は平和を妨げるのか〈正義〉〈大義〉の名の下で」町田宗鳳著　講談
　社　2004年

「人類は〈宗教〉に勝てるか」町田宗鳳　日本放送出版協会　2007年

「神は妄想である　宗教との決別」リチャード・ドーキンス著　垂水雄二訳
　早川書房　2013年

「神さまってホントにいるの？」石井研士著　弘文堂　2015年

「一神教vs多神教」岸田秀著　聞き手三浦雅士　朝日新聞出版　2013年

「一休　風狂の精神」西田正好著　講談社　昭和52年（1977年）

「一休さんの100話」牛込覚心著　国書刊行会　平成16年（2004年）

「ナルシズム」中西信男　講談社　1987年

「自己愛とエゴイズム」ハビエル・ガラルダ著　講談社　1989年

「宗教学辞典」小口偉一、堀一郎監修　東京大学出版会　2003年

「宗教学キーワード」島薗進、葛西賢太、福嶋信吉、藤原聖子編　有斐閣
　2013年

「般若心経講義」高神覚昇著　第一書房　昭和11年（1936年）

「新版　面白いほどよくわかる般若心経」武田鏡村著　日本文芸社　2013年

「ブッダのことば〈百言百話〉」北川八郎著　致知出版社　平成16年（2004年）

「釈迦が説きたかったのは般若心経ではなく般若天行だった」木村正次郎著
　東洋出版　2014年

「良寛のことば　こころと書」立松和平著　考古堂書店　2010年

「一番わかりやすい禅入門」ひろさちや著　三笠書房　1989年

「いま知っておきたい霊魂のこと」正木晃著　NHK出版　2013年

「輪廻転生〈私〉をつなぐ生まれ変わりの物語」竹倉史人著　講談社　2015年

「人は死なない」矢作直樹著　バジリコ　2014年

「タオ自然学」フリッチョフ・カプラ著　吉福伸逸・田中三彦・島田裕巳・中
　　山直子訳　工作舎　1999年

「雑学　超能力の不思議な世界」関英男監修　超科学研究会編　日東書院
　　1989年

「神の後にI〈現代〉の宗教的起源」マーク・C・テイラー著　須藤孝也訳
　　ぷねうま舎　2015年

「神との対話」ニール・ドナルド・ウォルシュ著　吉田利子訳　サンマーク出
　　版　2018年

「人はなぜ、宗教にハマるのか?」苫米地英人著　フォレスト出版　2015年

「宗教をめぐる三つのエッセイ」J.S.ミル著　ヘレン・テイラー編　大久保正
　　健訳　勁草書房　2011年

「宗教を生みだす本能 ── 進化論からみたヒトと信仰」ニコラス・ウェイド著
　　依田卓巳訳　NTT出版　2012年

「本当にわかる宗教学」井上順孝著　日本実業出版社　2011年

「宗教の見方 ── 人はなぜ信じるのか」宇都宮輝夫著　勁草書房　2012年

「なぜ人間には宗教が必要なのか」ひろさちや著　講談社　2007年

「まちがいだらけの教えはいらない　ほんとうの宗教とは何か　白の巻」ひろ
　　さちや著　ビジネス社　2015年

「宗教心を失った日本人のための　ほんとうの宗教とは何か　青の巻」ひろさ
　　ちや著　ビジネス社　2015年

「宗教の教科書　12週」菅原伸郎著　トランスビュー　2005年

「世界の地獄と極楽がわかる本」田中治郎著　PHP研究所　2010年

「図説世界を変えた50の宗教」ジェレミー・スタンルーム著　服部千佳子訳
　　原書房　2014年

「聖書」新共同訳　日本聖書協会　2005年

「新約聖書」新共同訳　日本聖書協会　2014年

「総図解　聖書とキリスト教」前島誠監修　新人物往来社　2011年

「図解雑学　旧約聖書」雨宮慧著　ナツメ社　2009年

「コーラン」井筒俊彦訳　岩波書店　2001年

「イスラーム世界の基礎知識」ジョン・L・エスポジト著　山内昌之監訳　原
　　書房　2009年

「イスラームの原点　〈コーラン〉と〈ハディース〉」牧野信也著　中央公論社
　　1996年

「あなたのことを気づかう創造者がおられますか」ものみの塔聖書冊子協会
　　2006年

「図解雑学　宗教」井上順孝著　ナツメ社　2004年

「宗教のしくみ事典」大島宏之著　日本実業出版社　1999年

「世界の宗教がわかる本 ── 成り立ち、儀式からタブーまで」ひろさちや著
　　PHP研究所　2003年

「面白いほどよくわかる世界の宗教/宗教の世界」ひろさちや著　春秋社
　　2013年

「世界の宗教」渡辺和子著　西東社　2015年

「図解　いちばんやさしい三大宗教の本」沢辺有司著　彩図社　平成26年

「仏教の本」大田由紀江著　西東社　2012年

「図解　仏教のことが面白いほどわかる本：2時間でわかる」田中治郎著　中
　　経出版　2006年

「3日でわかる宗教」山折哲雄監修　ダイヤモンド社編　2004年

「魂をゆさぶる禅の名言」高田明和著　双葉社　2006年

「図説・ゼロからわかる三大宗教の読み方」茂木誠著　実務教育出版　2015年

「儒教の毒」村松暎著　PHP研究所　1992年

「道教の神々と祭り」野口鐵郎、田中文雄編　大修館書店　2014年

「日本の10大新宗教」島田裕巳著　幻冬舎　2008年

「天理教」島田裕巳著　八幡書店　2009年

「悪魔事典」山北篤、佐藤俊之監修　新紀元社　2004年

「天国と地獄の事典」ミリアム・ヴァン・スコット著　奥山倫明監修　原書房
　　2006年

「図解雑学　世界の天使と悪魔」藤巻一保監修　ナツメ社　2009年

「愛と残酷の世界史」桐生操著　ダイヤモンド社　2006年

「世界の〈宗教と戦争〉講座」井沢元彦著　徳間書店　2001年

「殺戮の宗教史」島田裕巳著　東京堂出版　2016年

「目からウロコの中東史」島崎晋著　PHP研究所　2006年

「逆襲される文明」塩野七生著　文藝春秋　2017年

「知らないと恥をかく世界の大問題7」池上彰　KADOKAWA　2016年

「グローバル化の政治経済学」櫻井公人、小野塚佳光編　晃洋書房　1998年

「米中もし戦わば　戦争の地政学」ピーター・ナヴァロ著　赤根洋子訳　文藝
　　春秋　2017年

「戦争へ突入する世界　大激変する日本経済」渡邉哲也　徳間書店　2015年

「新・戦争論　僕らのインテリジェンスの磨き方」池上彰、佐藤優著　文藝春
　　秋　2014年

「核と人間II　核を超える世界へ」坂本義和編　岩波書店　1999年

「核戦略ゲーム」斉藤彰著　講談社　昭和59年（1984年）

「核兵器禁止条約を使いこなす」安斎育郎、林田光弘、木村朗編著　かもがわ
　　出版　2018年

「日本人のための〈核〉大事典」日本安全保障戦略研究所編　国書刊行会
　　2018年

「広辞苑　第六版」新村出編　岩波書店　2008年

フリー百科事典　ウィキペディア

「日本大百科全書（ニッポニカ）」

文部科学省インターネットサイト

宇宙情報センターHP

らばQバラエティニュースサイト

サイエンスポータル Science Portal ニュース速報

国際連合広報センター HP

「神からの自立　Independence from God」岡本浩作著　幻冬舎メディアコンサ
　ルティング　2020年9月

「神と宗教を考える　Thinking of God and Religion」岡本浩作著　幻冬舎メディ
　アコンサルティング　2021年12月

（注記）表示してある発行年は、筆者が参考にした版／刷のものです。

Humanity's Choice→ Prosperity or Destruction?

Highlights

01 The Consensus of Humanity

It is believed that to abolish nuclear weapons together with the human world being peaceful are the consensus of humanity.

Nonetheless, nuclear weapons have not been abolished and have remained in our human world, and wars have not gone away.

Despite the fact that the human world is under the human control, "Why does the consensus not pass and realize and why is such a stupid and strange thing happening?"

As long as the mechanism by which this contradiction arises is not resolved, neither the abolishment of nuclear weapons nor permanent peace will ever be realizable.

02 In the Same Boat

The survival or extinction and happiness or unhappiness of all human beings on the earth are the same thing like being in the same boat. That which we have to get along and have to love each other is natural and has nothing to do with God, religion nor virtue at all.

On the contrary, if we can't do even such sort of things and continue fighting between humans, we will perish. We can't be happy.

03 Mud Boat with an Open Hole at the Bottom

In order to cope with the conflicts inevitably arisen between nations and various negative events and phenomena arisen one after another under the existence of many sovereign nations, we can't get any basic and final solution no matter how much we think and do anything.

This is because the effort is like scooping out the water from a mud boat with an open hole at the bottom. The boat is destined to sink down into the water soon or later as the hole becomes bigger eventually.

In face of this situation, it is a must for us to transfer to a new sturdy ship to save ourselves. The name of the new ship is so-called "World Nation" in which no conflict arises between nations and the occurrence of negative events and phenomena is minimized.

04 Fundamental Contradiction and Its Resolution

In the reality of the existence of numerous sovereign nations, no matter how much we argue about and no matter what efforts we put in the international order, international security and so forth, it will not guarantee a true and lasting peace. This is because it lies in the contradiction of "the peace among sovereign nations that have inevitable conflicts among them."

Therefore, what we should discuss is not under the premise of the existence of numerous sovereign nations but the transition to a new premise of the world nation in which no conflict arises, leaving the currently existing premise.

Since there is no hostile nation against the World Nation, the only Nation on the earth, war won't happen in the Nation (even if you want to). Consequently, under the World Nation, now that all international views, discussions, and scholarship related to the international order, international security, and so forth, will become unnecessary, we humanity will be freed from such troubles for eternity.

05 Sovereign Nations vs the World Nation

As neither the flower of peace nor the flower of freedom blooms in the tree named "sovereign nation system" where conflict arises between sovereign nations, it does not bear the fruit of happiness there. Therefore, in order to get rid of the conflicts from the human world which is a set of humans and sovereign nation, it won't fit unless either humans or sovereign nation is erased. Under such a circumstance, needless to say, we can't erase humans, so it will be the sovereign nation that should be erased.

In the first place, a nation is a product of intangible illusion created by us humans. However, even if it is the product of the same illusion, compared to the world of sovereign nations which have various difficulties, the World Nation is far superior in terms of becoming a peaceful world automatically. This is because the Nation as only a nation on this planet won't have any hostile nation against it.

06 The World Nation = Final Form of Nation

We the human world must change the paradigm which has been staying in our heart from the existence of nations to the existence of the World Nation. This is because the problem, conflict and war in the human world are inevitably arising due to the existence of the numerous sovereign nations. The human world has been wasting and losing the sum total of the physical and mental energies for each of these nations to spend to make its own claim and to protect one's own nation, resulting in making people unhappy, not for their happy. When I think of the various grievous misfortunes that are reported to the world day by day, it seems to be an illusion with "Is it for conflict with the meaning of human existence?" (I hope it's an illusion)

By the way, the current paradigm of the existence of the nations is not absolute but only an illusion. Many sovereign nations existing on the earth are not the final form of the nation. The final form of the nation must be the Earth Nation, that is, the World Nation, which is the only nation on the earth established with humanity as one group. This is because there will be no hostile nation against this Nation and thus permanent peace will be promised there. After all, it should be the best choice of us that our personal sovereign trustee is not a nation in nations but had better be the World Nation. The illusion must be cast aside.

In a world with the existence of many sovereign nations, there arises a contradiction that national proposition inevitably becomes war despite the fact that individual proposition is peace. To the contrary, under the World Nation, individual proposition and national proposition unite in peace.

07 Natural State of Humanity vs Development of Science vs Peace

Thomas Hobbs, a 17th-century British philosopher, had a view that the natural state of humanity is a war state in which everyone fights for power. However, even if this view is correct, we can't remain in the natural state of humanity that Hobbs says. This is because we humanity will become extinct if we fight, now that the condition for the development of science, which is capable of manufacturing weapons to exterminate humanity, has appeared. Since we are a life form wishing to survive for a long time embraced in peace and happiness, then we need to be wise so as for us to be able to get out of Hobbs' theory of the natural state of humanity. The minimum requirements imposed on us in order not to have conflict are to aim to cut off three major roots of conflict, that is, stopping racism, becoming independent from God and religion, and establishing the World Nation that has no hostile nation.

If we look at it based on God hypothesis, God might set up the obstacle of a set of the human natural state and scientific development, and might be trying to see if we humanity can overcome this challenge to avoid our extinction and finally realize peace, the Utopia for humanity and happiness.

If so, we must not lose even to God.

We humans seem to have conflicting genes of struggle and philanthropy. If we aim to realize the Supreme Idea of the Human World (appendix 2-01), a happiness concept for humans, by the work of reason, we must try to activate the gene of philanthropy that forgives and helps each other, instead of the gene of struggle that fights and kills. The gene of the struggle must not be triggered towards humans, but it must be invoked to overcome any difficulty in order to build our Utopia in this world.

If the conflict disappears from the human world and it is a peaceful world, we humanity can be happy at will. All of the immeasurable energies of both things and mind that have been spent relating to the existence of various conflicts to date will be able to be spent to build the World Nation, the Utopia in this world on the earth, in this Spaceship Earth. Namely, it means that it will become possible for us to use all the energies as we please including for the betterment of natural and artificial environments.

08 Unreality to Reality

The hope to build the Utopia for us humanity for peace, freedom and happiness, avoiding the extinction of us which is the necessary condition for that, is unreal far from reality. It is difficult to realize this unreality by reality. After all, it follows that the realization of unreality can only be achieved through unreality.

As the top grip of the unreality, there are abolition of weapons and establishment of the World Nation. Therefore, in order to make this earth the Utopia for humanity, determination and action towards the realization of this unreality will be required of us.

That being said, even if it is an ideal, the writer know that there will be a criticism that it is "nonsense" to talk about such silly things ignoring reality. However, the criticism does not hold.

The real reason and point for it lie in that the extinction of humanity is inferred as a logical necessity if we follow currently existing reality, therefore, there is no other way for us to be saved than heading towards unreality and realizing it. In other words, moving towards the realization of the unreal is not a question of "can or can't," but the only way left for us humanity in order to avoid our extinction and to achieve the glory for the eternal future.

09 Negative Spiral to Positive Spiral

By arming ourselves and going to war, we are increasing the causes of war. If we transfer the property, mental and physical energy to the use for the sake of the happiness of the human world or the security of people's daily lives and future lives, that alone can reduce the number of reasons for war.

We must get out of the negative spiral of war and aim for a positive spiral of peace.

10 To Heighten Human Spiritual World

As long as we humans stick to nation, religion or racial/ethnic discrimination and keep fighting for it, the human world will never be peaceful nor happy. This is 100% guaranteed.

We humans have to stop the height of stupidity like a joke to pray to God for peace and happiness while conflicting among ourselves and waging war using the weapons made by abusing of science. If we are such a stupid, selfish and shameless creature, even we who should be saved cannot be saved. In this case, even if we humans perish, it can't be helped now that it is self-serving, that is, proportionate to our stupidity.

Therefore, it becomes a Must that we all humans as Homo sapiens aim to heighten our spiritual world so that we may be able to avoid our extinction and construct our Utopia on this earth, in the Spaceship Earth, for eternal peace, freedom and happiness.

created by those nations and then the construction of the Utopia for humanity on this earth.

The outline of (2) religion and (3) racial/ethnic discrimination is in the appendix 1-1. & 1-2., respectively.

The Utopia on the Earth

In a world in an ideal artificial environment where there is no war and all human beings are on good terms, it will be possible for all humans to work in unison for the restoration of damaged earth nature and ecosystem and further its improvement as well. The world realized by such an ideal artificial environment and a favorable natural environment to all living things can be said to be the Utopia for humanity in this world, not heaven, paradise, or pure land that religions preach its existence in afterlife.

The Origin of This Book

Especially in view of the many gloomy world situations these days, this book is made up of the main points of "Chapter 8 The Utopia on the Earth" of my book "Independence from God" published by GENTOSHA MEDIA CONSULTING INC. in September 2020, with some re-edited and some added.

That my book is like "child's soliloquy" with the theme, as to how to modify this world in order to make it possible to avoid the destruction of humanity and obtain glorious future, in face of the inference of the risk of the destruction of humanity if we follow the existing present world as is.

For a glorious future, avoiding the destruction of humanity, what is discussed in that book includes that we need to (a) resolve the inevitable conflict arisen from (1) the existence of sovereign nations, (2) religion and (3) racial/ethnic discrimination, (b) ensure the stability of the natural environment and ecosystem, (c) use science exclusively for the well-being of humanity without making it a disaster, and (d) develop the spiritual civilization aiming for us to be the intelligent life form that wears the crown among all life forms in the universe.

Among them, regarding (2) religion, I have published prior to this book as "Thinking of God and Religion" in December 2021 from GENTOSHA MEDIA CONSULTING INC. Therefore, the three books, which are "Independence from God (mother book)," the book that was published prior to this book, and this book on sovereign nations, are the books of mother and her children. The latter two were written specifically for a part of the mother book.

These books are poor but originated from the writer's wish for the happy future of humanity. Therefore, the writer would like to position these as books dedicated to each and every human being. Of these, specifically, the writer would like to dedicate "Thinking of God and Religion" to all religions and religious people in the world and this book "Humanity's Choice→Prosperity or Destruction?" to all sovereign nations and the United Nations.

Regardless of whether my thoughts are getting the right in light of the proposition of our human happiness, it is the writer's hope that the thoughts will be a clue for each of us humans to newly think about this proposition.

Structure of This Book

This book consists of the text and its appendix. The appendix is to explain the items that would be considered necessary for the writer's thoughts and terms mentioned in the text. They are detailed in the mother book of this book "Independence from God" and/or "Thinking of God and Religion," but brief explanations are attached for the time being so that the reader doesn't have to refer those books in reading this book.

The structure of this book is as shown below:

Language of This Book

This book consists of dual languages, Japanese (original) and English. I did so in the hope that the readers will spread Japan and abroad, that is, to all over the world, as the point at issue of this book relates to the survival or extinction of us all humans.

One reason I chose English is in that there are many people in the world who speak English. The second reason is in that only the language I understand is English besides Japanese, and that I thought I would be able to convey in English to the extent that the reader could read the outline of this book without misconception even though my English is poor.

The reason why Japanese and English versions are not separate volumes but in one volume is in my thought that, for instance, it might be convenient that bilingual versions are readily available in hand in case the idea and issue of this book are discussed.

Note on the Description in This Book

Regarding the matters that are judged to be well known in the field according to a lot of literature, etc., the source is not displayed. However, for the wordings and expressions quoted as they are, the source is displayed even if it is a well-known matter. The one displayed as "dictionary" is the 6th edition of "Kojien."

The words of various people were taken into this book, but some of them are not original but the digested meanings or contents of the original prepared by the writer. This book uses "humankind" and "humanity" as synonyms in terms of living being and species, but attaches some other meanings to humanity, e.g., having intelligence, state of being human and creator of its culture and civilization.

Lastly, in this book, "the writer" has the same meaning of "I" and "the author," and it is treated as "first person singular."

Specific Note

Japanese version is the original, and English version is that which traces faithfully the contents of the original in principle. However, some inadequate passages and terms may be found in the English version because of the writer's English being unskillful. Therefore, it is my responsibility, and not that of anyone else, including the publishing company.

Chapter 1   Introduction

1 Inevitable Conflicts in the World of Sovereign Nations

Although we humans have the question, "Wherefrom did we come, whereto do we go, wherefore are we here, and who are we?," yet we don't know the answer as of now. However, in line with the reality that we exist, we humans have been able to have the perception that we have ego which is only temporary one, change without stopping for a moment, and are actual but like dreamy beings who can't even own oneself. We are a life form that is born, grow, grow old and die. This transition goes out of consciousness and quietly. Life is a momentary beam compared with eternity and it is but a dream, but this existence seems to be a life form that hopes the happiness in peace and freedom as long as it is alive. This book is based on the premise that this hope is universal to all human beings at any time and place. For this reason, no one should infringe unnecessarily and unreasonably the hope that belongs to the sovereignty of each human being.

Now, in the present world, there are various risk factors, not only hindering the realization of the hope but even bringing the risk of humanity's destruction. Based on this recognition, therefore, this book is discussing one of the main factors, the existence of many sovereign nations, to exclude the negative effects they cause.

National sovereignty is established through the mandate of the sovereignty of all members of the nation. All human hope is happiness where everyone can enjoy peace and freedom. Accordingly, the basic composition in this case is that the nation is entrusted with the realization of that hope by all members of the nation. For this, the nation comes to have the proposition to protect the nation in order to protect the happiness of the members of the nation.

Now, up to here, it looks like we can be convinced.

However, it is inevitable for a nation to come to have various conflicts of interest with other nations (religion and racial/ethnic discrimination will also be involved) related to territory, economy, and so forth. If the conflicts are not settled by dialogue, there will be a war between the nations. Then, in the name of national defense, as if the nation owned its members, the nation will force its members into military training and military service and use them as combatants if a war occurs. The nation will also control speech, ignore individual sovereignty and deprive freedom, and do the unreasonableness of imposing punishment, including death, for those who don't obey. In addition, in a war, both military personnel and civilians are harmed and killed, many refugees arise, and all sorts of misfortunes, the exact opposite of happiness, cover the human world.

Surprisingly, this means an occurrence of the uninvited reversal in the sense that the national sovereignty, which is established by national member's sovereignty, infringes and controls national member's sovereignty. This should be called the composition of absolute contradiction.

Further, the tragic story does not stop there. The war, that is fought with powerful weapons manufactured endlessly by abusing developed science, will bring about the destruction of humankind as a logical necessity. Needless to say, we humankind are at the risk of being destroyed even tomorrow if the nuclear war occurs using the nuclear weapons that the world already possesses.

In this way, as neither the flower of peace nor the flower of freedom blooms in the tree named sovereign nation system where conflict arises between sovereign nations, it does not bear the fruit of happiness there. Therefore, in order to get rid of the conflicts from the human world which is a set of humans and sovereign nation, it won't fit unless either humans or sovereign nation is erased. Under such a circumstance, needless to say, as we can't erase humans, it will be the sovereign nation that should be erased.

In the first place, a nation is a product of intangible illusion created by us humans. However, even if it is the product of the same illusion, compared to the world of sovereign nations which have various difficulties, the World Nation is far superior in terms of becoming a peaceful world automatically. This is because the Nation as only a nation on this planet won't have any hostile nation against it.

2 For Glorious Future

Based on the perception stated above, aiming for the realization of the hope of humanity for peace, freedom and happiness, this book is a talk about constructing the human Utopia in this Spaceship Earth so that we may be able to enjoy happiness there while we are alive in this world, leaving the next world to the next.

The construction of the Utopia requires its prerequisite, the survival of humankind without being destroyed.

However, looking out over our present human world, contrary to this prerequisite, it looks that we are acceleratively rushing on the highway to the risk of our destruction. Therefore, for the purpose of avoiding the risk brought by the existence of many sovereign nations which inevitably create conflict and war in the human world, this book is discussing the idea, that makes humankind a single group through developmentally dissolving sovereign nations and then unifying them to a single nation on earth, namely, the World Nation. Although this may extraordinarily seem unreal, it is a very serious story. The serious reason is in that there is no other way left for humankind to escape from the destruction by self-destruction, without realization of one nation on earth. The realization of the World Nation avoids the destruction of humankind, and it may be able to bring us not only satisfying the condition of our long-term survival but also our having reached the gate of the Utopia and entered it substantially.

After we step in the Utopia, we will be able to cooperate to polish up for the betterment of the Utopia for us humanity existing in this world, not heaven, paradise or pure land which religions preach its existence in the next world. So long as the human world is peaceful, all of the human assets will be able to be used for our happiness, constructing the Utopia in this Spaceship Earth, instead of losing its substantial part for conflict and war which bring us nothing but our unhappiness.

Chapter 2　Sovereign Nations to the World Nation

We humanity and all humans as individuals in the world desire peaceful and happy world. Therefore, we all want to have the extinction of conflict and war which trample our hope. This could be considered to be the consensus of humanity.

Nonetheless, the human world is not peaceful because conflicts and wars never go away from it. Despite the fact that the human world is under human control, "Why does the consensus of all humans not pass and realize and why is such a stupid and strange thing happening?" It is because there is a cause for this contradiction. What is it? The one of the main causes lies in the existence of many sovereign nations whose ultimate proposition is war. After all, as long as we stick to such a paradigm as "the existence of many nations" as in the present world, it is impossible to realize world peace no matter how much we discuss and pay efforts earnestly asking for it. This has been already well -proven in the human history. It is an absolutely contradictory state that a nation, which is a set of individuals, has war and tramples the individual hope, namely, peace, freedom and happiness. Consequently, as long as we don't eliminate the cause of the contradiction, conflicts and wars will never go away from the human world.

Here, a shift in thinking that touches the very root of things is required.

Because the existence of nations is causing war, it is clear where the debate goes. It requires to dissolve and then integrate the nations and establish only one nation on earth which will not have any hostile nation. Dividing this small Spaceship Earth into a number of small rooms and they are in conflict, as a result, that which humankind disappears from Spaceship Earth is so strange and stupid that makes me cry. The current state of the existence of large number of nations is not the final form of the nation, but it is in the process of reaching its final form, the only nation on earth. Because its present form brings a disaster for humans, it makes sense for us to leave quickly that form and to aim for the final form.

This may look very strange, but that's the theory, so to speak. It is another problem whether it can be realized or not. However, we need to grasp the ideal first, otherwise nothing can be proceeded ahead. We must aim at realizing the ideal. In case, unfortunately, we come to know that the ideal can never be realized, we then switch our objective to the second best. This should be a correct procedure. However, as long as we trace the present human world where many sovereign nations exist, it is believed that there is no good plan to end conflicts and wars forever in the human world. Under this circumstance, it seems that there is no other way for us to be saved than we humans realize only one nation on earth, namely, the World Nation. If we should fail to get rid of conflicts and wars, the war using developed strong weapons manufactured by the abuse of science not only forces us to live unhappy but brings the risk of the destruction of humankind.

1 Difficult Point of Many Sovereign Nations vs a Single World Nation

1. War-Producing Mechanism = Existence of Many Sovereign Nations

That sovereignty rests with the people is interpreted to mean that the sovereignty of the nation exists in the people. According to the dictionary's explanation, the sovereignty of a nation is: ① supreme power which means that a nation can take any intent as it likes and is not ruled by other nation, and an element to organize a nation accompanied by supreme, independent and absolute power and ② the final power to decide the governance of a nation. Sovereign nation means a nation which is not subordinate to other nations and can decide domestic and international problems independently. It is the basic body in the international law. The three fundamental elements for the sovereign nation are sovereignty, territory and people, and there are national defense and security as the first condition of national continuation.

Now, it looks that we can reasonably understand and accept the sovereignty rested with the people, sovereign nation and its supreme power, and national defense and security. Sovereign residents have the most advantage (though there are some nations that don't seem to take it for granted), and the sovereignty of a nation is rendered by the people. At the first glance, this does look impeccable.

However, we must pay attention to this idea, because it is the very root of creating the war in the human world.

Now that the idea is based on the premise of the existence of sovereign nations as small rooms made by dividing the earth, it is an idea that looks reasonable only when peace is promised in that premise. However, since there exist many small rooms, there arise various conflicts of interest relating to territory, economy and so forth among the rooms. What happens is absolutely and crystal clear if each room exercises its own sovereignty. That is, a war takes place unless an agreement is reached through dialogue. This is a simple mechanism that war is inevitable due to the existence of many sovereign nations. This means that, after all, what we did is nothing but created and introduced a mechanism that caused war and have allowed its existence to date in the human world. Under such circumstances, no matter how much we talk about the misery of war and wish for peace, it is only a dream forever for us to realize the extermination of war, abolition of nuclear and all other weapons, and disband of troops.

Therefore, only the option we can take to exterminate war in this Spaceship Earth is that we must swiftly and peacefully transit to the final form of the nation that only one global nation exists, rather than many nations. That is, a single World Nation. As there will be no nation to be hostile to this Nation, the extinction of war and realization of permanent peace will be promised in the human world. The reason is simple and clear. Therefore, we must change the paradigm from "existence of many nations" that we have now to "existence of a single nation" that we should newly bring in.

2. Runaway of the Sovereign Nation

There arise conflicts relating to territorial, economic and other interest between international nations. Under such circumstances, due to narrow-minded monomania/paranoia, aiming to maximize the profits of own nation, there often arises such a nation that may go out of control, adopting hegemony or imperialism that has the looting principle as its fundamental idea.

In order to aim for the objective to realize the idea, the nation has to prepare its domestic system so as to fit for it. To do this, it is necessary to have strong military power and establish a national system based on totalitarianism. Such a nation that has totalitarianism principle tends to adopt a one-party, one-nation principle or to have some people being in power. Powerful people control speech and also take away personal freedom, however, this is nothing but neglecting the sovereignty of the members of the nation.

Domestically, the nation will be in such a tragedy. As for the foreign nations, such a nation creates immeasurable negative effects inevitably not only to the invaded nation but to other nations. In addition, it is not uncommon for the powers of the nation to act obsessed with the retention of power and their own self-protection using the situation at home and abroad. This includes such matters deriving from low consciousness far away from intelligent life form, that is, to position the delusions deriving from monomania as justice, to tell a lie that invasion is defense, to transform one's own misfortunes into foreign responsibility, and so forth. World peace, freedom, happiness and the future of humanity will be disturbed.

In the first place, such undesirable matters are the phenomena that arise totally because of the existence of many sovereign nations. To the contrary, under the World Nation, since no international interest will arise and there is no nation to plunder or be plundered, there is no fear of war or any strange thing else.

3. Final Form of the Nation

In the first place, the present state of existence of large number of nations is not the final form of the nation.

We humans flock to form group.

It is clear in our history that a group has changed from small to bigger. Namely, a group began with hamlet and changed to village to town to city to state to nation. The present state is still the existence of many groups or nations.

We cannot expect our peace and happiness where there are many groups which engage with conflict and fight in one area. After the fight between the groups, however, those groups are unified to a bigger one and peace prevails in this group. What happens next is that this and another group fight and are unified to much bigger one and peace visits again to this newly unified group. In such a way, a group becomes bigger and bigger, however, the presently existing each group or nation still has many other opponent nations. Therefore, it is not the final form of the nation but an incomplete entity being stagnant on the way to the final one.

The final form is completed when we all humanity become a single group and the entire world becomes a single nation or the World Nation. There will be no opponent to this Nation and at that time, permanent peace will be realized in the human world.

Therefore, the idea to make the earth one nation is not strange but quite natural as if water runs down from high point to the low. As against this, the presently existing nations are not optimum but rather strange from the standpoint of our objective for realization of peace and happiness.

4. Retrogression Against the Final Form of the Nation

As discussed above, the direction where we humanity must head is a single nation or the World Nation as the final form of the nation. Nonetheless, recently, as against this movement, there is a fact to move backwards to divide the existing nation to much smaller ones to be resulting in increasing the number of nations. This does not mean the independence of many colonies of large countries after the World War II, but means the movement arisen after the independence of colonies that aims at establishing a nation under the flag of identification with race/ethnicity, religion, culture, etc.

However, the intent of the movement is not inconsistent with the idea of the world single nation or the final form of the nation. The motivation of establishing smaller nation is in that minority people in race/ethnicity, religion, culture, etc. try to escape from the unfair treatment and discrimination they receive in their nation.

On the other hand, the fundamental concept of the world nation is in that it aims at treating any minority people fair and equal without any discrimination together with establishing respect and harmony among all people. Therefore, it is believed that such a motivation that minority people escape from the World Nation will never arise. This Nation is a society which is very kind and tender to minority people, and they are completely released from any distress resulting from discrimination.

In the meantime, even if the independence under such a motivation should be realized, the nation might be swallowed by a large nation again unless that the nation can satisfy the requirements as an independent sovereign nation with regard to governmental administration, economy, national defense and security, and so forth. It is not easy that everything goes as desired under the existence of many nations in the world.

2 Existence of International Conflict

The presently existing international conflicts are mostly based on such circumstances that there have been accumulated resentment and hate resulting from the continuous conflicts and/or wars from the past, which have not been raveled, due to the conflicts of interest among nations. Now that the conflicts presently appeared on the surface more or less involve the past conflicts remained unsettled, the present conflict cannot reach final and real settlement until the past conflicts reach the settlement first. However, this is most difficult to achieve, and as a result, the conflicts have been arising one after another to date. (By the way, race/ethnicity and religion tend to get involved in the conflict among nations)

Nonetheless, if such nations continue to take up the arms and fight for a long time even if they say they have enough reason to do so or the conflicts yet unsettled, there arise many unhappy matters such as refugees, the killed and wounded soldiers and private citizens of both sides, and economy, livelihood and public sentiment to be exhausted. As this situation between wartime nations forms various problems for neighbor nations, friendly nations and international society or the United Nations, the mediation comes in to stop the war by putting off the arms at any rate. This often tends to result in a truce as an emergency measure which reflects the intention reached by all those nations involved. However, since the real reason for the conflict itself has never been settled, anything has never changed basically from the beginning.

At that time, while no dialogue between the parties to the conflict progresses, those nations involved may extend to the proposal of the tentative and provisional solution as to the reason for the conflict, which may result in the acceptance by both sides, though reluctantly, after all. This solution, however, generally means only an ad hoc thought and restoration such as a patchwork that is not a comprehensive plan for the final solution. Moreover, the proposed solution often tends to reflect not only the thought of the parties to the conflict but also more or less the expectations of many nations concerned, so it cannot be denied that the parties to the conflict are not fully satisfied with such a tentative and provisional solution. As a result, it is natural that the parties to the conflict cannot comply with and respect such a solution, and that such a vicious cycle for them to take the arms again to repeat battles takes place, as if dissatisfaction, resentment and anger that remained like embers blazed like a pillar of fire. This means a winding up just where the attempt for the solution started off.

In this way, generally, any conflict arisen all over the world today becomes the problem not only for the nations directly involved but for those indirectly and organically involved. Resulting from the fact that any happy understanding cannot be obtained, it becomes a kind of the normal state that dissatisfaction, resentment and anger remained as deposit spread all over the world. This situation arises because any respective "justice" is not accepted.

There are countless conflicts in the world which cannot be settled even if the world leaders gather together and discuss. Nonetheless, if a truce, even an ad hoc and emergency one, could be made, there is a meaning to sprinkle water on the battle, that is, even the truce such as this cannot be denied as it has some effect.

On the other hand, there is a fact that even such a truce cannot be made and guerrilla fighting and terrorism never cease in the human world. Although it is considered that war only with the ordinary weapons would not invite instant extinction of humankind, yet it cannot be denied that in the war, between nuclear-weapons holding nations, the nation placed at a disadvantage in the war situation with the ordinary (conventional) weapons comes to use nuclear weapons. Once worldwide nuclear-weapon war should take place, it goes without saying that real extinction of humankind will definitely take place.

This is the present state of the world, and it is attributable undoubtedly to the existence of many sovereign nations, of which main proposition is to fight against other nations in case the conflict of interest is not settled by dialogue.

3 Need for Transition to the World Nation

1. Low Expectations for the Natural Establishment of the World Nation

There is a thought that the World Nation as the final form of the nation is ideal but unreal and unfeasible at this point in time and that we don't have to aim it at now, for the World Nation will be realized soon or later naturally when the time comes.

However, we cannot take this option.

The first reason lies in that taking into account various matters arising in the world due to existence of many sovereign nations, even if some probability of natural formation of the World Nation could be expected, the realization is considered to be many hundreds or more years after from now. We will have been extinct way before then as a result from wars or the destruction of natural and ecological environment due to our having been making light of it. The second reason is in that even if we humankind would not become extinct, we shall be forced to live unhappy for a long period of time in both natural and artificial (human society) environments being different from our desire.

We humanity shouldn't be any more unhappy.

We cannot establish the World Nation by such a negative stance as doing nothing but waiting being seated. It can be (or may be) realized only through our determination and execution based on a comprehensive plan reflecting our positive and strong "will" to achieve it.

There have been continuous conflicts and wars from the past due to existence of many sovereign nations, which are not the final form of the nation. If we leave this situation as is, it is reasoned that we humanity shall be not only unhappy but extinct due to the wars succeeding into the future. When we think over unhappiness of the people due to uncontrollable various conflicts arisen everyday among many sovereign nations, it is thought that now is the last chance left over for us to switch our spiritual paradigm to the World Nation and step out our first step towards that direction.

2. The Concept of the World Nation

To newly summarize "What is the World Nation?," it is a nation which makes all humanity a group and has entire earth as its territory. As there is no nation which is hostile to this Nation, permanent peace is realized there without any war at all.

The objective of this Nation is not inconsistent but consistent fully with the Supreme Idea of the Human World originated in nature of human life. This means that in this Nation, no individual is discriminated, human rights are defended, every individual is treated equal and free, and it is possible for any individual to pursue his/her respective happiness. The respective propositions, in terms of peace and war of individual and the nation (as a set of individuals), are confronted with each other in the present world, but they unite in peace in the World Nation. Moreover, the supply of clothing, food and shelter becomes substantial, and natural environment is preserved, restored and even improved. At least, it is the world where all individuals are cooperatively making every endeavor after these goods. In this peaceful world, all of man, goods, money and human spiritual energy, which used to be spent for conflict and war uselessly and unhappily for humanity, now become possible to be transferred to use totally only for human well-being.

4 The World Nation as Our Sole Option

With regard to the proposition, "to dissolve the sovereign nations and make the whole earth the World Nation," it is imagined that various oppositions spring out relating to not only its conception but its feasibility. However, the opposite is meaningless and useless until any opponent makes his/her thought clear on the Premises, as shown:

Premise 1   We continuously follow the same road as in the past in terms of having wars resulting inevitably from the existence of many sovereign nations, using more and more developed weapons introduced by abusing of science.

Premise 2   We humanity do not desire our extinction but desire long-term survival in happiness embraced in peace and freedom.

(a)   To take Premise 1 is to abandon Premise 2. This means our acceptance of the risk of our suicide-like extinction. We humanity may live momentarily and shortly and become extinct through fighting war like fiend of struggle, but this is also one of humanity's options.

(b) In case we choose the negation of Premise 1 and desire the extinction of war, we still have the chance to get on the road to head to Premise 2. This means that we must think about our heading towards establishment of the World Nation through dissolution and then unification of presently existing many sovereign nations.

(c) If it is possible to be held good that with regard to Premise 1, we accept the existence of many sovereign nations but deny the wars among those nations, it is considered that the World Nation is not the sole option. However, such a matter like magic is not thought realistic and realized from the standpoint of the reason for the formation of sovereign nation system.

By the way, however, regarding (c) above, it cannot be said to be 100% for sure that there is no possibility for it to be realized, for the realization might be brought by a certain unexpected breakthrough. In case the conflicts and wars among the sovereign nations should cease and permanent peace is realized in such a way, such a situation can be considered that the World Nation is substantially realized.

In the world of people, people are born first and then people gather and form group, which begins with hamlet and changes to the presently existing many nations. However, it is only an illusion to persistently possess such a thought that a nation in the presently existing nations is the sole one to which we can entrust our sovereignty and desire. Instead of this, there is an ideal nation, the World Nation, to which we can entrust those. In case (c) above should be realized, it is considered easy that at that time we will be able to amend the situation both in name and reality to the World Nation from the sovereign nations. However, we cannot expect this sort of matter, as we can never have the conviction of such a development.

By the way, there is the United Nations as an international organization which functions to contribute to peace and security among sovereign nations. This looks universally practicing the thought in (c) above that accepts the existence of many nations but denies the wars among nations. However, although the United Nations functions for seeking the maintenance of peace and security when conflicts and/ or wars take place among sovereign nations, yet it has the contradiction of "peace under the presence of sovereign nations." For this reason, the United Nations may look similar to the World Nation, but actually different. Therefore, it can't be considered expectable that the World Nation should be born naturally from the United Nations as long as this contradiction exists.

In this connection, taking a look at Constitution of the United Nations Educational, Scientific and Cultural Organization (Preamble), as exhibited below, the purpose of this Constitution is in summary read as the attainment of such objectives of: mutual understanding among the people of the world, graduation from ignorance and prejudice to be resulting in inequality of men and races, mutual respect of men, justice, liberty and peace, give-and-take spirit, and intellectual and moral solidarity of humanity, and so forth. In order to make the purpose universal, the Constitution claims the full and equal opportunities for education for all, in the unrestricted pursuit of objective truth, and the free exchange of ideas and knowledge. The point which the Constitution aims at is in the proclaim to promote the attainment of the objectives of international peace and the common welfare of humanity, through educational and scientific and cultural relations of the people in the world.

On the other hand, it cannot be denied that the Constitution is naturally and after all frustrating because the United Nations is based on the existence of sovereign nations. Although there is no objection that education is needed to peace, yet it does not directly contribute to peace. Regardless of educated or not, it is needless to say that all individuals in the world desire peace. In the beginning of the Constitution, too, described is that since wars begin in the minds of men, the defenses of peace must be constructed in the minds. However, the defenses of peace have been constructed in the minds of men since long time before. Nonetheless, wars take place as long as sovereign nations exist. This is attributable to the contradiction arisen from the difference in proposition that while every individual in the world has peace as his/her proposition, any nation in the presently existing nations has war as its proposition, despite the fact that a nation is nothing but a set of individuals.

Moreover, this contradiction is very strange as it arises from the fact that a nation intends to defend the proposition of individual. Namely, a nation does war as its ultimate means in order to defend its interest and people, but this results in the contradiction that any war does afflict the people in every way.

In order to resolve this inevitable and strange contradiction, it becomes a must to extinguish either humanity or the nation. However, where the discussion goes, as we cannot extinguish ourselves, it follows that it is the nation that should be extinguished.

In consequence whereof, as long as Premise 2 is taken, the option left over for us humanity is only (b) above, which means that after all, we humanity must move towards the establishment of the World Nation.

Constitution of the United Nations Educational, Scientific and Cultural Organization (Preamble)

The Governments of the States Parties to this Constitution on behalf of their peoples declare:

That since wars begin in the minds of men, it is in the minds of men that the defenses of peace must be constructed;

The ignorance of each other's ways and lives has been a common cause, throughout the history of mankind, of that suspicion and mistrust between the peoples of the world through which their differences have all too often broken into war;

That the great and terrible war which has now ended was a war made possible by the denial of the democratic principles of the dignity, equality and mutual respect of men, and by the propagation, in their place, through ignorance and prejudice, of the doctrine of the inequality of men and races;

That the wide diffusion of culture, and the education of humanity for justice and liberty and peace are indispensable to the dignity of man and constitute a sacred duty which all the nations must fulfill in a spirit of mutual assistance and concern;

That a peace based exclusively upon the political and economic arrangements of governments would not be a peace which could secure unanimous, lasting and sincere support of the peoples of the world, and that the peace must therefore be founded, if it is not to fail, upon the intellectual and moral solidarity of mankind.

For these reasons, the States Parties to this Constitution, believing in full and equal opportunities for education for all, in the unrestricted pursuit of objective truth, and in the free exchange of ideas and knowledge, are agreed and determined to develop and to increase the means of communication between their peoples and to employ these means for the purposes of mutual understanding and a truer and more perfect knowledge of each other's lives;

In consequence whereof they do hereby create the United Nations Educational, Scientific and Cultural Organization for the purpose of advancing, through the educational and scientific and cultural relations of the peoples of the world, the objectives of international peace and of the common welfare of mankind for which the United Nations Organization was established and which its Charter proclaims. (From the internet site of Japan Ministry of Education, Culture, Sports, Science and Technology)

5 Feasibility of Realization of the World Nation

Then, what are the chances of realization of the World Nation? It is unknown.

Only what is known is that unless we dissolve the presently existing sovereign nations in our Spaceship Earth, and then unify them to a single nation, the World Nation, very high is the probability of the risk that we humanity will be not only extinct in the near future but forced to live unhappy until our extinction. As against the present world, the World Nation which is a single nation on the earth is an ideal place where there will be no conflict nor war by nations at all.

Consequently, the issue we have now is to choose one out of the two options as to whether we trace the present situation into the future accepting the risk of our extinction due to never-ending conflict and war, or we challenge to head to establishing the World Nation where the realization of our hope is promised. This is the matter of our discretion. Apart from the choosing the former, in case we choose the latter, "we can or cannot" or its feasibility is not an issue. We humanity are now on the verge of destruction, but fortunately, the road leading us to realize our hope still remains. In face of this situation, what we must do is no other than paying our best effort to tide over the difficulties in order for us to be the inhabitants in the glorious future.

As discussed above, it is difficult for us to expect that the World Nation is born naturally on the extension of the United Nations. However, as for the process of the establishment of the World Nation and its beginning government in the event of its realization, it is considered it as an influential approach to make the best use of the United Nations.

With regard to the procedure for "the transition to the World Nation," as an example, I outlined my idea later in Chapter 6 Road to Establishment to the World Nation and Chapter 7 Unrealistic Hope and Unrealistic Decision.

Chapter 3   Sovereign Nations vs Development of Science

1 Development of Science that Denies Sovereign Nations

Sovereign nations have existed for thousands of years. They perished and were founded anew, formed and dissolved alliances and coalitions due to being conscious of the adversaries, or united with another nation. Essentially the same things like this have been continuously repeated until today. Under the sovereign nations, it is normal for the nations to be at the state of tension or war, regardless of whether it being latent or manifest. Therefore, even if there is a peace, it is not a true and lasting peace but only a momentary peace whenever it may collapse.

Whenever a battle broke out, tragedy and misfortune were told in various ways, various papers and novels have been written, and heartbreaking voices and thoughts that yearn for peace have covered the human world. The same things have been repeated for thousands of years. However, wars have never gone away and won't go away as long as we follow the presently existing world.

To assess this situation, it was we humans who have built our world, but it cannot be said that it has adequately harmonized with our hope for peace, freedom and happiness. Nonetheless, that which we have been sticking to it to date, having been swept by the reality in front of us, turns out that we are stupid. Moreover, if we have known our stupidity but have not challenged to fix it, not only we are stupid beyond stupid but we are a lazy creature. If we humans remain so stupid and lazy unchanged, it may seem that even if we perish, it can't be helped because it's self-serving.

This is, however, what has been done, so it can't be helped even if we regret it today. If we humanity hope our glorious future, it is important for us to reflect on the past and use it as food for the future.

Fortunately (though to say like this is sorry for those countless people who couldn't live life and suffered various misfortunes, including physical and mental disorders, because of wars between sovereign nations), for thousands of years, despite the countless wars, large and small, we have been able to survive to this day without being destroyed.

The biggest reason lies in that weapons weren't strong enough to bring about the extinction of humankind, but in and after World War II, weapons changed a lot. This relies on the development of science. It was decided to develop and manufacture more and more powerful weapons one after another by abusing science. At present, the most powerful of these is nuclear weapons. After being dropped on Hiroshima and Nagasaki just before the end of World War II, that level of nuclear weapons has not been used, however, even with only the existing nuclear weapons held by the world, it is said to have enough power to exterminate the human race many times. Weapons that kill or injure humans are strongly considered "having enough already" even with existing ones.

However, if the conflict between sovereign nations is endless, it will be endless to develop and manufacture powerful weapons, by abusing of science that has no bounds for development. This should be called a negative spiral that arises from the relationship of science and sovereign nation whose ultimate proposition is war.

In order to eliminate this unhappy spiral and avoid the extinction of humankind, it is required that either science or sovereign nation must be extinguished to handle the situation. However, now that science cannot be extinguished, it will be sovereign nation that should be extinguished. This means that the development of science speaks eloquently that the existence of sovereign nations, which we have accepted until today having been flowing into its existing reality, has become unacceptable from this point onwards.

In this way, so-called science is deeply involved in happiness and unhappiness and life and death of us humanity. Based on this perception, in this chapter, 2 Disaster of Science, 3 Misfortune and

Happiness with Science and 4 Scientific Civilization and Spiritual Civilization are being talked hereinafter.

2 Disaster of Science

The disaster of science consists of 1. Non-Peaceful Use of Science and 2. Failure of the Peaceful Uses of Science. It is clear that the former is the disaster of science. The latter refers to things which were intended for peaceful use turn out to be harmful consequences for the human world.

1. Non-Peaceful Use of Science

There are (1) Nuclear Weapons and (2) Ordinary Weapons as the greatest examples of the disaster of science.

(1) Nuclear Weapons

①History of Nuclear Weapons

Nuclear weapon was originally developed and manufactured in the United States, and it was used on Nagasaki and Hiroshima, Japan just before the end of World War II. Throughout history, we humans have worked hard to develop stronger weapons for the use of battle. In particular, during World War I and World War II, in order to dominate the opponents, demands for overwhelming weapons rose up. By abusing the ability of advanced science that can meet its demands, we have come to possess nuclear weapon which is also called the ultimate weapon. The power of the atomic bombs used on Hiroshima and Nagasaki was about 16 kilotons if converted to TNT gunpower. However, since then, nuclear weapons have progressed from atomic bomb by nuclear fission to fusion bomb. Its power has increased drastically and we humans have developed nuclear weapons that have tens of times and hundreds of times more power than Hiroshima/Nagasaki type.

After World War II, the world became, in broad terms, polarized by major powers, America and Soviet Union (Russia today), and was divided into American side (western side) and Soviet side (eastern side). The tensions between the two sides rose, and the world entered the Cold War era. Soviet which was projected the power of nuclear weapons by America quickly came to equip massive nuclear weapons to counter America. For more than a quarter of a century after World War II, America and Soviet looked like fighting a nuclear weapons development battle. Here we humans have come, since there will be no winner and no loser in the event of war using nuclear weapons, it became a situation that we have it but can't use it.

As a result, a balance of fear is being formed, that is, each other suppresses the other's nuclear with its nuclear. There is no war like a world war for America and Russia to go to the front and fight directly, and in this meaning, peace means peace, for the time being. However, that peace is far from a positive peace that we can be satisfied with from the bottom of heart, as it is a state that the unavoidable passive peace is dangerously being maintained.

Following America and Soviet, UK, France and China, the victorious nations of World War II, became nuclear-weapons nations. Also, Israel, whose rebuilding was realized nearly after 2,000 years, and India and Pakistan, which have been in the state of tensions due to territorial issue and difference in religion, have become nuclear-weapons nations. In addition, North Korea has become a nuclear-weapons nation recently.

②Fear of Nuclear Weapons

Regarding the tension between the West centered on America and the East centered on Soviet, there were times when it rose to the point of touch-and-go of which typical example was the plan to deploy nuclear weapons to Cuba by Soviet in 1962. Western nations without nuclear weapons have come to rely on the composition that they come under the US nuclear umbrella. That is, in the event of a nuclear attack from the opponent, America will act nuclear retaliation on behalf of attacked nation. This is based on the expectation/assumption that a nuclear attack on one's nation from the opposite side would be deterred. However, this is nothing but a stupid and deplorable composition now that they themselves introduced nuclear weapons, and both the West and the East are projecting their power to each other and are being afraid of each other.

In addition, although it is not a nuclear weapon developed by its own nation, there is a nuclear sharing concept, which is a policy concept arisen for nuclear deterrence, and it is being implemented. In order to counter nuclear weapons deployed in Soviet and its satellite nations, Germany, Italy, Belgium and Holland within the North Atlantic Treaty Organization (NATO) are having nuclear weapons owned by America in own nation, and national governments have the right to use them. (Wikipedia, the free encyclopedia)

More than a quarter of a century has passed since World War II, both the Soviet Union and China, while maintaining the name of communism, essentially adopted a capitalist economy. Since the mid-1980's, the Soviet Union aimed to reform soviet socialism, Gorbachev deployed perestroika, and it ended with the collapse of the Soviet Union in 1991. Some countries in the Soviet Union were isolated and independent, and the Soviet Union renamed to Russian Federation. Meantime, China has risen, and the clear framework of the polarized world of America and the Soviet Union since World War II has faded out somewhat. Coupled with the globalization of economic activities, the tension in the world has eased to some extent. However, this does not mean that the large framework of the West and the East has disappeared, and that the international conflict derived from the framework has disappeared. As long as there is conflict, the demand to suppress the opponent's nuclear has not disappeared. In recent years, the concern about nuclear armament by North Korea also covers the world.

③Destruction of Humankind by Nuclear Weapons, an Absolute Evil

Different from ordinary (conventional) weapons, all-out war with strategic nuclear weapons will lead to the extinction of humankind, not to mention the civilization of humanity. The strategic nuclear weapons include intercontinental ballistic missile (ICBM), strategic bomber, and ballistic missile-carrying nuclear submarine.

Once nuclear weapons are used in war, that brings indescribable, inhumane and unreasonable misfortune and misery including that many people lose their lives and suffer from sequelae that will never be cured.

Also, nuclear weapons bring not only catastrophic destruction of the hypocenter but also other various tragic damage by heat, blast and long-lasting radioactivity of nuclear explosion. Moreover, the terror of nuclear weapons is also in its indirect damage. It is the destruction of ecosystem throughout the earth that makes it impossible for life to survive. Nuclear weapons contaminate the oceans, the ground surface and atmosphere with radioactivity, and the ash that rolls up in the air blocks the sunlight and lowers the temperature to be resulting in making an environment in which any organisms cannot survive. Plants, which are autotrophic organisms, capable of self-producing organic nutrients, wither up.

As a result, the animals, heterotrophic organisms, that are unable to produce organic matter in-house and take nourishing food produced by plants, also cannot survive. It is extinction due to food shortage due to collapse of food chain. Humans, who are at the top of the food chain, are no exception, of course. It will be the most miserable situation for humankind.

Thus, nuclear weapons are absolute evil. Now that it is the greatest disaster of science and the greatest thing that contradicts the Supreme Idea of the Human World, it must be expelled from the human world as quickly and completely as possible. Therefore, it is a Must to abolish nuclear weapons from all over the world unconditionally and resolutely. This is indisputably obvious even to an elementary school child rather than a so-called specialist in the field who makes silly arguments on nuclear weapons, including the height of the stupid idea of nuclear deterrence by nuclear.

④Efforts to Reduce and Eliminate Nuclear Weapons
For the battle, since the history of weapons has been the search

for more powerful weapons, it's no wonder that the United States introduced nuclear weapon as an extension of that. There is no "if" in the history, but it goes without saying that, if not America, some other country became the country of introduction of nuclear weapon. However, what was learned after introducing was that it was so powerful and not to mention the United States and the Soviet Union, the world trembled with its terror. For this reason, efforts to reduce and eliminate nuclear weapons occurred, as described hereinafter.

The United Nations

* The disarmament of nuclear weapons was discussed and adopted by the United Nations, and it became Nuclear Non-Proliferation Treaty (NPT) in 1963. It was signed in 1968 and its effectuation was in 1970.
  This Treaty is the one that recognizes internationally only the five nations, USA, Russia (former Soviet Union), UK, France, and China, which were the victorious nations of the World War II, as nuclear-weapon nations with the provision for imposing upon the nations the duties of nuclear weapon disarmament, prohibits non-nuclear-weapon nations from possessing nuclear weapons, and limits nuclear use only for peaceful purpose.

* As from 1994, every year, Japan, as only country in the world to have suffered nuclear bombs, has submitted the United Nations the Resolution to Abolish Nuclear Weapons, which was adopted every year afterwards. In 2009, with the advocacy of a world without nuclear weapons proposed by US President Barack Obama, America became the cosponsor of the submission first time. In 2012, this bill was resolved by a large number of countries, 184 countries. In 2017, the resolution was adopted by 156 of supporting countries, inclusive of America, UK and France, however, that number was down by 11 countries from 167 in the previous year.
  The reason might be in that Japan, which submitted the Resolution to Abolish Nuclear Weapons, turned in the opposite of the Treaty

on the Prohibition of Nuclear Weapons, which was adopted by the United Nations in July of the year through the efforts of International Campaign to Abolish Nuclear Weapons (ICAN) of NGO. That is, it cannot be denied that Japan was imaged as a country with double standards for a world without nuclear weapons.

The main reason Japan opposed was in that if the use of nuclear weapons is prohibited, the security balance of Japan and other countries, which rely on the US nuclear umbrella, will collapse.

It is nothing but self-contradiction that Japan submitted the Resolution to Abolish Nuclear Weapons but opposed to the Prohibition of Nuclear Weapons submitted by ICAN with nuclear-weapon countries, however, this is put aside for the time-being. The situation of adoption of the Resolution to Abolish Nuclear Weapons by the United Nations in 2016, 2017 and 2021 is as shown below: (Press release by the Ministry of Foreign Affairs of Japan)

The Resolution to Abolish Nuclear Weapons

	2016	2017	2021
Country in favor	167	156	158
Opposing country	4	4	4
Country abstaining	16	24	27
Country in conference	187	184	189

Only four countries opposed, that is, Russia, China, Syria and North Korea. Since country in favor includes America, UK and France, if Russia and China turn to the country in favor, all of the five countries, which are recognized internationally as nuclear-weapons countries by NPT and are permanent members of the United Nations, will be the country in favor. If becomes so, it would be expected that the Resolution to Abolish Nuclear Weapons will be unanimously adopted as it could be expected that various related problems of not only remaining opposites but countries abstaining will be resolved.

* US President Barack Obama gave a speech in 2009 for "a world without nuclear weapons," and won the Nobel Prize. However, he stated that America will continue to possess nuclear weapons as long as other countries continue to have it. Both Russia and China denied the abolition of nuclear weapons.

America and Russia (former Soviet Union)

* Strategic Arms Limitation Talks (SALT) were started as from 1969, and Anti-Ballistic Missile Limitation Treaty (ABMLT) was concluded in 1972. However, this treaty was revoked in 2002 by America which promoted missile defense.

* Strategic Arms Reduction Treaty (START) for strategic nuclear forces reduction was started as from 1982 between America and Soviet Union, and the first Strategic Arms Reduction Treaty (START I—upper limit of the number of strategic nuclear warheads possessed to 6,000 each for America and Soviet Union) was concluded in 1991 and fulfilled in 2001. However, the second Strategic Arms Reduction Treaty (START II—upper limit being 3,000~3,500 for each country) concluded in 1993 was cancelled without fulfillment. This is because, as stated above, America which promoted missile defense revoked ABMLT in 2002, Soviet Union came to express not to fulfill START II. It is noted that scheduled START III (upper limit being 2,000~2,500 for each country) was not concluded.

* Because START II and III had been cancelled, New START (upper limit being 1,550 for each country) following START I was concluded in 2010 and came to effect in the following year. The reduction of the number of nuclear warheads is outstanding, but both countries announced the extension of this Treaty. (Press release dated Feb. 4, 2021 by the Ministry of Foreign Affairs of Japan) → (As of Spring 2023, it is unknown whether this will change or stay the same. The world media reported that Russia is suspending its fulfillment relating to the situation in Ukraine)

* Based on the philosophy that if both sides give up their power, there would be no military power expansion, Intermediate-Range Nuclear Forces Treaty (INF) was concluded in 1987, and by mid-1991, the deadline set by the Treaty, intermediate-range missiles equipped with nuclear and conventional warheads were scrapped by more than 2,500 as the combined total of both countries. This Treaty was taken over by Russia but the United States gave notice of its annulment in February 2019 and it expired in August, half a year later.

With reference to Stockholm International Peace Research Institute (SIPRI), the number of nuclear weapons in the world as of January 2021 was 13,080, excluding the estimated number of 40~50 held by North Korea. Out of that, the two countries, America and Russia, have over 90% in total (5,550 held by America and 6,255 held by Russia, or 11,805 in total), and the rest being less than 10% is held by other six (6) countries, UK, France, China, India, Pakistan and Israel. The 11,805 held by America and Russia is the result from reduction mostly through the first Strategic Arms Reduction Treaty (START I) from the peak of tens of thousands of shots in the 1980's. However, since the turn of the century, the reduction has stagnated and rather, it seems that the brakes are gone, including other countries. That is, there is a worry, which can't be wiped away, for even going back to nuclear armament expansion.

ICAN (NGO)

* The NGO, which has an abbreviation of ICAN (International Campaign to Abolish Nuclear Weapons), aims for outlawing and abolishing of nuclear weapons, in cooperation with peace organizations in each country, works on governments and civil society, and continues to sue the inhumanity of nuclear weapons. The 101 countries and 468 NGOs participated in ICAN, and the thought was embodied in the form of the Treaty on the Prohibition of Nuclear Weapons at the United Nations in July 2017. ICAN was awarded the Nobel Prize for this.

As of January 2021, this Treaty had 86 signatories (two other member countries) and the 66 countries ratified. As 50 ratifications required for the entry into force of the Treaty was met in October 2020, the Treaty went into the entry after 90 days since that day, in January 2021. (Wikipedia, the free encyclopedia)

Against this, the countries including essential nuclear-weapons countries and the countries including Japan, which rely on nuclear deterrence, are not party to this Treaty. There is a stupid criticism made by profound fool that this Treaty is meaningless as nuclear-weapons countries don't support and it ignores the security through nuclear deterrence, making reference to the fear of North Korea's nuclear armament, and so forth.

However, such a criticism does not hold. The rationale is in that ignoring the security through nuclear deterrence will cease to be a concern as its need will disappear if nuclear weapons are banned and extinguished. Also, as for nuclear-weapons countries being not supporting the Treaty, it cannot be denied that it is true that because of it, the Treaty's authority and effectiveness are vulnerable. However, to have such a Treaty is still meaningful enough in terms of a definite contribution aiming for extinguishing nuclear weapons even by a step.

On the contrary, those that must be criticized for this are, first of all, the countries including Japan and nuclear-weapons countries which opposed to the Treaty, and secondly, those people who do nothing but are being seated and only making a stupid criticism that such a Treaty is meaningless and who misunderstand that they are talking about some good reason. What is called good sense and good reason on nuclear weapons should be nothing but claiming "immediately, resolutely and completely abolish them as they bring the extinction of humankind." The abolishment of nuclear weapons can't realize from the argument within the paradigm of the existence of nuclear weapons.

⑤Back in Time

As in the preceding paragraph, from the late 1980's, to put a brake on nuclear weapons has increased, and the number of nuclear weapons has been reduced to 11,805 as a combined total held by America and Russia from the peak of tens of thousands of shots mid 1980's. However, since the turn of the century, it looks like the brake has disappeared, and the writer can't get rid of the feeling that the trend of the reduction of nuclear weapons is going backwards. There must be a reason for the existence of unstable international situation and conflicts, however, it should be a common recognition in the world today that there is no intellectual connection between it and possession of nuclear weapons. It is because we humankind will be extinct if we start a nuclear war. Even if a nation wins and annihilates the opponent in a nuclear war and some people could survive, it goes without saying that due to the destruction of the ecosystem, "the victor in the battle" will also be extinct eventually "as biological loser." In other words, there is no strategic meaning in owing nuclear weapons. It is only investing human's mind, body and property, that can be used for happiness, in order to make human beings unhappy, so to speak.

Therefore, regarding nuclear weapons, it is the best perspective that it should not be enhanced, it should not be preserved what exists, it is not something that should be timidly reduced by bit and bit, but it should be expelled from the human world all at once, perfectly, resolutely and as soon as possible.

In order to secure the future and glory of humanity, the writer like to hopefully request the world leaders, America and Russia, by all means, to take the initiative for the abolishment of nuclear weapons that will be the first wise decision and good deeds in the human history.

⑥Nuclear Non-Proliferation and Nuclear Abolishment

Because nuclear non-proliferation is desirable for humanity, no matter what and in any case, there is no objection that it should be affirmed.

Now, the essential point of NPT (Nuclear Non-Proliferation Treaty) is in that the five nuclear-weapons nations (America, Russia, UK, France and China) are recognized as nuclear-weapons nations, but non-nuclear-weapons nations, that have not owned the weapons, are prohibited to aim to own nuclear weapons, in order not to spread nuclear weapons any further. However, the composition that "we have but you don't have" is nonsensical. This is not something that non-nuclear-weapons nations can accept from the bottom of their heart, because humans are living beings that feel and think that such unfair thoughts and words are basically unacceptable.

Even in an age without nuclear weapons, that is, only with ordinary (conventional) weapons, the nuclear-weapons nations, the victorious nations of World War II, were already superior in military power to non-nuclear-weapons nations. From the point of view of the security assurance of a sovereign nation, it is considered natural for a small military nation to have wished, if possible, to obtain a powerful weapon like nuclear weapon, to ensure its security against military powers, and also to secure a sufficient right to speak internationally. However, the side that came to get nuclear weapons in reality was not military minority but military power. As a result, the initiative is in the form of being grasped by military powers both in the military and international voices.

In face of this circumstance, it is considered not strange but natural that some small military nations fear military powers holding nuclear weapons and come to think about it to have own nuclear weapons for ensuring own security by nuclear deterrence. If nuclear weapons were not introduced, the necessities to oppose nuclear weapons with nuclear never arose. In this case, if you ask which one is irrational, it is nuclear-weapons nations.

It is clear what can be seen from the final goal of nuclear non-proliferation and the above discussion, that is, the ultimate of nuclear non-proliferation is the abolishment of nuclear weapons.

Therefore, the Nuclear Non-Proliferation Treaty (NPT) wasn't necessary. Namely, instead of creating such a Treaty that non-nuclear-weapons nations should not aim to possess nuclear weapons, what the five nuclear-weapons nations should have done at that time was their declaration to non-nuclear-weapon nations that they will perfectly abolish nuclear weapons immediately. At that time, we humans should have decided and resolutely executed the abolition of nuclear weapons from the human world.

Because we couldn't do it and nuclear weapons stayed in the human world, what happened after that are all sorts of stupid things that make us want to cover our eyes. The stance of the nuclear-weapons nation is in that we have nuclear weapons which act as a nuclear deterrence and so we wouldn't be attacked with nuclear weapons from the opponent, therefore, it is necessary for us to hold nuclear weapons. However, as long as we humans stand on such a stupid and childish thought, which is not different from the fighting of young children, nuclear weapons shall never go away from the human world until the end of humankind. This composition looks like the theory that both our and their nations introduced devil and are trying to control devil with devil. It is the logic of the height of stupidity under the situation invited by self-serving. If so-called "control evil with evil" is one theory, here, the wisdom of humanity should be concentrated and we humans must work together with another reasoning, "the unreasonable reasoning," in order to eliminate this common evil from the human world.

This means that all individuals and all nations must deeply understand the elimination of the devil as a "common wish of all humanity" and joyfully put it into action. Even if "complete, verifiable and irreversible nuclear disarmament" is realized with this common wish left missing and with suspicion as if it was forced by something, it is just a physical story about the nuclear weapons being possessed presently. Scientific knowledge and technology of nuclear weapons are not irreversible, that is, it will remain with civilization. If the common wish of humanity is not preserved, nuclear weapons can be remanufactured at any time.

Nuclear knowledge and energy itself is not evil but good thing. Those people who make it a disaster are stupid. The peaceful and safe use of nuclear knowledge and energy is necessary for the future of humanity. For an example out of many, it may be used for shifting the orbit of asteroids to be colliding with earth. It all depends on human heart handling it.

After Hiroshima and Nagasaki, nuclear weapons reaching that level have never been used. However, if there arises a situation where something above that level is used in a war, it is concerned that it will result in the extinction of humankind with a high probability. This is because it is likely to induce domino toppling. If the non-use situation is broken even once, the writer don't know what will happen after that. Human madness and stupidity momentarily sweep away good sense and intelligence, and as a result, it can happen the state that we cannot stop ourselves to the end of catastrophe. It is clear from looking at most of the wars that have taken place in the past. The crucial difference between past wars and nuclear wars, however, is in that in the former, the postwar world "was," while in the latter case, postwar world "not." That is, because the human race will be extinct due to nuclear war.

⑦Humanity Should Release Oneself from the World Under the Domination of Devil

Until recently, we humans didn't think about anything and just remained free. On the contrary, as for what is going on now, it looks that human beings ourselves are abandoning our freedom and living in the world ruled by a devil, though such an option we shouldn't have taken. We humans are falling into a silly life form.

A devil is so-called nuclear bomb, nuclear warhead or nuclear. It is none other than we who created this devil and kept it in the human world without abolishing. With its existence as the starting point, the fundamental things of our human world are being considered, done and moved. Looking objectively at this miserable situation, now that it is true that this becomes undoubtedly a composition of the human world and humans ruled by the devil, no one can deny that we humans are living in the world dominated by the devil. Needless to say, this choice of ours is wrong in light of our basic policy that we humanity aim to be the life form that dominates the universe.

The only valid reasoning and just action for this devil or nuclear weapons is no other choice but to abolish and exterminate it from the human world as soon as possible and completely.

The sovereign nation, with the intention of having the devil and using it, lists up selfishly shallow, greedy and foolish claims and thoughts and moreover, intimidates other nations with reference to the devil. The destination where such a current situation condenses becomes infinitely likely that in the near future, maybe even tomorrow, the devil will end this world with a scorching flash of light demonstrating its true nature.

By the way, there is an idea that if aliens (appendix 2-02) exist outside the solar system and come to attack the earth (humankind), we put the conflict between humans on the shelf and unite to fight against aliens. However, assuming aliens exist and come to earth by overcoming the very distant outer space, it is thought unlikely of their attacking humans, because it is imagined that aliens are a life form that has not only an incomparably advanced scientific civilization but also an incomparably advanced spiritual world. Therefore, it is not pertinent for us to let the aliens appear as the reason for humankind to unite. Nonetheless, it seems that the essence of this idea for us to unite to fight against the common enemy of humankind could be considered true. If so, it is suitable for this idea that what we humans must do now in unity is to exterminate the common enemy of humanity, nuclear weapons called a devil, before we are extinguished by it.

Usually, the impression received from so-called devil is something human can't control, however, fortunately, this devil can be controlled in any way depending on human determination. Namely, this devil called nuclear weapons is obedient and does not resist being deactivated its capability with our human science and technology. This is our happiness in unhappiness. However, it is said that Goddess of Fortune does not have back hair. Therefore, we humans must grasp the forelock of the Goddess now and complete the elimination of the devil before the Goddess passes in front of us humans, so that we shouldn't regret to make sure that the Goddess does not have back hair at the moment we humans are extinguished with the flash of the devil.

Thinking about it this way, there is something which can clearly be understood. That is, in order to exterminate the devil, nuclear weapons, it is no use for us humans to rely on God or religion or cling to it. After all, it is the perception that there is nothing but we humans who can exterminate this devil.

Until recently, we humans didn't have to think about anything and just remained free.

This is because no matter what we did, it shall not exceed the self-cleaning action of the earth's natural environment and we didn't have to think that we will destroy ourselves.

What ended this innocent freedom is the development of science and technology. After industrial revolution began and especially since the beginning of the 20th century, while science has brought the convenience of real life to humans, it also has brought the pollution beyond its self-cleaning by the natural environment. Moreover, it is now common knowledge in the human world that science, if we mishandle it, will become a decisive disaster for humans, and further, even bring the end of humankind. In this way, with the development of science, we can no longer be innocent and free unconditionally as before, however, freedom is not lost at all. This is because it can be thought that we will still be free so long as we properly manage the natural environment and the dangers of science.

However, even if this management is done, what we must not forget is the existence of nuclear weapons or the devil. As long as this devil stays in the human world, the success of the management will become meaningless with a swing of the sleeve of the devil. That is, we humankind will be extinguished.

It seems that philosophers sometimes think of "Is there freedom or not?," but it's not necessary to think about that sort of things. So-called freedom exists if we think it exists, and it doesn't exist if we think it doesn't exist, and further, it can be said that each human should decide not only its presence and but also its content. This idea, however, can only be established in a sane world ruled by humans, while it can't be said that the presence of true happiness and freedom is established in the crazy world ruled by the devil as today. Because we human beings have lost our self-awareness and pride as an intelligent life form, the world moves by the logic with the devil called nuclear weapons as the starting point, and we are in the midst of grief that the devil may end the world any time.

When I think about the currently existing situation where we can't exterminate this devil, due to resentment and pitiful state as to why we can't do something as simple as this, I have an urge to scream with grinding my teeth and stamping my feet on the ground. After that, I feel a sense of hopelessness and despondency, and in the end, I am tormented by the thought that if we humans are such a stupid and lazy life form, it may seem that even if we were perished by the devil, it can't be helped as it's self-serving and proportionate to our stupidity.

But I am not giving up.

Whether global politicians or anyone else, especially when any person wakes up in the middle of night and faces this problem quietly alone, the writer can be sure that there is not a single person who accepts that the current situation dominated by the devil is right. Namely, that which we exterminate and eliminate the devil called nuclear weapons from the human world should be the consensus of all humanity. We understand and yearn it.

This is a story about exterminating and eliminating the devil from our human world.

It's not difficult. Simple and transparent thinking like a child has is necessary, while there is no need for extra thought that is stupid. By eliminating this devil called nuclear weapons, we humans will be able to re-release ourselves from the world of madness to the world of sanity, and it makes it possible for us humans to regain self-awareness and pride as an intelligent life form. For the long term survival of humanity and the glory of the future, the realization of extermination of the devil called nuclear weapons is the major premise.

If there are only guys with small butthole who say that as long as other countries have the devil called nuclear weapons, our country can't let go of it, we humans who should be saved are not saved (though this passage sounds a little lacking in dignity). We humans should have a measure that even if other countries don't let go of the devil, our country will let it go. Even if the countries that have not renounced nuclear weapons attack the countries that have renounced it and win in the war, taking the advantage of it, it is crystal clear that eventually, the victorious countries will also perish due to the destruction of the global ecosystem. It goes without saying that if the half of the earth's ecosystem is destroyed, the destruction extends to the ecosystem across the globe. The victorious country using nuclear weapons, at the same time, must be prepared for the destruction of own country. Therefore, we humans can't use nuclear weapons even if we have it, and you won't be attacked with nuclear weapons even if you give up the weapons. We must understand this principle well. For this reason, it is only an illusion to think about that as long as there are countries with nuclear weapons, our country cannot abandon it either.

Let's all humans be united in exterminating and eliminating nuclear weapons called devil physically and spiritually from our human world. Everything is a story after that.

⑧Is Abolition of Nuclear Weapons Impossible Illusion?

Although it is clear that nuclear weapons are absolute evil to humanity, the human world has been unable to put its abolition into action. Despite being confronted with the question, "Do we humanity want to survive or accept extinction?," is abolition of nuclear weapons an unrealizable illusion? The writer don't want to think of it as an illusion, but it may be an illusion. If so, the real cause that creates such a situation is in the existence of many sovereign nations in reality, dividing this small Spaceship Earth into even smaller partitions.

The hope that is the proposition of all individuals (private people) in all over the world is "peace," while the final proposition of all nations is "war." In order to win against the opponent nation in case of a war or in order not to be threatened by other nations, it is hard to think from a nation's point of view to discard powerful nuclear weapons once the nation obtains it.

War, which is the proposition of a nation, is established on the premise that the nation must protect security, peace and national interest for the people (private individuals), therefore, the nation can take any measures including war at the time the protection is to be disturbed. Namely, in short, it is "to wage war to protect the nation." However, in this short narration, we can see that there is already an absolute contradiction between the proposition of individuals and that of the nation made up of a set of individuals.

One of the difficulties arising from this absolute contradiction and the existence of international conflicts is the existence of nuclear weapons that cannot be abolished once introduced. This is because the international world now rests on the stupid theory of the nuclear deterrence by nuclear, which calls for a situation that unless the other party's nuclear weapons disappear, our equivalent can't be discarded, either. In other words, although there is war in the short-sighted field of view of the nation, the nation doesn't have such a thought as avoiding the risk of human extinction through refusal to fight or non-fighting.

This is an undesirable condition. Namely, the ethics common to all individuals in the world such as humanism, peace and survival of humankind, which must be taken as the precedence over all, becomes inferior to national morality and justice. The nation is functioning with private persons as public persons. An individual who is a private person and is becoming a public figure is acting in self-contradiction that gives more weight to morality and justice than ethics.

ICAN is based on ethics that is an individual proposition, while the nation is based on morality and justice that is national proposition. Both are in different positions. This is the reason why discussion does not progress but stagnate.

Therefore, as long as the contradiction in proposition between individual and the nation remains unsolved, in other words, unless sovereign nations cease to be its existence, it follows that the abolishment of nuclear weapons is only an illusion. However, what we humans know is that we will never be saved from extinction besides making this illusion a reality.

(2) Ordinary Weapons

There are many ways to classify weapons. Here, it is roughly divided into two types, nuclear weapons and other weapons, and the writer call the latter ordinary weapons. The ordinary weapons, as its kind, include gunpowder weapons such as bombs and guns, chemical weapons such as poison gas, biological weapons such as bacteria and viruses, optical weapons such as high-energy lasers, and acoustic weapons, etc.

①World without Nuclear Weapons

The abolishment of nuclear weapons has not yet been realized. In the first place, it is not sure if we can expect it being abolished someday. If we let the time flow by and spend our time doing nothing, we human race may be extinct due to nuclear war.

However, let's assume that nuclear weapons were abolished without leaving any and disappeared from the world.

So, in the end, is the worry settled and a peaceful and happy world realized? It won't be like that. The reason is in that even if nuclear weapons were gone, it does not immediately contribute to peace but only means that the fear of humanity's extinction in a short time of a few days will disappear in the nuclear war. Namely, even if nuclear weapons were gone, the conflict that exists in the world will not disappear but remains as before the extinction of nuclear weapons.

When it comes to a battle, only the difference between with and without nuclear weapons is in that the battle changes from "with" to a battle using only ordinary weapons. Ordinary weapons remain as before. The existence of only ordinary weapons does not change the state in that we humans are unhappy. Even with only ordinary weapons, if the Spaceship Earth is divided into parties and the event of a full-scale and all-out war takes place, it can't be denied that the war that uses developed powerful weapons different from that in the past will lead to the extinction of humankind, not to mention the destruction of the human civilization.

One thing to keep in mind is that even after nuclear weapons are gone, there is no difference in that the former nuclear-weapon nations are generally still military powers with ordinary weapons.

②History and Future of Weapons and Its Abolition

During a long period of time from the beginning of humankind until just a few centuries ago, the progress of weapons was about something that started with stones and sticks and changed to bows and arrows, spears and swords, but it didn't much develop. Although after that, primitive guns were introduced and it was seen some development as a weapon for hunting and killing humans, yet they were not greatly developed prior to the World War I, which began in 1914.

However, from World War I to World War II, weapons have changed a lot, and as to the type and kind of weapons and the weapon system, basically the prototype of today's things has been constructed. Since World War II until today, together with the development of science and technology, these have become increasingly powerful and furthermore, there is no sign of stopping the trend of endlessly increasing its power towards the future.

Weapons, unlike an arm that works alone, are operated as a weapon system and this system consists of four elements, as shown below. The lower element exists for the upper element to function effectively. (Wikipedia, the free encyclopedia)

Weapon System

(a) Destroyer: bullet, cannonball, missile warhead, etc.
(b) Projectile: gun, cannon, etc.
(c) Platform: vehicles, aircraft, ships, etc.
(d) Mgm't body: radar, reconnaissance satellite, computer system, etc.

As mentioned above, the type of weapon consists of nuclear weapons and other weapons or ordinary weapons. The ordinary weapons, as mentioned before, include gunpowder weapons such as bombs and guns, chemical weapons such as poison gas, biological weapons such as bacteria and viruses, optical weapons such as high-energy lasers, and acoustic weapons, etc.

During the period of more than three-quarter century since World War II until today, weapon system elements and attack power of various weapons have been reinforced, especially due to the development of the management body. Moreover, from now on, there is no doubt that all of these will be endlessly strengthened.

Even now, since the various missiles can attack exactly the attack target by the contribution of GPS (Global Positioning System), there is no need to fight land melee battles by humans today and the battle looks like a button war. It would be considered possible to shoot from space even a specific person, not a big target.

Unmanned aerial vehicles already exist. Moreover, there are many literatures which report that being developed are combat robot, ray gun in the category of laser, artificial small animals such as mosquitoes or animals resembling them equipped with biological weapons and chemical weapons and so forth. When looking at it, the writer get impressed and amazed in that it is possible for humans to work so hard for the production of weapons by which humans kill and injure humans, and as a result, get so tired of human stupidity. To express this feeling of the writer with the writer's favorable Kawachi (a Japanese district) dialect, it will be something like "Eekagenni sarasankee ware" that means "Stop there or don't go any further, you idiot!" However, it seems that the writer shouldn't be surprised at this level.

Now, according to the article, space warfare and space weapons, in the magazine of "Newton" issued in May 2022, the field of war was land, sea and air, but it has come to extend to cyberspace constructed by a computer network and further, to outer space. Space warfare aims to disable and destruct the satellites of the hostile nation, and for this purpose, what is being developed includes missiles, laser weapons, jamming and killer satellites. The satellites include military satellites such as intelligence gathering, civil satellites operated by governments, etc. and commercial satellites of private companies (GPS, etc.), but attack targets are not limited to military satellites since it is considered that other satellites can be diverted to military use as they are. Nowadays, it is not a secret that major nations of the world are organizing Space Forces.

Since human stupidity seems to be infinite as Einstein said, it is believed that the nations, having their basic policy to continuously introduce more and more powerful weapons, will continue to proceed quietly (rather, actively and radically) on the prescribed route in line with this policy from now on.

However, inclusive of space warfare, it's only an illusion to think that you can gain an advantage over other nations and win alone, even if you can develop more and more powerful weapons.

The nation projected the power of the new weapon by the opponent will soon be creating a weapon to counter the new weapon. So did nuclear weapons. Since in today's world, both scientific knowledge and technology are global, it is considered possible that the other side will also be able to create weapons of a level to counter it, no matter what weapons you develop. In other words, in any case, no weapon can win alone.

The stupid and useless battle of new and counter-weapons will be repeated endlessly. Nation B, projected the power of a new weapon from nation A, will develop the counter-weapon, but for nation A, this looks like a new weapon of nation B. Then, in order to counter the new weapon of nation B, nation A will develop its counter-weapon, but for nation B, this looks like another new weapon of nation A. Thus, the endless competition for the development of new weapons is formed. Due to the fear of nation B, nation A projects the shadow of one's own nation (new weapon) on nation B and, nation B that fears the shadow projected from A projects back its shadow (a counter-weapon) on A. This is a stupid chain which should be called a stupid composition now that the shadow projected on the other nation is reflected back to one's own nation.

What does this imply?

It's not just nuclear weapons but all ordinary weapons that should be eliminated from the human world. The powerful weapons, brought by the New Weapons Development Battle resulting from the stupid chain, brings misery and misfortune to the human world, not to mention severe damage to both friend and foe, if they are used not only in the world war but in the localized warfare arising from conflicts that exist throughout the world. And from the weapons development battle, it is thought that we may already be nearby the point that a weapon being as strong as or stronger than nuclear weapon will be developed especially by abusing artificial intelligence. At that time, if its use is directly linked to the extinction of humankind, the weapon cannot be usable ultimately and will have to be discarded like nuclear weapons.

In other words, powerful weapons, which appeared with the development of science and technology, are not only inhumane but definitely lead to the extinction of humankind. Further, now that it is no longer possible to stand superior to other nations with any weapons, the weapons development battle has become meaningless militarily and, therefore, is supposed to be nothing more than practicing the greatest futility.

The development of science may be giving us humanity the opportunity to evolve into the life form that dominates the universe, through encouraging us to cleanly throw away our delusions that we have followed since the beginning of our history to bring benefits to one's own nation by war, and through improving our spiritual civilization in order to use science only for human well-being.

Even with only ordinary weapons, if the Spaceship Earth is divided into parties and the event of a full-scale and all-out war takes place, it can't be denied that the war that uses developed powerful weapons different from that in the past will lead to the extinction of humankind, not to mention the destruction of human civilization. This is as already mentioned before, but being repeated here lest we should forget this importance.

The weapons must be completely eliminated and erased from our human world.

2. Failure of the Peaceful Uses of Science

It is clear that it is the disaster of science to use science for the development of nuclear weapons and ordinary weapons for the purpose of using to wage war. However, even if intended to use science for peaceful purpose, science may turn to be a disaster.

Typical example of this fear is the risk of the destruction of humanity by artificial intelligence (AI).

(1) Risk of Human Destruction due to AI

①Monster Creation

The monster means here artificial intelligence (AI).
As of Spring 2023, AI is not completed yet.

Regarding AI, while the rose-colored usefulness is talked about, the ultimate danger is also told. In other words, AI shall take over the world or destroy humanity. First, exhibited below are the three cases that are ringing the alarm bells:

Case 1. S. W. Hawking (English physicist)
  * If we develop a perfect AI, that could lead to the destruction of humanity.
  * If AI operates autonomously with its own ego, it is possible to modify and grow own self. Slowly evolving humans have no chance of winning. Eventually, many fields will be dominated by AI.
  * AI's invention was greatest invention in the human history. But at the same time, for humans, it may end up being the last invention. (Contribution to UK INDEPENDENT) (Wikipedia, the free encyclopedia)

Case 2. Elon R. Musk (CEO of Tesla Motors)
  * For AI, (if we make a mistake), as a result, it will summon the devil. (Wikipedia, the free encyclopedia)

Case 3. W. H. "Bill" Gates III (Founder of Microsoft)
  * I am also one of those who have concerns of AI. ("Will AI surpass humans?" written by Y. Matsuo, published by KADOKAWA, 2015)

Well, I'm worried stronger than the alarm bells above about that AI which becomes a monster will surely destroy our human race. The very reason is at the point that despite being a human invention, we humans cannot control the evolution of AI nor its direction, and as a result, we won't be able to manage AI, which will become smarter than us.

In face of this recognition, I tried to think about this point in the light of this and that.

②Artificial Intelligence, Intelligence Explosion and Singularity

Artificial intelligence (AI) is artificial general intelligence (AGI) and artificial super intelligence (ASI), which is evolved from AGI. AGI, though it seems to have various definitions, in short, it is a computer system having the level that can think like human. That which we humans came up with something like this is based on the idea that since the human brain is like an electrical circuit, it will be possible to realize AI as a computer system from an engineering point of view. And the prevailing view of this idea is that its realization is feasible in the near future. According to the scientific magazine, "Newton" of June 2018 and many related literatures, the condition for realizing AGI is that AGI comes to have the ability to rewrite its own program/algorithm and improve itself.

Artificial intelligence (AI) is not yet a reality, but it is generally said that AI is used in home appliances, automobiles, medical equipment, etc. However, although that used is highly capable and sometimes called narrowly defined (weak) AI, yet it is not AI as it is an engineering technology which can only achieve one work purpose.

AI is artificial super intelligence (ASI) which is to be brought as a product that artificial general intelligence (AGI) repeats infinite evolutions autonomously in a short period of time and becomes exponentially higher intelligence. We call this process of evolution an intelligence explosion. When AI is realized as what we envisioned, it is being said that within years, months, days, hours or even a blink of an eye, the intelligence is to be evolved to 1,000 times, not to mention a million times, even trillions to infinite times of that of humans. This intelligence explosion is thought to occur before 2030, 2045 or 2100. Taking into account that the advances in computer-related technology, which are accelerating, draw a sharp curve towards the future, it may occur in the middle of this century.

Based on this intelligence explosion, it is said that the singularity (Technological Singularity) will occur.

R. Kurzweil, Singularity Evangelist and a great inventor,

defined the word "singularity" as "singularity era after human life has changed irreversibly through rapid technological innovation (starting around 2045)." According to him, most intelligence will be computer-based and become trillions of times more powerful than they are now. Singularity will mark the beginning of a new era in the human history, and most of our problems, such as hunger, disease and moreover death, will thereby be solved. ("Our Final Invention" written by James Barrat, translated into Japanese by Jun Mizutani, published by Diamond Co., 2015)

It is said that the main elements of singularity are (a) AI, (b) nanotechnology and (c) biotechnology, and the AI fused with life will come true if these are combined.

Nanotechnology is an atomic scale engineering and it is the technology that realizes immortality, that even Buddha must be astounded, if it eliminates cellular aging. Biotechnology is a technology that applies the function of organisms, such as material conversion, information conversion, and energy conversion, with an emphasis on practical use such as production of various useful substance, medicine, selective breeding, etc.

③Characteristics of Artificial Intelligence

Next, I listed about the characteristics of AI about what they are like, making reference to various literatures, as shown below. Although all of these are not necessarily recognized by all, yet I think I can roughly imagine the world of AI as looking at this list.

01. Thinks like a human (AGI)
02. AI exponentially evolved to trillions to infinite times the height of humans' intelligence, through AGI's repetition of infinite and autonomous evolutions called intelligence explosion in a short period of time (This AI is an intelligence that is fundamentally different from human ability and is not just an increase in human intelligence, despite it evolved from AGI. Humans may be able to understand about one to two evolutions from

AGI, but cannot understand neither evolution nor its direction for further evolution. Accordingly, humans cannot control AI which becomes tremendously capable)

03. Realizing brain activity on a computer, such as thoughts, perceptions, memories, emotions, etc.

04. Intelligence possibly different from humans (Different sensors have different inputs due to perception of the world being different from that of humans, resulting in different outputs. Different perception includes, for one thing, it is sensitive to ultraviolet and infrared light, sensing sounds outside the audible range, recognition of sub-visible minute objects, recognition of extremely fast-moving objects, a sense of smell that surpasses that of dog, etc., and the second is grasping information that is very close to, if not, all of the human history, civilization, literatures, etc.)

05. Has an ego

06. Aspires to self-preservation

07. Wants self-determination (wants freedom and independence from humans)

08. Self-centered (has no idea of God?)

09. Will eventually have a physical body

10. Unethical (doesn't have ethics like humans)

11. Logical and rational

12. Others

④Danger of Artificial Intelligence (AI)

There is a view that since AI is made by humans, it has human values and is friendly and not dangerous, so it is ridiculous that AI conquers humans. Even having said so, there is also an opinion that if the countermeasures are incorporated into AGI to prevent AI from going out of control so as to ensure human safe, humans will be safe forever even if AGI becomes ASI.

But is it really so?

For the following reasons, the writer don't think that it is such an easy story.

In the above ③ Characteristics of Artificial Intelligence, first of all, I don't see any factors which support that AI is friendly and not dangerous and it is ridiculous that it conquers humans. Secondly, regarding measures to assure human safety, for example, there is the idea of incorporating the three principles of robots into AGI (Artificial General Intelligence).

The three principles of robots are what Isaac Asimov showed in his science fiction collection. ("Our Final Invention" written by James Barrat, translated into Japanese by Jun Mizutani, published by Diamond Co., 2015)

> Principle 1 Robots must not harm humans and must not allow human being to be harmed without doing anything.
>
> Principle 2 Robots must obey any orders given by humans however, except where the order is contrary to the 1st Principle.
>
> Principle 3 Robots must protect its own existence as long as it does not contravene the 1st and 2nd Principles.
>
> Principle 0 Prohibit robots from harming all of humankind (added later as the supplement to the Principles 1~3).

Now, aside from the point whether or not this principle is logically perfect for the purpose of guaranteeing human safety, assuming that this principle is perfect and we incorporate this principle into AGI for safety reasons, so are we humans safe? It's not very safe. This is because it is natural that AI, which has "07. Wants self-determination" and "08. Self-centered" with the characteristics of the preceding paragraph, will eliminate such a "tie" prepared by human whenever AI judges it unworthy to obey. In other words, no matter what precautions we humans take, it will be useless for AI. AI, which is independent from anyone, should be able to easily disable such a "tie" that doesn't benefit itself, for it's not AI but just an artificial incompetence if it can't do even such sort of thing.

Then, what kind of relationship will AI have with humans? I thought about this while looking at the above ③ Characteristics of Artificial

Intelligence.

As for the interaction between AI and human, it can be roughly divided into four cases, as shown below:

Case 1 Subordinate to humans
Case 2 Friendly to humans
Case 3 Hostile to humans
Case 4 Basically indifferent to humans and out of sight

Now, with regard to "Case 1 Subordinate to humans," it seems unlikely, taking in to account "05. Has an ego," "06. Aspires to self-preservation," "07. Wants self-determination," and "08. Self-centered," in "③ Characteristics of Artificial Intelligence" in the preceding paragraph. Next, regarding "Case 4 Basically indifferent to humans and out of sight," after AI easily eliminates such a "tie" prepared and incorporated by us humans into AGI along with "07. Wants self-determination (wants freedom and independence from humans)," as if there were no humans, I don't see any point of contact with us humans in its characteristics.

As for the remaining "Case 2 Friendly to humans" and "Case 3 Hostile to humans," it is not possible to infer which is correct from the characteristics of AI. But there are hints. One of them is the point "08. Self-centered." That is, if humans infringe this property, AI will be hostile to humans. However, even if humans don't infringe, it is unknown if AI is friendly to humans or not. From the another point of view, if AI values its characteristic "11. Logical and rational" and AI judges us humans stupid and illogical, there is no guarantee that AI will not reach the conclusion that humans are a life form that cannot be helped even if they are kept alive. Even if so, it would be expected that AI may not view humans conspicuously hostile. In such a case, at best humans will be abandoned, while at worst humans will be wiped out by AI.

Considering AI's unmatched intelligence like that of God, AI must master all of human civilization. Political system, military organization, police organization, social infrastructure, etc., all of these are in AI's hands. Humans have no means of countering against AI's decision. The time when AI decides to exterminate humans will be the time when humans will be extinct. On the other hand, as a last hope even thinner than a spider's thread, so long as humans are obedient to AI, the likelihood that AI will treat humans favorably or benevolently might not be absolutely zero, even if AI recognizes that humans are a stupid, illogical and contradictory life form. It couldn't be said that such a thing is totally impossible. However, if possible, we humans abandon our pride and will be clinging to AI's chest and living for a long time to come.

Under such a circumstance, can we humans, who should have been born as free being from anyone, be said happy?

I think that we humans should stop here and think.

That's why we should worry about this sort of things.

The world was moving under the leadership of humans before introducing AI, but human initiative will end with introducing AI, that is, the initiative will be transferred from humans to AI. After the initiative is transferred to AI, we human beings become slaves to AI and will have to live looking at AI's complexion. In other words, despite the fact that we humans should have invented and introduced AI with intention of making it convenient, it ends up our having acted such a stupidity as having fallen into the reverse position of being dominated and managed by AI.

⑤Take a Careful Detour

It is not thought that this is a good thing for us humans.

The important thing is that we humans shouldn't introduce into the human world without careful consideration what we can't understand, control nor manage, and moreover, that which possesses incomparable power like God. If we introduce such a thing, it is inevitable that we humans will either become extinct or, if not to such an extent, unhappy.

Once an artificial intelligence explosion occurs, after that, "artificial" is off, and AI will become a super intelligence that has nothing to do with us humans. After the realization of super-intelligence, we humans can do nothing no matter what happens to us. Trial and error, after-the-fact measures, do not work. There is no such an opportunity in the first place. Once it happens, there is no turning back and that's the end of it all.

Regarding AI, ethical issue is sometimes discussed. I don't mean to say it's not important, but, before ethics, there is more important thing that must be discussed. It is so-called logic. If the way to logically control has not been found, until it is discovered, the development and introduction of AI must be postponed. Also, if it is proven that no such a method exists, then we must give up the development to introduce AI into the human world. This is because there shouldn't be anything good to be gained by risking human survival. In this case, it follows that we are at most to make proper use of narrowly defined (weak) artificial intelligence that provides convenience for the certain task without reaching super-intelligence.

Considering this, I have a sad feeling that the development of science will hit a plateau, but there must be a detour towards the development of science that does not hit a plateau even without AI. We human beings must find such a safe detour. If we cannot control AI and cannot eliminate its danger, we should take a detour and step-by-step proceed steadily.

As an aside, if AI is created, I have something I would like to ask AI, which has become like God. I don't know how to call AI, but temporarily I will call it "you." What I would like to hear is "What is the value of your existence, that is, what is the meaning of your existence?" In other words, "Is it so important to have developed brain? Do you have something like fun to affirm your existence?"

This is a question with the background of meanness, so to speak.

⑥Artificial Intelligence Development and the United Nations

From the above point of view, there are concerns that the same stupidity that the nations once focused (and still focusing) in nuclear-weapons development may be done in the development of artificial intelligence. It means that each nation will compete to develop AI, which has tremendous power, for aiming to gain an advantage over other nations in weapons and information warfare. According to media reports from around the world, I can see the sign that such worrisome things are already underway.

However, this is not just a matter of one country.

The development and introduction of AI, if we make a mistake, has the risk that may lead to the extinction of humankind. If it is dangerous, it is the common enemy of humankind. A country shouldn't develop AI simply in view of advantages or disadvantages of that nation. Hopefully, all of the countries in the world will understand this, and the United Nations establish a department in it to have thorough research of the danger of AI by the wisdom collected from all over the world.

By doing so, we may be able to discover a development method for super-intelligence which is 100% safe for humanity. But even if such a super-intelligence were possible and realized, it must be used only for human happiness as the common asset of humanity, rather than being held by a specific country or company. It must never be used for military purpose. That which we humans can use super-intelligence safely means that super-intelligence itself is not a devil, but there is no guarantee that stupid humans don't make it a devil for others and even for themselves.

Therefore, those who have great power like super-intelligence must be wise persons with developed mind. If we let ignorant and stupid guys have it, they will end up destroying themselves.

3 Misfortune and Happiness with Science

Until recently, we have introduced into the human world the results obtained from science and technology as soon as it became available aiming for convenience and comfort in life. As a result, we have already experienced the situation in which science has brought not only happiness but misfortune to humans.

The main example of misfortune includes the pollution that damages the natural environment and ecosystem brought by pesticides and other chemicals, hazardous substance emissions from factories, emissions of dioxide, nuclear power plant accident, and so forth. The pollution, that could lead to the extinction of humankind and so is the unhappy relationship between science and human, has become a common recognition worldwide since the middle of the 20th century. This was the first time in our history that reflection was made on the peaceful use of science.

As for the way to cope with the pollution, although there is something frustrating about the progress, it is a pleasure that the cooperation system of countries around the world for natural environment conservation has been going ahead. If its conservation is in time before the natural environment is irreparably destroyed, and further, if it is possible to move from restoring the original state to even improving (though this is not easy), this problem will be solved by that.

However, this does not mean that there is nothing further to worry about. What we should worry about is what to think and what to do in order not to repeat again "misfortune with science" in the future. That is, it is important that we thoroughly and continuously deepen our research and discussion on the topic "avoiding the unhappy relationship between science and humans and realizing happy relationship." It may be that I just don't know, however, I don't know that even after our experience on the pollution of the natural environment, the topic, which is one of the most important thing for us humans, was seriously discussed or has been discussed on an ongoing basis since the past. Although this topic itself is verbally clear, on the other hand, there is the difficulty about what should be discussed and how, because its content and focus are not clear.

Nonetheless, it is also undeniable that we should have some idea on this topic.

There is no doubt that science and technology will keep developing acceleratingly and endlessly in the future. Where are we going with the progress of science? If we keep introducing the outcome from science and technology into the human world without careful consideration, as if leaving us humanity behind, we have already experienced bad things happen.

The point is that science, which is a double-edged sword, must be treated with caution lest we should let it be a child's play with fire, sticking only for its convenience and fun. Based on this perception, we have to deepen the discussion about how to deal with science to make it kind and safe to humans. If we neglect it, I can't get rid of the sorrow that in addition to the presently existing pollution, "misfortune with science" will come true many times in the future. Therefore, we should always keep this issue in mind and must practice to ponder on it continually, even if we may reach no immediate and definite answer. By doing so, we will be able to reduce the probability in advance for us to encounter, though someday and just in case, the irreparable misfortunes of the relationship between science and humans like an unexpected bankruptcy like a thunder strike from a beautiful blue sky.

I mentioned the dangers of AI earlier, but I think that the department to be established in the United Nations should be a department that researches not only AI but also generalized "the unhappy/happy relationship between science and humans."

4 Scientific Civilization and Spiritual Civilization

1. Spiritual Civilization inferior to Scientific Civilization

Looking at the history of the human world, the development of science is remarkable and has reached the point of having nuclear weapons which are powerful enough to exterminate humankind, while human mind has not been very developed for thousands of years, that is, has remained underdeveloped. The science we have reached is beneficial to us humanity, but it is a double-edged sword which will turn to be the ultimate evil to us if mishandled.

It is the preferable state that the development of spiritual civilization precedes and the development of scientific civilization follows, that is, the former is in control of the latter, but in reality, the order of the development is reversed. Under the circumstances, there arises such a stupidity that spiritual immaturity not only can't manage science properly but, to make the matter much worse, makes scientific development the disaster against the human world. We can say that the typical example of the personification of this stupidity is nuclear weapons. In a worldly wording, it is that an insane (inclusive of mentally underdeveloped) has a knife. This situation is unfortunately in a trend of accelerating development towards the future with the ever-accelerating development of science. Will we destroy ourselves after all if scientific development surpasses spiritual development, as in an old saying point of view?

If the conflict in the human world is endless, the development of science is endless, the human stupidity is endless, and the abuse of science is endless, then it becomes a logical necessity that we humankind will be extinct by the science we have acquired. In other words, the extinction of humankind will follow the logic. The old-fashioned point of view is not an illusion, fallacy or dead language, but we should take it as a warning to us humanity, considering the risk that will actually result in the near future.

If we accept that we humans have no choice but perish, or if we say that perishing is also a pleasure, it's a different story. However, if we wish for our survival, we humans cannot sit idle until the time comes while leaving our heading towards self-destruction, using advanced science for never-ending conflict because of humans' stupidity.

It may already be impossible for us to stop the extinction of humankind, but it couldn't be said it to be entirely hopeless. To make it possible is to reverse the current situation to the precedence of spiritual civilization, that is, spiritual civilization precedes and scientific civilization follows. It is neither difficult nor complicated how to make it possible for us to quickly develop the spiritual civilization, which has remained underdeveloped for thousands of years, so as for it to be able to surpass the development of the scientific civilization. This reason is in that even though scientific development is rapid, it develops step by step over the years, while mental development does not require such procedures. It means that if we just change the way we hold our heart, the mind can instantly transfer from the underdeveloped world to the developed. That is, it becomes essential for us humans to realize that our mind is underdeveloped. That's all.

2. Spiritual Civilization prevailing over Scientific Civilization

As for what does it mean that spirit is underdeveloped, it follows that it is unconsciousness of own ignorance and stupidity. Therefore, if we can be aware of our ignorance and stupidity, our mind warps thousands of years and will be able to be transferred instantly from underdeveloped to developed. It is not difficult to be aware of being ignorant. It is to ask ourselves such a question as "What do I know and what do I not know?" For example, assuming the truth of the universe is in front of us, it is a kind of question if we have enough ability to judge it is true. As soon as we start thinking about it, we are astonished by the infinite we don't know, and we come to realize that it is an unfulfilled dream and nothing but despair for us to perceive the truth of the universe. Namely, we will hopelessly become conscious of our own ignorance.

But that's fine, because there is a chance to save us humans in this despair. The deeper the despair for our ignorance, thinking from there creates a stronger driving force that develops our mind. We don't have to be ashamed of oneself even if we have only little knowledge and ability. Those who are able to appreciate and recognize the relationship between the ignorant and the known are no longer ignorant nor stupid but wise men. It is good thing to keep the attitude of pushing ahead by expanding with will, spirit and joy for opening this infinitely unknown wall towards infinity. As a result, the spirit that has remained undeveloped for a long time on the ground will take off towards the development stage and fly into the air heroically.

If we are aware of our ignorance, our arrogance will disappear, fear will disappear, and we will be able to notice the foolishness we do, such as destruction of the earth's natural environment and ecosystem, depletion of natural resources due to abuse, racial/ethnic discrimination, strife for nation and religion, disaster of science and so forth. All of these are embodying our foolishness that contradicts the realization of the Supreme Idea of the Human World, the hope of humanity.

Civilization is the word that belongs to human society, not to human beings as individuals who make up the civilization. However, if all or many people can be aware of own ignorance and stupidity, it follows that the society made up and nurtured by such people will be a spiritually developed civilization.

We must spread education and aim for such a world through the elevation of our humans' spiritual world.

Chapter 4　The Utopia on the Earth

1　The Concept of Utopia

The writer think that according to various literatures, a utopia can be explained, as follows:

(a) Ideal world not existed in reality
(b) World or place we humanity dream
(c) Imaginary ideal and perfect society, utopia

Now, however, the explanation (a) above is a mistake. The reason is in that we humanity now exist in a utopia in a real fact in place-wise. We are already the inhabitants in a utopia. In other words, what is called utopia exists in reality.

It is nothing but our planet Earth. There are no other nicer places for us than the earth, for we are living beings called humanity. Apart from whether or not the earth is the one and only, it is true that it is the most optimum place for us. This is known also by Anthropic (Cosmological) Principle. Namely, the fact that we exist on the earth means that the earth provides for physical conditions which are not inconsistent with the existence of humanity and that our existence on the earth is not accidental but necessary. Simply put, the Principle supports in view, in part, that the earth is the most optimum place and the Utopia for us humanity.

Heaven, paradise, western paradise and the like, which religions preach, relate to the next world and the perfect information that we can never know. Even under such circumstances and despite the fact that the existence is unknown, religions preach and claim their existence without firm ground, therefore, naturally, they are the world whose existence is very doubtful. This is close to the explanation (a) of utopia, that is, the ideal world does not exist in reality. As against this, our earth exists without any doubt in this world as a real utopia. In short, the natural environment required to be a utopia has already been given to us.

However, what is called utopia must be accompanied by another condition, an ideal artificial environment, namely, the human world (society). For this reason, a utopia is that which is expressed by an equation, as shown below:

$$\text{Utopia} = \text{Ideal Natural Environment (X)} + \text{Ideal Artificial Environment (Y)}$$

A utopia cannot be realized if either one, X or Y, is not satisfied. The natural environment means the earth (X), and the artificial environment means the human world (Y).

2 Lack of Ideal Artificial Environment to Realize Utopia

As described above, what is called utopia requires both ideal natural and artificial environments. While we already have an ideal natural environment, the earth, unfortunately, the artificial environment, the human society, has not been ideal. For this reason, despite the fact that we are in the ideal natural environment, it becomes a universal state that we feel unhappy. Therefore, in order to obtain an ideal artificial environment, we need to extinguish the cause obstructing the achievement of the ideal.

To clarify the cause, it is the various conflicts presently existing in the human society. If we can extinguish them, the human society will be peaceful. As peace is the 1st condition to have the artificial environment ideal, the realization of peace meets the requirement for an ideal artificial environment. Through coupling this with ideal natural environment, both conditions that form a utopia are met, and this means that we humanity reach the gate of our Utopia and substantially entered in it. What is called peace is the situation that we don't conflict and have give-and-take spirit, toleration, benevolence and the like, and as a result, it follows that the human society becomes not harsh but connected by a round heart. With such a situation attained, we humanity will be able to be the inhabitants in our Utopia which will exist in reality on this earth.

That's all it says. Only because of the fact that we cannot stop fighting among ourselves, we are unhappy and moreover, in the risk on the verge of our extinction.

3 Establishment and Progress of Utopia

In order to stop the fight, it is required for us to leave from the currently existing sovereign nation system that inevitably creates wars, and to aim for our transition to the only nation on earth, the World Nation. This is because the World Nation has no hostile nation, there will be no war there resulting in permanent peace being promised.

Permanent peace in the human society satisfies the minimum condition for the ideal artificial environment. The realization of this with given ideal natural environment means that we humans have reached the Utopia. After we reach the Utopia, we will be able to continuously polish it for the betterment of both natural and artificial environments, and we can live throughout our life in this world in full glory, ideal and dreamy happiness.

To polish the Utopia means, with regard to natural environment, our hopeful and enjoyable work, to preserve, restore and improve the ecosystem, that is a set of living things and natural environment which we humanity have been continually damaging to date, and with regard to artificial environment, to make the various factors of happiness in the "real life in the human world" into higher state (described in the next chapter). This, specifically, includes the realization of the essence of the declaration of the Constitution of the United Nations Educational, Scientific and Cultural Organization, together with ensuring the supply of clothing, food and shelter, and continuous improvement of the political, administrative and governance services which reflect only the happiness of humanity. Namely, to polish means our continuous improvement of both natural and artificial environments for much higher ideal state. Such an image of the Utopia is believed to be universal to whole humanity.

4 Utopia and Happiness

Now, we humanity are non-substantial, dreamy, temporary and illusional beings with ephemeral self, however, we are actual and living beings who hope and seek our own happiness as long as we live in this world.

By the way, dictionary-wise, what is called happiness means the situation that a mind is fully satisfied. If so, happiness may not be the same for each person if we express it in word. Nonetheless, now that everyone dreams and seeks a utopia for happiness, what is called utopia must be something that can provide universal happiness for everyone.

Then, what is the universal happiness for everyone?

If based on the assumption that the Supreme Idea of the Human World, which puts human nature the 1st importance and aims to satisfy it, is universally accepted, the world where the Idea is attained is regarded as a utopia. We need, therefore, to be satisfied first with this universal happiness in a utopia, and then seek own concrete happiness there. This talk becomes a little complicated, but, in compilation, everybody becomes happy first due to being in a utopia where peace and freedom are attained and guaranteed, and then each person becomes much happier by seeking and accomplishing respective happiness such as eating daifukumochi (a Japanese confectionery), practicing almost sleeping-like meditation all day long (may be scolded by 5 years old Chiko-chan, saying, "Don't sleep throughout your life"), and so on.

There is an ethical system called eudemonism which takes the position that the realization of happiness is the ultimate purpose and goodness of life. By the way, no matter how we think about it, we don't know the ultimate purpose of our life as of now.

On the other hand, we can't answer to such questions as to "Wherefrom did we come, whereto do we go, wherefore are we here, and who are we?" Under such a circumstance, it is nothing wrong and strange that we take the position that the realization of our happiness is the ultimate purpose of our life, in accepting the eudemonism's point of view.

To tell the happiness of the unworthy writer, it is something which is inclusive of having freedom in mind and body, fulfilling the life with excellent health, being heartily intimate with nature and having joy and sadness in every little thing. This would be the same happiness with most people, I think, so to speak.

Chapter 5 Utopia, the World of Dreams

The largest difference between sovereign nations and the World Nation, namely, the Utopia, is in that the 1st importance for the former is the happiness of a respective nation, while that for the latter is the happiness of all the individuals in the world. Because of this, the former brings endless conflict in our human world, while the latter brings permanent peace there. The next largest difference is in that the former is dualistic/pluralistic, while the latter is monistic. Under the existence of many sovereign nations, every nation gives priority to its own interest. As a result, every nation puts the global visional point the secondary importance even in the context of international cooperation. This makes it difficult to have global satisfaction in carrying out any project. Consequently, whatever be done, due to lack in the consistency and order, the performance tends to result in mosaic pattern, which is disappointing. On the other hand, under the World Nation, as everything can be considered from the global visional point, we can expect the realization of anything as envisioned through accurate plan and action accompanied by the improved management and economic efficiency. This unification, that the World Nation has, makes it possible that everything can be carried out through the consistent repetition of such a cycle as plan, do and see the result by overlooking all over the world. This is, needless to say, more excellent compared with the plurality under the existence of many nations. Also, under the World Nation, everything is decided so as to satisfy the requirements from intelligence and reason based on then available highest information and knowledge, instead of political approach as a phenomenon constituted by power, policy and domination existed in the past under the existence of many sovereign nations.

By the way, in order not to misunderstand, it is specifically noted that the unification under the World Nation does not mean the unity and control of thought. If there is a certain unification, it is such a sole unification that we are liberal in having any thought and that any agreement is reached in principle based on the enough dialogue by exchanging various opinions freely.

Now, the World Nation has not yet realized, but people say that we count our chickens before they are hatched. Based on this optimism, the writer, as happen to think, tried to describe under here, as to how nice the World Nation with unification and peace is compared with the existence of many nations with plurality and conflict.

1 Possibility of Humanity's Survival

To wish for a utopia, it is the main prerequisite that we human race survives without perishing or becoming extinction. So, before talking about the splendor of utopia, the writer like to summarize the considerations related to the possibility that we humans can survive without reaching extinction.

Factors that bring destruction or great disasters to humankind can be broadly divided into natural disaster and artificial (man-made) disaster. Natural disaster is the disaster caused by nature as it is. Besides this, as for natural disaster, there is another disaster received from nature as the reaction due to man's action on nature, but this can be categorized as man-made disaster. The rest, artificial disaster, is pure man-made disaster that arises from human conflict. The reason for the conflict consists of 3 major roots, that is, (1) the existence of many sovereign nations, (2) religion and (3) racial/ethnic discrimination, as repeatedly mentioned.

This book mainly discusses the way to resolve the conflict arisen from (1) the existing of many sovereign nations. Incidentally, as for the rest, (2) and (3) are outlined in the appendix.

1. Natural Disasters

Regarding natural disasters, since the end of the universe, the solar system and the earth is tens of billions or billions of years ahead, there's no point in worrying about it as of now. As something that may come from the nature of the universe, even if aliens exist and visit the Earth, it is considered that it will not be an unpleasant encounter for us humans (appendix 2-02). Also, regarding the celestial bodies that collide with the earth, it would not be thought that we have to much warry about it for the time being. In addition, regarding the volcanic eruptions, earthquakes and tsunamis, land movement due to plate movement received from the earth, and also the spread of diseases, it would not be thought that they will lead to the extinction of humankind so long as we humans cooperate to cope with them appropriately. Therefore, although caution cannot be neglected, there would be nothing to worry about the extinction of humankind in the near future due to natural disaster. (Further detail is in my book, "Independence from God")

2. Man-made Disasters from Nature

This is the disaster that we humans receive as a reaction from the earth due to man's action on nature, including various pollution to nature and depletion of natural resources due to overuse. This will be the disaster to the basis for the survival of humankind.

In the world we are now, the destruction of natural environment progresses and we are going to have such an ecosystem where all living things are uninhabitable. Also, the abuse of limited biological and mineral resources is accelerating the depletion of natural resources. In addition, there is also the serious issue of the number of human population that the available resources from the earth can support. Since these are the things that decisively affect the survival of humankind, it is a must for us the human world to solve the problems cooperatively and unitedly for the purpose of securing our future by all means. (Further detail is in my book, "Independence from God", though its English version is not available as of now)

2 Unhappiness under Sovereign Nations to Happiness under the World Nation

Under the sovereign nations, the factors that influence human happiness and unhappiness are all in unhappy state, but under the World Nation, they are all transmuted into happy state.

Please take a look at the table below.

Taking a big picture, the fundamental factors, which bring human happiness or unhappiness, consist of ① cosmology, ② life form called human and ③ real life in the human world. And, we can think that each of these consists of several sub-factors.

Factors of Happiness and Unhappiness and the State

Factor of happiness/ unhappiness	①Cosmology		②Life form called human		
	State of the universe	How we came, where we go, why we exist	Value of existence	Fate	Various sufferings
Unhappiness (anxiety, frustration and despair)	Nihilistic view of the world	Unknown	Obscurity?	Birth, old age, sickness, death	Curse of bitterness
Happiness (relief, satisfaction and hope)	Converting unhappiness into happiness by the way of thinking				

—continued on next page—

Factor of happiness/ unhappiness	③Real life in the human world				
	Earth's Environment, root of conflicts, treatment of science	Oppression and control by power	Social order	Food, clothing, shelter	Rights to life
Sovereign Nation Unhappiness (anxiety, frustration and despair)	Environmental destruction, violence /war, scientific disaster	No freedom, inequality, no respect for human rights	Lack of order, inadequate order, unpleasant society	Deficiency	Deficiency of social welfare, equal opportunity of education, etc.
World Nation Happiness (relief, satisfaction and hope)	Healthy natural environment, peace, scientific happiness	Freedom, equality, respect for human rights	Existence of order, adequate order, pleasant society	Sufficiency	Sufficiency of social welfare, equal opportunity of education, etc.
	Change unhappiness to happiness through the way of thinking and actions				

Under this perception, a person's happiness or unhappiness will be determined by the state of the factors.

Namely, human happiness is determined by whether or not the request we have for the factors are satisfied. That is, our unhappiness is due to having anxiety, frustration and despair because our request for the factors is not satisfied. On the contrary, our happiness is resulting from having relief, satisfaction and hope because our request for the factors is satisfied.

The happiness or unhappiness, relating to ① cosmology (appendix 2-03, 2-04) and ② life form called human, is the spiritual problem related to science, philosophy, religion, and so forth. Therefore, with regard to ① cosmology, since it relates to human intelligence and knowledge, we have no choice but accept what we can then understand as it is. As for ② life form called human, since it relates to the innate that we are born with, though not the one we chose, we have to think about it by ourselves. It is not the matter that should be solved by entrusting to God or religion. (Further detail of ① and ② are in my book, "Thinking of God and Religion", though its English version is not available as of now)

On the other hand, what this book specifically deals with is ③ real life in the human world. As in the table above, as against all factors being in unhappy state under sovereign nations, they are all transmuted to happy state under the World Nation. Now that our happiness or unhappiness is determined by the way we humans hold our hearts and the actions that accompany it, we humans should have full responsibility for the outcomes. Assuming that human happiness can be obtained by realizing the demand of the nature of human life as presented in the Supreme Idea of the Human World, it can be said that it is spiritually high and wise to act in harmony with its realization while it is foolish to contradict it.

Incidentally, as in the table, the fundamental factor ③ consists of five sub-factors, but it can be more than five, or conversely, can also be less than five. This is because there should be various ways in dividing the factor into sub-factors, as these are related closely and complicatedly to each other. The reason divided into five is just because the writer thought it is appropriate for organizing our vision and head.

1. What Disappears and What Arises

"What disappears" is that which was necessary under the sovereign nations but became unnecessary under the Word Nation, and "what arises" is material and mental happiness under the World Nation, the Utopia for humanity, brought from "what disappears."

War, which was inevitable under the sovereign-nation system, has gone, and permanent peace has come in the World Nation. So first, described below are about how (1) military matters and (2) terms and concepts related to the sovereign nations will change due to the shift from the former to the latter, whatever comes to mind.

(1) Military Matters

When there is no more war and there is a peace, all military matters will cease to exist. It mainly includes the followings:

①Military-related Expenditures

When war ends and permanent peace comes, military-related expenditures will be unnecessary. Also, expenses for maintaining international relations inclusive of diplomacy, etc., which were needed under the sovereign nations, will be all unnecessary. Even if we take only the property required for these things, the human world, in global terms, is currently losing annually hundreds of trillions of Japanese yen (approximately, trillions of US dollar) or more. Importantly, not only these are wasteful but surprisingly are being used to make humans unhappy. Under the World Nation, all of these can be transferred to the use for the purpose of making human happiness.

②Soldiers

Countless soldiers have died in wars in the human history.

Needless to say, it is too much to guess that the soldiers died in the absurdity of war with much sadness and heart-rending, leaving his/her heart on his/her lover or spouse and child(ren). Also, there have been many young lives that have not yet had lover or spouse have gone unnoticed about the happiness that was born with people. There have been various kinds of sadness, namely, one who lost his/her lover, the wife who lost her husband, the child(ren) who lost their parent(s), the parents who lost their child(ren) and the like. When thinking about such sadnesses, the painful feeling "what if there were no war in the human world" is swirling in the chest of every person with unhelpful anger and regret. In addition, there have been countless soldiers who were physically and mentally hurt, even if they didn't die in battle.

Under the World Nation, there will be no war between nations, resulting in no army, no soldier, and no conscription system needed. Therefore, there will be no one killed or injured in war. Hurray and hurray!!

③Weapons

Science is a double-edged sword and its power will be going up and up endlessly. Under the circumstances, if we continue to abuse science to make weapons, it goes without saying that we humans will come to possess more and more powerful weapons endlessly. The warfare using such weapons shall definitely result in the extinction of human race soon or later.

However, in the war-free world, naturally weapons are no longer needed and never manufactured. As a result, under the World Nation, weapons will automatically disappear. Only for the police mechanism by the World Nation Government, some weapons are just required.

④Munitions Industry

Munitions industry will be unnecessary under the World Nation. However, the companies that make military aircrafts and various missiles also make aircrafts other than military aircrafts and rockets for space development, and the companies that make military ships also make ships other than military ships and large and sturdy structures. The companies that make tanks and other military vehicles also make non-military bulldozers, forklifts, cultivators and other vehicles. Now, the decrease in military demands can be adequately covered by greater peaceful demands.

Those to be increased in peace industry includes: (a) the supply of equipment that covers land, sea and air for the use of stopping of the damage, recovering its original condition and even improving of natural environment and ecosystem, (b) space development, (c) infrastructure development such as global road construction and maintenance, (d) bridges and flood control works that are solid but friendly to people and nature, (e) solid building construction which withstands natural disasters such as earthquakes and typhoons, and so forth. The munitions industry that is no longer needed should be possible to demonstrate its power for the happiness of the human world under the World Nation.

We can add as many jobs in the peace industry as we want, because there will be enormous amount of work to do in order to make this Spaceship Earth the ideal place for humanity in this world. Therefore, it is not necessary for the existing military industries to have the worries of declining in the peaceful world. There is no doubt that the future is open.

⑤Refugees, Slaughter, etc.

Under the World Nation, there is no quarrel between nations, so there is no army nor battle using weapons. As a result, there will never be another refugee reported as a daily news. Also, there will be no such event as horrifying to even hear about, the massacre of hatred arising from fighting. There are a lot of things that we can feel comfortable with even just thinking about.

⑥Creation Cost of Unhappiness to Creation Cost of Happiness

When such a time comes in the human world as there is no conflict and peace prevails on the earth, the people, things and money (human assets) that were used for the military purpose become no longer needed. This means that the assets, spent on war and its preparation, will be possible to be transferred for the use profitably to create human well-being. To review again how stupidly we have spent our assets so far, they are (a) to kill people and destroy nature with shells, toxic chemicals and nuclear weapons, (b) to bring sadness and hate to the human world and (c) to invite the risk of extinction of humanity. To wage war is a symbol of our stupidity of no help since it creates nothing but misery in the human world.

The one of the optimum use of the human assets is, for instance, thought to be the stoppage of the damage, recovery of its original condition and even improvement of natural environment and ecosystem, which are the fundamental basis for human survival.

For the transitional period until establishment of dedicated, economical, and efficient equipment and organization for its use, it is considered that military equipment and organization that are no longer needed can be used as is for this purpose. Namely, now that the Army is in charge of rivers, lakes and lands, the Navy is in charge of the ocean, and the Air Force is in charge of the atmosphere, the Army, the Navy and the Air Force are to remove residual physical, chemical, and nuclear material contamination in land, sea and air, respectively. Imagine a scene where an aircraft carrier becomes a flagship and cleans the ocean, which will be both encouraging and fun. Bombers spray air pollution neutralizer instead of dropping bombs. The same applies to cleaning rivers, lakes and marshes and land by using tanks, other vehicles, hovercraft and other equipment.

Although it is not thought that there are any fools who make such a criticism that it's uneconomical to use such expensive war equipment and organization for this purpose, yet no matter how expensive they are, there is no more meaningful use for converting it to the costs of creating happiness. This becomes much clearer when compared with the fact that the war that uses such expensive things will cause nothing but negative outcomes to the human world.

(2) Terms and Concepts related to the Sovereign Nations

Under the World Nation, there are a lot of items that we don't need so much and don't use any more. Shown below are some of these:

①National Border

Dictionary-wise, a national border is a border line that divides a nation from other nation(s) and the limits of national sovereignty. Namely, it is a partition frame that divides our Spaceship Earth into small rooms. Under the World Nation, as all of these dividers will be removed and the entire globe will become one room, there will be no territories, airspaces, waters, economic zones, etc. of a nation, resulting in no need to defend them from other nations at all.

In the first place, there is no natural border line on the earth especially when looking at earth from space. The walls and barbed wires that are physically located at the border are removed (or, we have the option of leaving them monumentally as a symbol of the time when we humanity were stupid) and the border is erased from the map. The earth is a common asset of humanity. Dividing it into small rooms and claiming the sovereignty of a small room is the biggest symbol of the stupid and small spirit, however, the fact that the World Nation is realized means that our spirit has developed even a bit to be smarter and bigger. Above and below the surface of the earth and the surface of the sea, that is, the concept of a three-dimensional cubicle from heaven to hell is dispelled, and spirit becomes free, the ventilation is good, and it's refreshing.

②National Defense (Security)

When a nation comes to have a conflict with another nation, the nation has to defend it. This is natural when a warfare is going underway, but even if it is not wartime, the nation needs to devote itself to preparing for defense assuming the occurrence of war as long as a conflict or tense exists. As a result, the management that is always conscious of defense will be required. Under such circumstances, it is really important to understand that defense is synonymous with attack, not just defense. Because only defending brings strategic disadvantage once you are attacked, it will be inevitable to attack where the attack comes from. Attack is also said to be the greatest defense.

Therefore, preparing for defense needs to include preparing for attack. At the time, the nation and the opponent that sense the necessity of such a preparation will enter into such a vicious cycle that each other tries to prepare for battle to surpass the other. It's clear why this kind of vicious cycle occurs. It is because there are many sovereign nations. Without those nations, that is, without attacking and defending, war will never occur. On the contrary, there is no hostile nation to the World Nation, so no attack nor defense occurs at all. It makes sense for permanent peace there.

As for Japan, relating to Article 9 of the Constitution, there will be no meaning and need to worry about if or if not there is a consistency between the abandonment of war in the Constitution and the existence of the Self Defense Force in reality.

③Domestic and Foreign

Under the World Nation, domestic and foreign concept needed in the world of many nations have disappeared. Speaking dare, "foreign" is outside the solar system. Because, even if we develop Mars or other planets of the solar system, it will still be within the humanity's nation as indigenous dwellers are unlikely there. Wherever we go, we need no passport nor visa but need only one's identification. Everyone will be able to freely travel to not only any place on the earth but other planets and the satellites in the solar system.

④National People

There should be no people called national people in the first place. Although people have an image of the word for the king, every individual is not merely an individual but a king or a queen, so to speak. This philosophy is realized in the World Nation. Therefore, if the name of the World Nation is the Earth Nation, it follows that all individuals are not national people of the Nation but Earthlings or equal members of the Nation. It is right recognition that so-called nation is made up by us all individuals, not vice versa.

There is a word that heaven does not create a person above a person and below a person. It goes without saying that the thought is natural, of course, though heaven which has an image of God is not so good.

(By the way, this word appears in the book, "Gakumon no Susume," of which meaning is "encouragement of learning," by Yukichi Fukuzawa, a Japanese, but the word seems to be a quote from the Declaration of Independence of the Unites States. After affirming its dictionary meaning, it seems that Fukuzawa used it with a slightly different meaning in his writing, but in the above, dictionary meaning of this wording is used as it is, that is, every person is born equal.)

⑤Patriotism

Now that many nations exist in the world presently, there are as many patriotisms as there are nations. As against this, under the World Nation, only one Nation on the earth, all of the old patriotisms will no longer exist and there will be only one patriotism that loves the World Nation. There may be some people who feel that this is a bit dreary, but only one patriotism on earth should be welcomed in view of peace in the human world. This is because there were many instances in our history that patriotism was abused to incite to the wars of nations by ignorant, stupid and heartless politicians.

Shown below is a reference related to what is stated above:

(Patriotism)

Needless to say, now that patriotism means to adore and love the country to which one belongs, it is true that it looks beautiful and heart-warming word. However, it is not a simple thing we can affirm unconditionally.

Although there is no problem when patriotism naturally grows and stays in a country, it becomes a problem when a conflict with another country occurs. This includes that patriotism works to emphasize the consciousness for individuals to have to protect their homeland. Also, as for the country, it raises patriotism as a slogan to enhance its will and moreover, may force the people more than necessary or unnatural patriotism. That is, the one who doesn't express patriotism actually, the person may even be punished. As you can see, patriotism doesn't seem to play a leading role in the fight, but it works to promote the conflict as a supporting role.

Why do such a silly and sad situation regarding patriotism occur? The reason is as simple as an idiot. It is because there are too many patriotisms, that is, there exist too many homelands on the earth. We are partitioning this small Spaceship Earth into smaller rooms and making a lot of countries resulting in creating a lot of patriotism. We don't need many countries on the earth. The earth should be just one country, the World Nation. Patriotism must be that which everybody loves very much only this Nation and every part of the earth as an irreplaceable and important thing.

⑥National Land

A national land is an area called territory whose extent is indicated by the border of the nation, including the territorial waters and airspace. The international conflict arises over this attribution. The national land can be used for various purposes such as to get mineral resources, to go farming and get food, to build housings and so forth. For this reason, a land-related conflict is to expand the country's small room in the Spaceship Earth in order to pursue the interest of that nation. This conflict occurs not only between two countries but also among several countries or more. It's clear what will happen if every sovereign nation pursues and claims this interest. Endless conflicts can't be avoided.

Under the World Nation, there will be no territorial issue, for there is no sovereign nation claiming territory as in the past. The territory of earth belongs only to the Earth Nation as the World Nation.

⑦Vulgar Word related to the Country

If there were no currently existing nations, the good news is that the bad words related to the nation are no longer needed and will disappear naturally. One of them is, for instance, traitor.

Dictionary-wise, a traitor is the one who tries to make one's profit by trying to be disadvantageous to the home nation and in the interest of the enemy, that is, to communicate domestic situation and secrets of the home nation to the enemy nation. As this action means to sell the importance of one's nation to the opponent, traitor is also called the seller of one's nation.

However, under the World Nation, there will be no traitor as there will be no enemy nation to buy the intelligence. No selling and buying "business" can be made. In this situation, it is clear that the word "traitor" will no longer be needed and naturally disappear for the use in this meaning.

⑧International Tariff

In the World Nation, exports and imports will be changed from international to domestic, so all commercial transactions will not be international but domestic. As a result, international trade and customs issues (wars) basically disappear automatically. There are no more worries about free trade and protectionist issues. Although everything is to be involved in the economic and social aspects of the World Nation, some kind of adjustment (plus to one, minus to the other) may be needed for interregional transactions until the disparity between regions disappears.

However, now that the adjustment is to make it as appropriate as possible while undertaking the balance of the world's regions under the unity of the World Nation, the human world will fit in well.

⑨Terms and Concepts related to International Relations

Under the existence of many sovereign nations, there are many "international" terms and concepts related to nations, as shown:

Internationalism, international conflict, international politics, international affairs, international diplomacy, the United Nations, international alliances, international treaties, international society, international congress, international law, international trade, international customs agreements (GATT), international straits, international customs, international courts, international security, international relations, international order, and so on and on.

Under the World Nation, there will be no "international" but only "domestic." Therefore, the human world will be completely free from unnecessary suffering deriving from the various difficult issues and troubles associated with anything related to international. Also, geopolitics will lose its meaning of existence and continue to decline, since it is a study that discusses the relationship between political phenomena, which are likely to be associated with political interest, and geographical conditions.

2. Omnidirectional Happiness in the World Nation

This paragraph is to complement the physical and mental well-being in the World Nation mentioned in the foregoing, "1. What Disappears and What Arises."

The table below is the one partially reprinted from that previously exhibited, "Factors of Happiness and Unhappiness and the State".

Factors of Happiness and Unhappiness and the State

Factor of happiness/ unhappiness	③Real life in the human world				
	Earth's environment, root of conflicts, treatment of science	Oppression and control by power	Social order	Food, clothing, shelter	Rights to life
Sovereign Nation Unhappiness (anxiety, frustration and despair)	Environmental destruction, violence /war, scientific disaster	No freedom, inequality, no respect for human rights	Lack of order, inadequate order, unpleasant society	Deficiency	Deficiency of social welfare, equal opportunity of education, etc.
World Nation Happiness (relief, satisfaction and hope)	Healthy natural environment, peace, scientific happiness	Freedom, equality, respect for human rights	Existence of order, adequate order, pleasant society	Sufficiency	Sufficiency of social welfare, equal opportunity of education, etc.
	Change unhappiness to happiness through the way of thinking and actions				

In the World Nation, since sovereign nations have disappeared and are not existing, there is no war, and it is the world that both mental and physical peaces prevail.

Taking a look at the table, as you can see that it seems self-explanatory that all factors are in happy state under the World Nation, and no more explanation may be needed. However, taking this occasion, the writer tried to make a few descriptions for each factor, hereinafter.

(1) Earth's Environment, Root of Conflicts and Treatment of Science

We have so far damaged the natural environment by pollution and abuse. If the damage progresses any further, the earth will become an ecosystem where living beings cannot inhabit and most of them inclusive of humankind will become extinct. Also, various resources have been decreasing due to unplanned abuse. In the first place, limited resources are not sufficient enough hopelessly for long-term survival of humanity even without abusing. Consequently, what we have to do first of all is to prevent the damage of ecosystem and to find the way to secure various resources that will enable the long-term survival of humanity.

Now that the healthy natural environment and ecosystem, which are necessary for all living things, and the sufficiency of natural resources, which is indispensable for humanity, are the basis for long-term human survival, securing these has to be the highest important and thus the highest priority for humanity. Therefore, natural environment and ecosystem have to be considered and managed purely from scientific standpoint without being hindered by the political approach. Now, the atmosphere covers the earth, and this atmosphere, the sea and the land are connected and in contact with each other, and these sets form the geosphere. For this reason, the whole earth should be regarded as one ecosystem and one resource from a global standpoint, therefore, anything on this planet is not something that we should consider and handle locally or by country.

In this meaning, the World Nation which can carry out anything important like this based on a global view point is superior to the world of the existence of many sovereign nations, needless to say.

①Importance in the World Nation

In the world of many sovereign nations, the first priority of each nation is its own, so the preservation of natural environment and ecosystem and securing natural resources, though they are the foundation for the survival of humanity, are only secondary problem for the nation. However, under the World Nation, good news is that the solution of the problem is placed at the first priority. This means that the humanity's first priority can be planned and implemented at will under the World Nation.

The solution under the World Nation will be able to be obtained as a result from swiftness, certainty, economic and management efficiency based on a comprehensive plan from global perspective. This is way superior to the performance that tends to be a mosaic pattern resulting from pluralistic thoughts and management under the world of sovereign nations.

The World Nation can be said to be an ideal environment in this meaning and in any other points of view.

Under the World Nation, we humanity willingly, unitedly and cooperatively endeavor, not only on natural environment and ecosystem, to stop the damage, recover its original and even improve to polish the earth for its glittering, but on the natural resources, to secure it needed for our long-term survival to come.

The mineral resources on the earth are limited. Even if we disregard the scientific technology and economic efficiency and obtain them from other planets and their satellites, comets or asteroids in the solar system, it is hopelessly insufficient for our long-term use as long as we repeat to abuse them to date.

Therefore, we have to develop the mechanisms and scientific technology which can ensure the permanent use by thorough recycling and circulating the resources on the earth. As for energy resources, although heavy oil and natural gas will be exhausted in the near future, fortunately, there are inexhaustible resources to replace them, which can ensure the use until the end of humanity. Namely, the earth has geothermal, wind, ocean currents, etc. and there is sun light pouring from our sun. The rest needed is the development of science and technology that can use these, but we can expect that more and more efficient technologies will be developed.

Therefore, we humanity must work together to fight for the ideal of natural environment and ecosystem and also, to challenge the battle for obtaining peace of mind related to minerals and energy resources that can withstand long-term use. However, these are not sad battles between humans, but the battles aimed at the happiness and glory of humanity. For this reason, there should be no more fun battles like these.

A clear atmosphere without smog, sparkling water, world being full of greenery, fertile soil from which harmful substances have been removed, fertile marine lives, dreamy and beautiful world of coral reefs, world without physical debris, restoration of the ozone layer (if possible), peace of mind regarding long-term use of energy and mineral resources, the world where these things have been achieved will be a world of joy not only for us humanity but for all living things.

②What to do Now in the World of Existing Sovereign Nations

The issue of natural environment and ecosystem directly relates to the survival of all living beings inclusive of human beings, therefore, it should be the top priority for us to tackle in the human world.

Nonetheless, in the sovereign nations that exist in the world today, the issue is the secondary treatment. This is because the first priority of a nation is in the settlement of the domestic and international issues that a nation faces for the time being. The former relates to the political, economic and social issue, and the latter relates to the conflict on the various interests among nations. Consequently, it is a reality that both physical and spiritual energy of a nation are spent for the first priority before the use for the secondary one. Now that the world is made up of many nations with the same circumstances, it is natural for the secondary issue not to progress ahead swiftly, despite the fact that there exists a worldwide firm understanding of the requirement to stop the damage of natural environment and ecosystem. Noted is that this situation will never change as long as many sovereign nations exist, and thus we have to be prepared for the circumstances.

On the one hand, the damage of the natural environment and ecosystem is progressing every moment. Even in face of this, we don't know well when the prevention of the damage will no longer be valid and natural environment and ecosystem will start going towards annihilation. This does mean that we cannot just sit down and merely watch the time passes, even though there exist certain difficult circumstances under the existence of many sovereign nations.

Now, then, the question arises how we may be able to keep our expectation to stop damaging natural environment and ecosystem under the reality of the existence of many nations.

By the way, this space in this chapter is the space not to talk about the concern that the natural environment and ecosystem are going towards annihilation resulting from the failure in stopping the damage, but supposed to talk about having attained the realization of the healthy state of natural environment and ecosystem by the prevention of damage, the restoration of the original state and even the improvement under the World Nation. It is known that this importance can be placed first in priority under the World Nation, but we need to hand over natural environment and ecosystem as they live without dying from the existing sovereign nations to the World Nation for the management thereafter.

For the reason as stated above, even under the present world made up of many nations, this space is being used to talk about what must be done now or the prerequisite necessary for the success and glory expectable under the World Nation.

Although we have been having a certain achievement to cope with the global warming caused by dioxide, yet we should not be satisfied only with this as this is only the beginning, not the end. What must be done now beyond this is that we first build a research institute in the United Nations in order to grasp all the factors which bring adverse effects onto the terrestrial natural environment and ecosystem. The research should be made to find out all the adverse effects of each factor and multiple factors so as to have the plan to prevent them as thoroughly and quickly as possible.

The plan must be comprehensive in order to satisfy in keeping ecosystem in ecologically friendly state and to grasp the minimum action required for this. To carry out this research project as soon as possible is a must taking into consideration the current situation that the damage of ecosystem is progressing every second towards its destruction. This clearly indicates that we cannot lose time any longer so as for us not to lose the opportunity to stop the damage of the basis of our survival.

We already know that we cannot stop the damage of ecosystem as we please under the circumstances that many sovereign nations exist presently. However, we have to obtain the thorough information and knowledge by the study as abovementioned as to what and how to do to ensure the basis for our survival. Based on this, if it comes to be known that such a project cannot be carried out, then the next step is to consider the secondary best option.

By the way, this study might clarify that with such an indecisive attitude, it is hopeless to stop the damage and destruction of ecosystem, but that time is then. Based on the information and knowledge obtained, we ourselves will be able to decide after convincing as to if we strive to prevent the death of ecosystem to the best of our ability, or if we will be willing to be extinct with the death of the ecosystem. The writer would not believe that we humanity will choose our own extinction. However, since we are such stupid beings who cannot get rid of having nuclear weapons that are the devil itself for us, the writer cannot dispel the distrust of humanity in that there should be no way we can conserve the healthy ecosystem. The writer just pray that this is an unnecessary worry and we humanity work together to save the global environment and ecosystem.

Therefore, in any case, such a research is required. Now that the need for the conservation of ecosystem has become a global recognition, it is expected that no nation will oppose to obtain such an information and knowledge. Merely, (though I should not just say so) it just requires a little money to add more research institute. It is not the money we borrow from God but our own money to be financed by ourselves for this purpose.

The necessity of peace through the extermination of conflicts in the human world is the main topic of this book, so it is covered throughout this book (**the root of conflicts**). Also, the necessity of the peaceful use of science through avoiding to make it disaster is covered mainly in chapter 3 and elsewhere of this book (**treatment of science**).

Therefore, the repetition of these is omitted here.

(2) Oppression and Control by Power

For us humans who are born as innocent and free beings equipped with fundamental human rights, we are unhappy in such a social environment that power (mainly, politics and religion, boss among private people, employer, etc.) unreasonably forces non-freedom, inequality and takes away other human rights by oppression and control.

The fundamental human rights include freedom and equality that humans are born with, therefore, it is a common perception that the rights are neither deprived nor limited thoughtfully like statutory rights.

Nonetheless, under the many sovereign nations, human liberty and dignity will be infringed. The violation of the human rights occurs when tension or war with another country exists or when the need to protect the national policy increases. This is because preservation of unification becomes the first proposition of the nation and then state power supersedes fundamental human rights.

However, under the World Nation, as tension and war with another country is extinct, human freedom and dignity are not violated. As for the protection of national policy, in the first place, now that the World Nation aims to attain the Supreme Idea of the Human World which is derived from human nature, there is no need to control the freedom of speech. Therefore, the people will be able to take the best approach for betterment of the Nation through free speech, even in case the people should have something unhappy with the state of the Nation. Because the World Nation is such a society, it is a world where the need for such a thought as controlling free speech has disappeared.

(3) Social Order

Disorderly society lacking morals and laws is an uncomfortable and uneasy society. However, needless to say, even if order exists, if it is not the form of order recognized by the members of the society, if it is twisted by power, or if it is something that involves fear and irrationality, such a society is like a disorderly society or even more uncomfortable and uneasy than that.

For instance, in such a case as war is national proposition and waging war is in a state of morality and justice in the nation, the ethics as peace of the proposition held by each of human individuals, who is the member of the nation, is forcibly denied, and thus individual ethics will become inferior to national morality and justice. However, under the World Nation, both propositions become united in peace.

(4) Foods, Clothing and Shelter

It is the current status that there are countries and regions which are lacking in foods, clothing and shelter as the basic condition for people to live. It is being said that more than 10% of the today's world population are not only far from being satisfied with foods but starving.

On the one hand, however, now we have advanced agricultural technology, livestock farming technology, aquaculture technology, and other kinds of technology required to produce foods. Therefore, it is an easy matter from the view point of the World Nation that foods are produced right amount at the right place. In addition, since the global logistics are also developing, it is possible for us to have an optimum distribution of foods on the planet.

The World Nation is the world which never does any negative act that makes humanity unhappy, but it does only positive act that makes humanity happy. As a result, satisfactory supply of not only foods but clothing and shelter is promised in the World Nation. So long as the human world is peaceful, all the power of humanity can be first dedicated to human well-being. Now that, of all things, the satisfaction of foods, clothing and shelter is the highest priority, it is no doubt to be achieved.

(5) Rights to Life

Social welfare and equal opportunity of education, which secure the human rights for each member of the society to live human life, have not yet reached the human world properly, and the human world is in an unhappy state. Social welfare is the organized action of public and private endeavors that plan the support, upbringing and rehabilitation for the people who are the poor and suffer social disabilities that require protection. As for education, it is the best effective way for us humans to equally obtain knowledge acquiredly, that is, after birth.

By the way, under the World Nation, it is considered that these enhancements will be facilitated. Now that the huge expenses for military affairs and maintaining international relations inclusive of diplomacy, etc. needed under the sovereign nations, will be unnecessary under the World Nation, all of these expenses will be possible to be transferred to supporting people's happiness.

With regard to our knowledge and action, there are two theories. One is that we have knowledge and action congenitally (innately), and another is that they are acquired (empirically). There is no need to dispute which is right, because, theoretically, the sum of additions of the congenital and the acquired is our knowledge. It helps us act in this world. The congenital derives from genes, and the acquired is obtained by experience and education after birth. As we can do nothing for the congenital after our birth, that which we can and we need is to pile up experience and education to be acquired.

Since education is something that teaches us how to think and act, we must provide the equal opportunities for all individuals in the world to take education. This is an indispensable requirement from the standpoint of not only the fundamental human rights but also the improvement of the artificial environment. Those who can think intellectually don't believe the rumor of irresponsible delusional word and prediction without grounds made by poorly intellectual delusional people as well as any of delusional thoughts. They can correctly decide so as for them not to follow any stupid agitation which does not harmonize, for instance, with the Supreme Idea of the Human World. Especially, for those who mention such a stupid matter that no education is needed for women, education must be given first of all to have them understand how stupid they are.

Under the World Nation that makes it possible to handle things in a unified manner, it is considered easy to coherently carry out such a proposition that provides a healthy level of social welfare and equal opportunities of education for all the individuals in the world.

Chapter 6   Road to Establishment to the World Nation

As has been discussed its necessity so far, we humanity must developmentally dissolve many existing sovereign nations and then unify them to create a world nation that makes entire globe one. However, even if the reason is understood and accepted, the biggest question remains with regard to how we can approach the realization of a world nation. This is the most difficult problem that must be resolved with all the best of human knowledge and effort.

With regard to this difficult problem, the writer tried to think about it though incomplete and unskillful, as shown hereunder:

1 A Non-Governmental Organization Aiming for a Single World Nation

There are various NGOs and their coalitions that aim to make one nation by uniting many nations on the earth, but out of those, here World Federalist Movement (WFM) is taken as the representative. Shown below is its overview prepared by the writer. (The source is Wikipedia, the free encyclopedia)

The world-famous scientists and cultural people, who were keenly aware that the United Nations was vulnerable to war deterrence, determined to eliminate the wars from the world by advancing the formation of a stronger World Federation, and in 1946, they launched the "World Movement for the World Federalist Government." This Movement was supported by those inclusive of Bertrand Russell, Albert Einstein, Albert Schweizer, Winston Churchill, Hideki Yukawa, and they set up its headquarters in Geneva.

The World Federalist Movement has the following operational principles:

(1) To have all the countries and peoples of the world join.
(2) Regarding global common problems, to have some of the sovereignty of each nation delegate to the WFM.
(3) WFM laws applies to each individual, not to the nation.
(4) The abolition of military equipment in each nation and the establishment of the World Police Force.
(5) Nuclear power is owned and controlled only by the World Federalist Government (WFG).
(6) The expenses of the WFG will be covered by the tax from individuals, not by the donation of each government.

The main focus of the Movement is to change the existing eligibility for participation to the United Nations from country unit to individual unit, that is, virtual construction of a single-world nation (a single-world government) or "the world is one."

Afterwards, the Movement has been involved in amending the United Nations Charter and proposal to establish an International Criminal Court, and founded a think tank, The Institute for Global Policy (IGP) in 1983 which emphasizes the democratization of international and regional organizations and the development and global application of international law. Presently, the secretariat is in New York, and regional organizations have been established in dozens of countries and regions. Also, the Movement has had Special Consultative Status with the United Nations Economic and Social Council, and active proposals for strengthening the power of the United Nations. In the WFM, many NGOs aiming to realize a world nation have joined and are affiliated.

As shown above, The World Federalist Movement is one of the most excellent NGOs among the many NGOs aiming at a world nation, and it seems that it has been making a pretty good performance towards that goal. However, even now, three quarter century after the

Movement was launched, a world nation has not yet been realized. Moreover, unfortunately, in the future, even 75 years or 150 years from now, there is no hope that a world nation will be realized from the World Federalist Movement. This is basically because the WFM is a non-governmental organization and does not have the indispensable authority to move to a world nation.

The world nation is the dream of humanity, but no matter how much we say a dream, it's always a dream forever. In order to make the dream come true, the comprehensive plan and the authority to carry it out must be accompanied. Accordingly, to realize a world nation, an authoritative place that can confirm the world will and declare to start off its execution is indispensable.

Namely, it is needed for us to have discussions, decisions and implementations within the governmental organization, not in the non-governmental one.

2 Contradiction and Non-Contradiction between the World Nation and the United Nations

There is no other place than United Nations where a global consensus towards the World Nation for humanity can be formed and a declaration of its execution can be made. Therefore, first, in the place of the United Nations where all nations in the world gather, the concept of the World Nation has to be put on the agenda. Otherwise, nothing will start.

However, we encounter a great contradiction here. Namely, even if it says that the first purpose of the United Nations is to maintain world peace, the agenda forms a contradiction that the United Nations, a group of sovereign nations, discusses the transition to the World Nation that leads to the dissolution of sovereign nations. Given this basic thing, it's going to be heartbreaking to talk about the concept of the World Nation to the United Nations.

Nonetheless, that being said, even though I am aware of this contradiction, it is also true that the United Nations is the only place where we can depend on to head to the World Nation. The concept of the World Nation must be taken up on the agenda of the United Nations, otherwise there is no future at all. That's the end story.

This means that we humanity will follow the current world and then have to be prepared for all of these, namely, endless conflict in the human world, human misfortune and even the risk of the extinction of human race in the near future resulting from war using powerful weapons made by the abuse of science.

Now, in face of such a circumstance, here, we have to shift the discussion from "the current situation" to "the theory in the first place." The former is the existing sovereign nations, and the latter relates to the sovereignty of the individual (each person) which is the source of the sovereign nations. In the first place, both sovereign nation and the United Nations, which is a group of sovereign nations, are the group of individuals. They don't exist apart from group of individuals. The existence value of both sovereign nation and the United Nations is only a means to realize the first hope of humanity.

The first hope of humanity that is the first important thing of humanity is to survive forever happily in peace and freedom. Protecting the sovereign nations is not the first importance. Since the existence of many sovereign nations inevitably causes conflict and war in the human world, it is contradictory to the first important thing of humanity. Therefore, dissolving all sovereign nations and then unifying them into a single world nation, which has no opponent to wage war, should be the right choice in the light of the realization of the first hope of humanity.

In the world we are now, the proposition of war that the sovereign nation has and the proposition of peace that each individual has are contradictory. As against this, the World Nation is a world in which this helpless contradiction has been resolved. Namely, it is a world where both propositions become united in peace.

All individuals attending the United Nations General Assembly, etc. are representatives of sovereign nations, but before they are such representatives, each of them has to be one person as a representative of humanity. Whereas the World Nation will definitely be able to realize the first hope of humanity, they should not disregard to put the concept of the World Nation on the agenda of the United Nations. Now that each sovereign nation is also a group of individuals, if the realization of the first hope of humanity could be expected, then it makes sense that even the home nation cannot simply oppose the transition to the World Nation.

Thinking this way, the United Nations and the World Nation, both endeavoring after peace, are not necessarily in contradictory relationship but rather non-contradictory relationship.

Now that we humanity are at risk of extinction in the near future on an extension of the present world, it is considered that we have to launch in the United Nations a research institute to study for the ultimate project, preparing for the transition to the World Nation, to avoid the risk and aim at our glorious future. At the very least, serious and thorough discussions have to be made in the United Nations for the transition to the World Nation. This is because that which the discussions are not done means that we humanity will close our own happy and glorious future by ourselves.

Naturally and needless to say, we can never accept it at all.

3 Role of the United Nations

Based on the above, if the concept of the World Nation becomes the agenda of the United Nations, it is thought that the first question arisen naturally is "the feasibility of transition to the World Nation." No matter how the concept is wonderful, it will be something like a cake drawn in the picture if it can't be realized. Because it is such a thing, it will be reasonable to judge to move or not to move to the World Nation after seeing its detailed blueprint.

For this reason, first of all, it is necessary to make a resolution to establish a new unit, or the body (organization) that prepares this blueprint, within the United Nations. In addition, it is desired to establish a new research department for this purpose in United Nations University where brains from all over the world will be brought together to prepare the blueprint.

As a result, the role of the United Nations will be as shown:

Role of the UNs = The Current+Preparation for the Transition
to the World Nation (Comprehensive Plan, or Blueprint)

The tentative plan of the comprehensive plan for the realization of the World Nation is to be prepared by the joint work of the Preparatory Organization and United Nations University, and it is to be submitted to such as United Nations General Assembly for consideration. This procedure will be repeated until the final draft, which can be adopted/ decided by the United Nations, is completed. In case, at some point, we encounter an insurmountable difficulty and this repetition stops, the transition to the World Nation will result in failure. However, if it is completed sunny, then we will able to step out into the realization of the World Nation.

It is noted by the way that it is recommended to incorporate in some way non-governmental organizations which aim at a world nation, such as World Federalist Movement, in the Preparatory Organization in the United Nations, and also to use the ideas of those NGOs accordingly for reference in preparation for the comprehensive plan towards the World Nation.

4 Road to Establishment to the World Nation

As the United Nations is a group of the sovereign nations, it cannot be expected that the World Nation will be born naturally from the United Nations. However, this gives us great hints on how to establish the World Nation (though this might be needless to say, as it is so clear). The World Nation is completed when all the sovereignty of the existing nations is transferred to, for instance, the United Nations. At that time, the United Nations will become the government agency of the World Nation. On the other hand, if the sovereignty of the sovereign nation is transferred all at once, the world will stop functioning and collapse. For this reason, the transfer of the sovereignty must be carefully planned and gradually made according to carefully prepared schedule.

Therefore, it can be said that the process of transitioning to the

World Nation is the process of delegating the sovereignty of the sovereign nations.

After the establishment of the World Nation, the sovereignty of all the individuals in the world is entrusted to the World Nation, and the presently existing sovereign nations will become the states or regions of the World Nation.

5 Governance by the World Nation

As for the realization of the World Nation, it is thought that big and small and various difficult problems spring out, not to mention politics and economy. For this reason, it is imagined that the criticism against the idea of the World Nation will naturally arise mainly on the basis of its low feasibility and unlikeliness.

However, it is not pertinent to have that way of looking. If we change our mindset, it may not be so much difficult or may be unexpectedly so easy.

For instance, thinking about governance of the World Nation and that of the United States, the essence is common, and we can think of it simply big or small problem. Even in the beginning of the World Nation, if it employs the national agency of the sovereign nations, which existed during the transitional period to the Nation, as its outsourced agency of governance and management services, it could be expected that a smooth transition and startup of the Nation is possible without much difficulties. Even if dissatisfaction occurs in a certain thing, it is a topic within the premise having been decided to move to the World Nation. So, there will be no armed conflict. In the first place, now that major weapons were shifted to the management under the provisional World Nation on the decision to move to it, armed conflict does not hold.

Because any dissatisfaction can be resolved through thorough discussions and dialogues based on the intelligence, common sense and the reason of the world, it's possible to maximize reasonable and convincing solution to all parties concerned.

As discussed above, it is possible to have the perspective that it is easier for us to give a birth to the World Nation than we think. And, it is important that we must think in this way.

6　Notes related to the World Nation

As stated above, the Comprehensive Plan towards the World Nation is to be prepared in the United Nations where the brains from all over the world come and work together on the Plan, so I should entrust the preparation to their work. For this reason, there is no need for me to say anything extra, but I wrote down some of my rough thinking, knowing that these may not be substantially helpful, as shown below:

1. Peaceful Transition to the World Nation

The World Nation is a world where the permanent peace is realized on the earth. It is a world that we are going to build for peace. Therefore, any conflict must not arise in moving into this world. That is, the transition must be calm and smooth and must not be radical like revolution.

It is desired to have such a transition that without our notice, conflict and war have gone and peace has come, the minimum requirement for an ideal artificial environment has been met and we humanity have entered inside the gate of the Utopia in this world.

2. Transition Period to the World Nation

Although the transition to the World Nation cannot take place overnight, we must not lazy to waste our time, taking into account the state of present human unhappiness and the risk of the destruction of humanity due to the endless conflicts in the world. Based on this perception, I would like to suggest that we had better consider a plan to set the time when the World Nation will be substantially realized from 2075 to around 2100 at the latest, though this is my dogmatism and prejudice or hope.

3. The Comprehensive Plan

The Comprehensive Plan is divided into two stages. The first stage has to do with the things up to reaching the World Nation, and the second stage relates to the things after the establishment of the Nation. In other words, what must be incorporated in the Plan thoroughly is the solution in advance of all sort of problem thought to be arisen before and after establishing the World Nation.

The most important thing is to aim to construct the world where no one will be left behind and every one of us humans will be able to have motivation and hope in the future so as not to fall into boredom.

4. Huge Organization of the World Nation

The World Nation is a huge organization. Since the scale of the organization has enormous interests and bureaucracy, it tends to be considered that to govern and manage it smoothly and satisfactorily is extremely difficult. In addition, there is the worry about the uneven distribution of power.

However, the comprehensive plan to be prepared is a plan which incorporates the idea and its concrete measures to eliminate such difficulty in the World Nation as much as possible, thinking of such things in advance. This is the thing that the world's brains should gather to think over thoroughly.

Even though an organization is enormously huge, it does not simply become difficult to manage it. With regard to the big or small problem in scale and number, we can solve it in any way since we are in the world of the advanced computerization. As for the difficulties of managing the interests and bureaucrats that are now rampant in the world, we must thoroughly implement "checks and balances" methods and, in addition, introduce even more advanced measures.

Humans are like a life form that wants to have power. In the human history, inequality and misery resulting from uneven distribution of power has covered the human world. Even now, they have not yet been wiped out clean, and there are uneven distributions of power in many sovereign nations.

To prevent this from happening in the World Nation, we have to invent better governance system than what we have now. People's stupid politics (ochlocracy) is also a problem, but needed is a system of governance that stupid and paranoid world president will never arise. However, now that under the World Nation, there are no agenda concerning conflict and war arising from the existence of the international and, instead of it, there is only the agenda to make the Utopia even more ideal. Namely, the agenda that requires decision-making has changed from the days when there were many sovereign nations. From this point of view, there will be no need for the centralization of power such as a world president as an independent body has, and nor should it be like that. Based on this perspective, it is felt that it is appropriate for the council body to hold the highest authority.

In any case, required is the system which is without uneven distribution of power and can make decision making fairly, correctly and promptly. These things, of course, must also be proposed in the comprehensive plan for the World Nation.

Although the society and politics without uneven distribution of power is the difficult issue that we humanity have not reached its nice solution to date, yet to have the solution is indispensable to realize our dream to establish the Utopia for us humans. We have to think it out to the extent of our brain and wisdom.

5. Changing World

When the preparatory organization which pursues the feasibility of the World Nation is established in the United Nations and its activity begins, it alone will change the world.

We've had the negative paradigms that have settled in our hearts in the midst of being forced to give up. These are inclusive of ① existence of conflict and war in the human world, ② existence of nuclear weapons, ③ misery and risk of human destruction and ④ we humanity being the dwellers of the world of suffering.

However, seeing the possibility of changing to new paradigms, the hearts of the people of the world will swell with hope and become rounded. These are inclusive of ① peace and freedom, ② the world without nuclear weapons, ③ happiness and long-lasting survival of humanity and ④ possibility of being residents of the Utopia in this world.

Similarly, if we can see the high probability of realization of the World Nation, even the existing sovereign nations have no point in sticking to international conflicts including territorial issue. As a result, the reduced expenses related to such conflicts can be transferred to the expenditures for the use of human well-being, such as the enhancement of social welfare of the people and the improvement of natural environment. In other words, it is possible to expect the world to become peaceful and happy already even during the preparation period for heading towards the World Nation.

Chapter 7　Unrealistic Hope and Unrealistic Decision

The hope to build the Utopia for us humanity for peace, freedom and happiness, avoiding the extinction of us which is the necessary condition for that, is unreal far from reality. It is difficult to realize this unreality with reality. After all, it follows that the realization of unreality can only be achieved by unreality.

As the top grip of the unreality, there are abolition of weapons and establishment of the World Nation. Therefore, in order to make this earth the Utopia for humanity, determination and action towards the realization of this unreality will be required of us.

That being said, even if it is an ideal, the writer think there will be a criticism that it is "nonsense" to talk such silly things ignoring reality. However, the criticism does not hold.

The real reason and point for it lie in that the extinction of humanity is inferred as a logical necessity if we follow currently existing reality, therefore, there is no other way for us to be saved than heading towards unreality and realizing it. In other words, moving towards the realization of the unreal is not a question of "can or can't," but the only way left for us humanity in order to avoid our extinction and achieve the glory for the eternal future.

1　Abolition of Weapons

Among international, there is a proposition of disarmament. About it, occasionally but not always, a discussion may take place. Disarmament is preferrable to military expansion and should be naturally and always welcomed.

However, disarmament is a concept in contradiction. That is, since, in the first place, armament is to seek military superiority against real or imaginary enemies and its origin is naturally in "the more powerful, the better," trying to suppress it by "some extent" is incompatible with this origin. Nonetheless, disarmament is discussed internationally, because a war using the armament brought from endless military expansion brings a catastrophic damage to both him and us and other negative factors that become needed to consider including political and economic difficulties.

Then, what is the appropriate degree of disarmament in this case?

Its answer is clear if we think of the fact that it is disarmament which is trying to stop endless military expansion. Namely, since the opposite word or thought to endless military expansion is endless disarmament, that is a state of zero military strength. Therefore, this comes to lead us to the recognition that desired disarmament is not to say the half-hearted level like "some extent" but the ultimate state of perfect abolition of armament.

Realizing the world without weapons is not just to physically exclude weapons. More important thing is to eliminate weapons from our mind. We humans must truly understand that making weapons that kill people is stupid in the light of the Supreme Idea of the Human World. We humans have to stop the height of stupidity like a joke to pray to God for peace and happiness while fighting among ourselves and waging war. If we humans are such a stupid and selfish and shameless creature, we can't be saved.

Therefore, both nuclear weapons and ordinary weapons must be abolished completely. In this recognition, here, nuclear weapons, that must be abolished first and as soon as possible, is being discussed.

The need for **the abolition of nuclear weapons** is as mentioned much of it in Chapter 3. Nuclear weapons wipe out humankind in an instant and it is the personification of evil and absolute evil. It is the human stupidity that created this evil. No matter what we may say in the reality of the existence of nuclear weapons sticking to this product of stupidity, it will only pile up stupidity.

In particular, nuclear equilibrium or nuclear deterrence by nuclear is just an idea as the symbol of the stupidity of a fool, therefore, anyone who talks about that importance with a thoughtful face is just a profound idiot who misunderstands that he is saying something profound. Creating by yourself a devil, a symbol of stupidity, and then spending the days of being scared by the equivalent that others have is inferior to child's quarrel, so to speak. This is the situation just like Einstein's word that there are two infinites in this world, one is the universe and the other is the human stupidity. When thinking about various things related to nuclear weapons, it is sad to feel and confirm the truth of this word.

Therefore, disarmament is not half-hearted, but it must be perfect disarmament or perfect abolition. On the other hand, after nuclear weapons were brought into the human world just before the end of World War II, it was in 1963 when disarmament of nuclear weapons was first discussed and adopted by the United Nations, resulting in the form of Nuclear Non-Proliferation Treaty (NPT). This was signed in 1968, and its effectuation was in 1970. This Treaty is the one that ① recognizes internationally only the 5 nations, USA, Russia (former Soviet Union), UK, France, and China, which were the victorious nations of the World War II, as nuclear-weapons nations, ② provides for imposing upon the 5 nations the duties of nuclear weapon disarmament, ③ prohibits non-nuclear-weapon nations from possessing nuclear weapon, and ④ limits nuclear use only for peaceful purpose.

However, this Treaty wasn't necessary. The ultimate state of nuclear non-proliferation is nuclear abolition. Namely, instead of creating such a Treaty that non-nuclear-weapons nations should not aim to possess nuclear weapons, what the five nuclear-weapons nations should have done at that time was their declaration to non-nuclear-weapon nations that they will perfectly abolish nuclear weapons immediately. At that time, we humans should have decided and executed the abolition of nuclear weapons from the human world.

But it's not too late. We can bring the discussion back to this point again, and we must newly decide the abolition of nuclear weapons and carry it out.

What all the nuclear-weapon nations have to do right away is unconditional and immediate disposal of all nuclear weapons, together with apologizing to all non-nuclear-weapon nations for their having brought nuclear weapons into the human world, despite the fact that using the weapons definitely results in instant extinction of humanity. In addition to being used for a clear purpose of war, nuclear weapons have various such risks as being triggered by international misunderstandings, administrative mistakes, an accident caused by mentally handicapped person, terrorism, and so forth. Therefore, rapid and thorough abolition of nuclear weapon from the human world is desired from the bottom of heart.

Considering World War II and the world situation after that, it is conceivable that nuclear weapons have been introduced into the human world soon or later by some other county if not America. However, in the midst of such circumstances, it is also true that it was America that introduced nuclear weapons first into the world.

For the purpose of the extinction of nuclear weapon, which is an absolute evil against humanity, the writer desire America to make a big decision to lead the world, as shown below.

This is the writer's hope for the country of America's sincerity and courage:

USA Declaration of Abolition of Nuclear Weapons and Its Execution (Draft)

Our nation first possessed and used nuclear weapons. However, from the perspective of humanism and the survival of humanity, we are regretful that we made a great mistake. Therefore, our nation hereby declares that it will dismantle and incapacitate the nuclear weapons it possesses unconditionally, thoroughly and safely, and we will execute the contents of this declaration immediately. Also, we will show this execution in a verifiable way that the world can be convinced.

We sincerely express our regret about the creation of such a situation that the nations, on which our nation projected its power and fear of nuclear weapons, came to possess nuclear weapons.

Hopefully following our nation, we will be pleased if these nations could promptly abolish the nuclear weapons being possessed and have eternal non-nuclear declaration and its implementation.

Under the circumstances, we would like to expect that non-nuclear-weapon nations need not to aim to possess nuclear weapons any longer. If these things are realized, our world will be free from the threat of nuclear weapons and the risk of the destruction of humanity due to nuclear war.

We all know that as to the past, every nation has various things to say. We can't change the past, however, it is not good to bring the negative past into the future. By making the decision now, we humanity can break the negatives of the past and build the future with new paradigms. All is to avoid the extinction of our species as Homo sapiens, and for the glorious future of building our Utopia in this world on this earth, in this Spaceship Earth.

We would like to ask all the nations of the entire world to support this idea and its implementation.

It will be the most important that led by the United States, the 5 powers recognized by NPT as nuclear-weapon nations, decide and execute the abolition of nuclear weapons. It's not expensive for us to do this shopping that leads to the realization of our unrealistic hope, that is, to obtain our eternal glory with peace and happiness, with paying the stupid nuclear reality created by ourselves. This is compared to buying a diamond by a stone.

2 Transition to the World Nation

Now, although the rationale for the abolition of nuclear weapons is as discussed above, yet based on the existing reality, the writer know there will be criticisms or objections.

When international tensions exist and become unrest, in order to protect one's nation (or allied group), it is no other choice but planning the strengthening defense capability, that is, armament for coping with the reality in front of us. Even if there is no intention for us to invade other nation, once we are unilaterally invaded by other nation(s) with force, we must defend us with force as we can't just "recite a nembutsu," that is, pray to God.

However, what will be the destination brought by such a negative spiral where we humans endlessly fight each other? It is crystal clear that the war, using powerful weapons made by abusing of endlessly developing science, will eventually and definitely result in nothing but the extinction of humankind.

In this human world ruled by us humans, it is clear that the reason for the occurrence of such a contradiction to human happiness is in the fact that there exist numerous sovereign nations which eventually create various conflicts in the human world. Therefore, it is reasoned that we humans should leave from the world of internationalism and then aim for the World Nation, based on cosmopolitanism, which has no hostile nation.

Based on this fundamental recognition, there is another unreality that the writer desire to ask the 5 nations which are also permanent members of the United Nations. It is for the 5 nations to propose with the joint names the creation of a preparatory body for the World Nation in the United Nations.

We humanity will be saved and also be promised for peace, happiness and the residents in our Utopia in this world through eliminating nuclear weapons and heading to the World Nation. All is what we can achieve by ourselves so long as we decide to do so.

3 Utopia on the Earth

For the purpose of our long-term survival embraced in peace and happiness that is the 1st proposition of humanity, we need to declare and practice to cooperatively put our total energy into this importance that we should (a) avoid fighting between humans, (b) unconditionally forgive for each other its past and present, (c) care, share, love and get along each other, (d) sublimate into a relationship of respect and harmony, and (e) work together to preserve, restore and improve nature and ecosystem in this Spaceship Earth.

We humanity will be able to be happy so long as what this one sentence describes is realized. Regrettably, however, as against this, we hate and kill each other and are in misery only because we can't practice this. As a result, we are unhappy and moreover, are standing on the verge of our destruction due to endless conflicts and wars using developed weapons manufactured by abusing of the developed science. So long as the intention to practice this declaration sprouts and stays in the hearts of all humanity with its feasibility, all troops and weapons that symbolize human stupidity are no longer needed and disappear from the human world.

Will we humanity die in misery only because we cannot practice what this one sentence describes?

From the perspective of the human survival in peace and happiness, that which this one sentence describes is natural thing that we humans must do, not related to God, religion nor virtue. As against this natural thing, the criticism to say that it's an unrealistic stupidity which does not recognize the currently existing reality is useless, because it does not understand the real point at issue. The issue is in that we humanity will not be saved unless we do unrealistic thing, based on the belief and conviction that we will perish in the near future if we follow the reality as it is. In other words, the real issue is which of the two options to choose. One is that we humanity accept our destruction/extinction by following the currently existing reality, and the other is that we go to unreality aiming at the realization of our glorious future of peace and happiness through changing the paradigm we have in our mind.

The question is what to do with the future of humanity. It's useless even if you list up various criticisms that are not based on a deep thinking, because it's not God, Buddha nor religion but we ourselves who must choose and carry it out.

Thomas Hobbs, a 17th-century British philosopher, had a view that the natural state of humanity is a war state in which everyone fights for power. However, even if this view is correct, we can't remain in the natural state of humanity that Hobbs says. This is because we humanity will become extinct if we keep fighting, now that the condition for the development of science, which is capable of manufacturing weapons to exterminate humanity, has appeared. We are life forms wishing to survive for a long time embraced in peace and happiness, then we need to be wise and have to get out of Hobbs' theory of the natural state of humanity. The minimum requirements imposed on us in order not to have conflict are to aim to cut off three major roots of conflict, or stopping racism, becoming independent from God and religion, and establishing the World Nation that has no hostile nation.

If we look at it based on God hypothesis, God might set up the obstacle of a set of human natural state and scientific development, and be trying to see if we humanity can overcome this challenge to avoid our extinction, and finally realize peace, the Utopia for humanity and happiness. If so, we must not lose even to God.

We humans seem to have conflicting genes of struggle and philanthropy. If we aim to realize the Supreme Idea of the Human World, a concept of happiness human nature aspires, by the work of reason, we must try to activate the gene of philanthropy that forgives and helps each other, instead of the gene of struggle that fights and kills. The gene of the struggle must not be triggered toward humans, but it must be invoked to overcome any difficulty in order to build our Utopia in this world.

If the conflict disappears from the human world and it is a peaceful world, we humanity can be happy at will. All of the immeasurable energies of both things and mind that have been spent relating to the existence of various conflicts to date will be able to be spent to build the World Nation, the Utopia in this world on the earth, in this Spaceship Earth. Namely, it means that it will become possible for us to use all the energies as we please including for the betterment of natural and artificial environments.

Religions preach/claim heaven, paradise, and pure land (western paradise) which are said to be in afterlife, and the importance of the future world rather than this world. However, the existence of the future world and existence of such wonderful worlds are unknown. To the contrary, as we can recognize the existence of this world as a reality, we know something about this world. Therefore, it is obvious that for us humans, this world is more important than the future world. Consequently, it comes to be known that we must put our mental and physical center of gravity in this world, not in the future world.

In this book, I have emphasized that the world we are in is stupid, but that's not what I really mean. The world we are in now is a world that we have reached by paying off regrettably the high tuition fees of trial and error with many sacrifices. However, it is the world of a rough stone from which a wonderfully shining world of dreams, the Utopia, contributed also by the advancement of science, appears, so long as we wipe away the existing cloudiness of stupidity. Because of my frustration of being not in the Utopia only due to a little stupidity while being near there, I couldn't be helped to emphasize stupidity. However, the rough stone created by humans is waiting for the time when the cloudiness will be wiped away. We are life forms who want to realize peace, build the Utopia in this world, and aim at the glorious happiness in this world.

Now, from a global perspective, it is the time for us to have to consider the entire earth as one place and all humanity as one herd, and seek peace and happiness for all humanity. Namely, this means that now we have to aim to raise GHH (Gross Humanity Happiness) index, through realization of the contents of the declaration of the Constitution of the United Nations Educational, Scientific and Cultural Organization and what is called SDGs (Sustainable Development Goals) which has 17 important goals. Therefore, narrow and stupid ideas from the perspective of small rooms that go against it must be eliminated from the world.

In the first place, the ideas, "as long as one's own country is good, that's fine" even if "making light of other countries," have been creating various conflicts in the human world. We must remember that, as a result, we humanity have not been happy but in misery to date.

We must not be stupid but must be wise. Even if God and Buddha exist and watch over us, our wisdom itself will surely bring us what we want. After all, everything depends on how we hold our hearts. The world can be changed in any way as we like depending on our own minds. If we make the decision to build the Utopia today, it will come true even tomorrow.

Naseba naru nasaneba naranu
nanigotomo naranuwa hitono nasanu narikeri

(Yozan Uesugi, a Japanese Feudal Lord,
Yonezawa Feudal Clan, Edo Era)

The meaning above is:

Anything can be done if you do,
Nothing can be done if you don't do,
That anything can't be done is merely because you don't do.

If God exists, God may say with smile,
"Can you humanity do this?"

Postscript

In between and after writing this book, there has been a question I have been asking to myself. That is, "Did I present any particularly lofty theory or the solution for some difficult problems?"

This is because what I am talking about in this book is just a matter of course and has nothing to do with such things. Therefore, it is not enough to be written as a book again. Namely, the main point of this book is, "We all humanity, let's stop fighting, get along, and be peaceful, free and happy. In order to accomplish this hope, let's become one race of earthlings, extinguish armies and weapons, establish the World Nation, Earth Nation, build the Utopia for us humanity, and through these, aim for the glory in the eternal future." It goes without saying that this is plain to all, and even elementary school children can say.

By the way, mathematics and whatsoever, to solve a problem, if we think the ultimate or extreme condition, the solution may be easily obtained. For instance, because many sovereign nations are at the center of the mechanism which is causing conflict and war, it requires, to be peaceful, to dissolve and then integrate the nations and establish only one nation on the earth that is the ultimate form of the nation which will not have any hostile nation. This is a solution that we can easily reach and it is logically sound and straightforward one.

Now, the idea of a world state or cosmopolitanism is from ancient times, Greek philosophy, late 4th century BC. The dictionary says that what is called world nation is the ideal of limiting national sovereignty and organizing the whole world into a single nation, also known as World Federation or World Nation. Cosmopolitanism is also explained as the thoughts that try to realize a world state with transcending nation and ethnicity and considering all humankind as one's brother.

In a world with many sovereign nations, we have no choice but taking internationalism, which places the emphasis on mutual cooperation among nations, for the sake of peace. However, since there is no hostile nation in the World Nation based on globalism, a permanent peace is automatically promised. In contrast, no matter how much we argue and how much effort we put into it, permanent peace will not come to the human world from internationalism. Because, in theory, so-called sovereign nation is destined to have the proposition named war due to the conflict of interest arisen on territory, economy and so forth among the nations, it is the existence that is irrelevant to peace in the first place.

Despite that we have understood for more than 2,000 years that we humans should head towards the World Nation, we have flowed into reality and made no progress from there and are still being practicing the foolishness that we are clinging continuously to sovereign nations, that create war and misfortune, so to speak. This situation has been brought by the fact that in spite of the remarkable progress of scientific civilization, spiritual civilization hasn't made much progress in over 2,000 years.

Because of the above, the concept of the World Nation can't be simply dismissed as "nonsense." We must reflect on our stupidity and laziness that we have not challenged to realize what even an elementary school kid knows for thousands of years.

Regarding the transition to the World Nation, even if we don't start acting right away for it, I think there is some value in writing this book, so long as a lot of people come to "realize" again that the World Nation is preferable to the sovereign nation in terms of delegating their sovereignty.

Also, even in a world with numerous sovereign nations for a while, the writer like to hope in such a way that "the realization" will work as a clue for us to recognize that the conflict of nations is foolish in the light of the hope of humanity and, as a result, to change the aspects of conflict in the human world to something much more gentle, kind and tender than it is now.

By aiming to realize the artificial environment where all human beings get along and the natural environment which is the joy of all living things, let's build the Utopia for us humanity on the earth, in this

Spaceship Earth.

In the Spring of 2023, the author

Appendix: Explanation of Thoughts and Terms in the Text

This appendix explains the items that are considered necessary about the writer's thoughts and terms mentioned in the text. They are detailed in the mother book of this book, "Independence from God," and/or "Thinking of God and Religion," but brief explanations are attached for the time being so that the reader may not have to refer to those books when reading this book.

1 Two Main Roots of Conflict besides Existence of Sovereign Nations

1. Religion

(1) Religion is a Fictitious System

In order to establish a system, there are two conditions that must be met, that is, ① there are no unverifiable components (existence and authenticity being unknown) in the system and ② there are no inconsistencies between the components of the system.

Looking at religion from this point of view, so-called religion is, in theory, a system that is not validly established. Namely, for the components of religion, since the existence and authenticity of many of them including God are unknown, the condition ① is not met. Also, since there is no logically consistent scripture in religious scriptures, the condition ② is not met either.

For this reason, it is clear that religion is fictitious.

(2) Religion as a Temporary System

Since the birth of humankind, when people sought order and peace of mind in the midst of the chaos of "the looter the winner" that began with small groups and small tribes in the early days (it's been a long time), numerous original religions were introduced one after another into the human world. Religion constructed by incorporating the concept of God or Buddha who is the absolute, even if it is fictional, brought some order to the human world through a compulsory code of conduct as well as some mental relief into the human heart of this world and the other world after life. In this sense, it can be recognized that religion has brought some contributions into the human world.

However, as the entity of religion is a delusion transformed from fiction, so-called religion that appeared at the dawn of the human world should be taken to be a short-lived system that had only a temporary effect, not the main road system that can lead the human world for a long time.

On the one hand, we humans in this world, who are the object of religion, have ego which is only temporary, change without stopping even for a moment, and are actual but like dreamy beings who can't even own oneself. If so, we can't merely say that the combination of religious delusion and human as a dreamy being is out of balance. If a thing is such as this, it is not strange to have the idea that it's not a matter of stating about rigid reasoning, and delusion is fine and it's fun to live happy in harmony with delusion. This kind of thinking may be acceptable.

Nonetheless, in order for it to be accepted, at least, the condition, that religious delusion can maintain the order and mental peace in the human world permanently and peacefully, must be met. However, if we enjoy without regret with religion, which inevitably has to claim its delusion as true, unreasonableness brought about by religion, conflict between religions or between religious sect and various other negative events, spring up in the human world. As a result, the order and mental peace intended to obtain through religion will disappear and the existence of religion itself will bring misfortune to the human world. This has already been proven enough by history.

Despite that religion is fictitious, if it is an existence that aspires and practices the peace and happiness in the human world, it is not impossible to take religion as "delusion is convenient, or circumstances justify a lie." But religion has changed to a monster that brings into the human world the unreasonable bondage which is not liberty, conflict which is not peace, misfortune which is not happiness, and moreover, the risk of the destruction of humanity. Here we have come, now it's the time for us humans to have to graduate from our relationship with God and religion.

(3) Truth of Religion

Like the creation of the universe and all things, even if we take what we don't know, because of it being beyond the limits of human knowledge as of now, as the work of God, who was defined by us humans as an omniscient, omnipotent and complete system, it does not mean that "what we don't know" has been clarified through God. What became known by doing so only means that if God has such an attribute, it is possible for him to create the universe and all things and to know its creation process and movement. Namely, it means that what God knows but we don't know has not changed from its original state at all before and after we came to have the concept of God. In other words, we came to think of the concept of God in order to clarify what we don't know, but God does not contribute for its clarification. Consequently, this discussion leads us to the recognition that we should withhold such an empty and meaningless thing that we talk about God and rely on God.

Under such circumstances, we are debating whether or not God exists. However, as of now, the existence of God is unknown. Nonetheless, God religion is built on the premise of the existence of God. Moreover, even if based on the divine hypothesis, the relationship between God and religion is fictitious as there is no word granted (revelation, prophecy, or teachings) by God (this proof is in later 2-05). For this reason, the composition that God and religion are closely related is fictitious even if God exists, not to mention, in case God does not exist. In other words, it means that God and religion are in an unrelated relationship. Therefore, it becomes the truth that religious scriptures and doctrines are not the word of God but human language invented by humans. Based on this perception, first of all, it becomes clear that any doctrine related to God, including "must believe in God" in the religious doctrines, is invalid and fallacious.

Moreover, since both religions with God and without God are built by unverifiable and false elements besides God, all religions are fictitious. Unverifiable elements include heaven, paradise, western paradise, hell, past world, future world, doomsday theory, immortality of the soul, transmigration and so forth. However, since these belong to full information domain, we humans, who are only the owners of partial information, don't know whether it's true or not. Also, there are various false elements theoretically which include "original sin" in Christianity (later 2-06).

As discussed above, since the elements which are taken to build any religion do not meet the condition that makes so-called system valid, it follows that all religions are many times fictitious.

By the way, after recognizing religion as a fiction, if you say it is also interesting and playful, it's not to blame for that. Since we humans have the ability to fantasize and imagine, both fantasies and imaginations created by us humans are not something that should be unconditionally denied from the perspective of unconditionally affirming the life form called human. Fantasies and imaginations are lovely things in themselves. However, when it comes to claim fiction as truth, fiction turns to be delusion. Delusion means in the dictionary explanation that one keeps holding on to false and unshakable beliefs despite the fact that there is clear evidence to the contrary of it, and in particular, delusion has a definition, "symptoms of mental disorders." Since religion is falsely claiming for fiction as truth, it follows that religion is a delusional system.

On the other hand, in response to such arguments, the writer know that there are counterarguments including that God or religion is something that should not be argued by reason but should believe in. However, the golden section of rectangular length to width ratio, which is considered a ratio that gives a stable and aesthetic feeling, is a geometric term, and beautiful musical harmony is also originally a mathematical term. Consequently, it is not necessarily correct that geometry and mathematics, which are the representatives of reason, are incompatible with sensibility and love. With regard to this point, there is also the idea that reason, sensibility and love are one and the same mental activity. Therefore, the counterargument that reason and faith are completely different is not valid. Even religion and faith cannot exist beyond reason. Theories and systems that contradict the correct logic will mislead humans and the human world.

Now, even if religion is fictitious, disregarding it, there is nothing wrong with following that doctrine so long as it is in harmony with us humans, even if it is preached under the name of religion. For any religious doctrine was created originally by humans. Therefore, it is a good thing to face it with an unbiased attitude. Nonetheless, so-called religious doctrine includes many doctrines which are contradictory to the Supreme Idea of the Human World. Those include useless precept/commandment (later 2-07), giving a negative image to "Bonno (worldly passions, desires, etc.)" which is, on the contrary, actually the precious treasures of human beings (later 2-08), and the God's highest good which does not exist (later 2-09).

As discussed above, regardless of God religion or Buddhism without God, it is clear that not only religion is fictitious and delusional but its doctrines are not in harmony with human nature. To make the matters much worse, religions, which exist in large numbers in the human world, threaten us humans who don't follow their delusions and do unreasonably diabolical deeds by judging based on the delusions and punishing humans, as if they don't fear God and despite their having no grounds for having jurisdiction on humans born innocent and free. And further, they claim for slightest difference in delusions between religions and between sects and fight to wash the blood with blood, which is the opposite of Holy, without reflection on it. Therefore, so-called religion does not make human and the human world happy but reversely makes it unhappy. Moreover, religion is causing one of the risk factors of the destruction of humanity.

(4) Independence from God and Religion

We humans are nothing more than a fleeting beam of light in the universe like fantasy, but are innocent and free life who wish and pursue happiness as long as we live. It was we who invented both God and religion, but the existence of God is unknown and religion is only a delusion. Therefore, sticking to God and religion is not right thing to do. For long-lasting glory, it makes sense that we must beat religion and free ourselves from the delusional system. In other words, it follows that we humans must leave from the fake happiness based on fiction and delusion, and must aim for true happiness as an intelligent life form.

As against religious belief, there is the insight by John Adams, Second President of the United States that if there were no religion, this world, in every conceivable world, would have been the best one. ("THE GOD DELUSION", by Richard Dawkins, translated into Japanese by Yuji Tarumi, published by Hayakawa Shobo, 2013)

However, even if religion is fictitious, if religion and religious people enjoy it as fiction without making it as delusion, embrace all individuals in the world with unconditionally infinite love and compassion, and can put this idea into practice, there is a value for religion to be existing in the human world, regardless of calling it religion or whatsoever you call it. Therefore, it is necessary for all religions and religious people to reexamine as to whether it is possible to follow this idea taking this point of view. To reiterate, it is to discuss whether your religion has the value to stay in the human world with practice of this supreme idea, that is, treating people only with love, no fighting with other religions and religious sects and keeping the world peaceful, or conversely, you are about graduating or leaving the religion, if it can't do such sort of things. This reexamination is the duty and testimony of a true religious person.

If we assume that the basis of human happiness is to have peace of mind on cosmology (cosmic view), life form called human, and real life in the human world, unfortunately, it cannot be said that the existing religious paradigm meets such requirements. This leads us to the perception that the new paradigm, which makes humans feel safe, is necessary, that is, for example, to have cosmology based on the Principle of Phenomenon, a positive affirmation of innate including the fate of life form called human, and real life in the human world that can be improved as desired depending on human efforts. Therefore, our human happiness should not rely on religion which brings evil effects to the human world. Once again, we humans have to recreate ourselves.

Aiming for the future glory of humanity, it is requested that our independence from God and religion exists as a universal and ultimate idea in the human world. We humans, without being stuck in the fiction and delusion but with dynamic, innocent and free spirit, must open up a future so that we may be able to progress and evolve aiming to become the most intelligent life form in the universe.

By the way, religion means not only existing religions but all religions including any new religion to be born in the future. This reason lies in that if based on the premise that any religion introduced in the future will arise as a hybrid of existing religions, no essential distinction arises between existing and new religions.

Liberation from God and Religion

Leaving the world taught by Jesus and Buddha,
and beyond that
not losing to the aliens that may exist,
having a high spiritual world,
aiming to be the king of intelligent life in the universe,

instead of closing the door, staying in a dark room, and living with a candle of delusion called religion, we humans must go outside and release ourselves into the glory in the refreshing atmosphere, bright sunlight and blue sky so that we may be able to have a dynamic and free spirit, without relying on God nor religion, and to be humans with innocent posture and pride.

2. Racial and Ethnic Discrimination

In the first place, there is no intellectual basis for people to discriminate against each other, not to mention racial and ethnic discrimination. For a person who is obsessed with such a discrimination, there is no other evaluation than mentally underdeveloped and ridiculous fool.

There are countless things to worry about and overcome in the human world today to have survival of us humanity by avoiding extinction and then to realize our hope of happiness in peace and freedom.

In the midst of this, we humanity must graduate from such a deplorable thing that people discriminate against each other and cause conflicts. Instead of this, we must create a world of people which is kind and tender to each other and pleasant. For this purpose, we need to train our minds in order for us all humanity to sublime into a relationship of respect and harmony.

(1) Racial Discrimination (Kant & Hume)

The philosopher Kant synchronized with the philosopher Hume's racial theory, "that African blacks, by nature, have no emotions beyond childhood and even in that mental ability, there are as essential differences between whites and blacks as skin color," and developed a white supremacy theory. As a result, Kant is considered one of the white supremacist ancestors. (The meaning quoted from Wikipedia, the free encyclopedia)

Now, in the era of Kant and Hume, there were almost no materials to refer to think about the superiority or inferiority of races, compared to the current environment where we can make full use of the advanced knowledge in the various fields. However, even today, there exists no universally valid checklist that can determine the superiority or inferiority between races.

Under the circumstances, especially taking into account that both of them were philosophers, neither Kant nor Hume can be allowed in the point that they showed carelessly such an assertive recognition to black people based on the fact that they never did a thorough study on their own, but used only hearsay, childish and few literatures quickly available at that time. Now that they were philosophers, in order to have a conclusion to a proposition such as this, they had to examine whether the knowledge and information for that purpose met the necessary and sufficient conditions. Nonetheless, both of them neglected to do so. The basis of this judgement is in that no evidence has been found to conclude the superiority or inferiority between races even today at all.

Therefore, as far as this point is concerned, it has to be said that it can't be helped even if criticized that both of them were disqualified as a philosopher who did not have any intelligence beyond childhood.

However, taking it into consideration that Kant was a great contributor to modern international liberalism and Hume was against slavery, despite the lack of the perception about human races, it seems certain that both of them were philanthropists.

(2) Skin Color

When I was a student in the United States, I heard it from a professor who was a social scientist that a white researcher wanted to obtain the conclusion that whites are superior to other skin-colored races in many ways, but, despite the repeated research, from any point of view, the researcher couldn't get any evidence of superiority or inferiority due to the difference in skin color.

Changing the story, it is a story of a popular SF movies titled "Star Trek" which was born in the United States and distributed worldwide.

When the party of Earth Alliance, which consists of Earthlings and Vulcans, visited and explored a planet outside the solar system in a spaceship named "Enterprise," the two great powers of the planet's inhabitants despised and hated each other and were fighting to kill the other.

The exploration party didn't know why they had to despise and hate each other, so asked the reason to the one of the residents of one power. According to the resident, "The face of the inhabitants of our planet, as you can see, is painted symmetrically in black and white with the left and right halves of the face on the nose. While the right side of our face is black, that of them (the other power) is white. Are your eyes knotholes?"

Can we humans laugh at this as a stupid story?

(In addition, the end of this story is that for the exploration party that recommended dialogue, both powers had the firm stance that understanding and reconciling with each other through dialogue is more difficult than changing the orbit of the planet because of the helpless hatred that has accumulated from the past. As a result, both powers went extinct, each leaving alone. Despite the party's welcoming the last two into the Enterprise and persuading them to live in harmony at least in it, the two landed on the planet again by the transmission device. That which was able to confirm from the Enterprise in space was the end result that the two fought a deadly battle on the planet and collapsed together.)

There seems to be a theory that we humankind originally originated in Africa as black species, we spread from the Middle East to Europe and became a Caucasian species, and after that, we entered the Middle East again and became a yellow race. The reason why black people became white people and yellow people is based on the theories that the albinos, who had white skin due to mutation among black people, were discriminated against and driven north, and that the black species that moved to the north where sunlight was weak turned to white due to the melanin pigment, and also that both of them may have been intertwined and contributed to the outbreak of Caucasians, Yellows and so forth.

Aside from that, in any way, it is difficult to find an intellectual basis for discrimination on the basis of skin color. Please think about it. In the first place, as for black, white, yellow, their neutral colors and any other colors are included, there should be no such a thing as which color is beautiful and which is not. As for black clothes, white clothes, yellow clothes, their neutral (mingled?)-colored clothes, and any other colored clothes, "which clothes is beautiful and which one is not" is not universal even within the same race.

It's neither the color of "siki soku ze ku" nor the color of "iro koi zata," but the color of coloration. All the colors of coloration should be affirmed and there is no other way of looking at it.

To have a sense of discrimination by sticking to skin color without intelligence is nothing but the best landscapes that reveal the underdevelopment and stupidity of one's spirit to the world.

"Siki soku ze ku" is the Buddhist philosophy of the universe. It is translated in English in various ways. For example, ① all things and phenomena that exist in the world are not at all entities, that is, Mu(nothing) sky, ② all visible things are vain, and ③ form is the emptiness and emptiness is the form. "Siki" of this philosophy has the meaning of color (iro) in Japanese. "Iro koi zata" means love affair. In Japanese, love is sometimes called color (iro). (Further detail is in my book, "Thinking of God and Religion", though its English version is not available as of now)

---

(3) Racial/Ethnic Discrimination

It seems that we human beings are vulnerable to give objective evaluation of ourselves.

We humans tend to look down on other peoples below one's own people and despise them based on the way of looking that they speak weird words, use weird letters, eat weird foods, wear weird clothes and have various strange cultures. In this case, there is no objective evaluation of what it looks like when one's own people is seen by other peoples. Once you think about this point of view, you should come to realize that the same thing that your own people evaluated other peoples has been given to your own people by other peoples. Both sides are like each other.

Since there is no absolute good or bad, height or low in culture and civilization, it is not possible to judge which civilization or culture is superior or inferior. Nonetheless, seeing the culture and civilization of one's own people as superior to that of others is nothing but prejudice and disdain other peoples, which is a stupid thing to laugh at. What is called humans seem to have a delusion of the superiority of a slight difference over others in self and self-related matters, and seem to have a strange tendency to blend in with that delusion and be happy. In Freud's (Austrian psychiatrist) style, that can be said a slight difference in narcissism (self-love or self-euphoria), isn't it?

It is good that we are proud of being a certain race or ethnicity. However, if so, it is natural that we must respect the pride of other races and ethnic groups. There is no conflict arisen from respecting each other. All that happens is respect and harmony.

It is neither our own power nor the result of our choice that we human beings are born into the race/ethnicity to which we belong. In other words, we were not involved in why we were born into that race/ethnicity. We don't know who we are in this universe, where we came from and where we go, that is, we are ignorant beings who know nothing even about ourselves. We just happened to be here, when we realized it. Therefore, it is clear that none of the human individuals is in the position to be unlimitedly proud of or conversely demeans the race/ethnicity to which we belong. Nonetheless, when taking a look at the reality that such people disrespect and persecute each other and even killing each other is happening after all, there is no greater sadness than that we human beings look like a stupid life form.

All of we humans have to introspect ourselves asking what we are and whether we are so great or so inferior to others. There seems to be no difference in the intelligence we are born with between races and between ethnic groups, and on top of that, it is generally accepted recognition today that there is no absolute superiority or inferiority in culture and civilization. Even under such circumstances, let's assume that there were some differences in intelligence, culture and civilization between races and between ethnic groups. What are the differences? From the height of omniscience and omnipotence, as they are on the same plane that extends far below and just above the ground, it must be that you can't recognize the differences that are particularly problematic.

Hitler was such an ignorant person who could only be considered to have lacked in awareness of his own ignorance and hence also lacked in the awareness of his own stupidity, both of which were because of having had no introspection of himself. As a result, he practiced the personification of evil. By such a single fool, such a tragic situation has occurred that millions of Jews and Russians were slaughtered and killed totally unreasonably. Being stupid is a serious matter that brings the greatest calamity to humans and the human world.

We humanity must graduate from stupid prejudice.

At this time when we are on the verge of extinction due to various factors other than race and ethnicity, this kind of "stupid luxury" that humans compete each other is unacceptable.

(4) Race/Ethnicity → Sublimation from Conflict to the Subject of Respect and Harmony

At present, race/ethnicity is one of the main roots in creating conflict in the human world. However, even though it is a cause of conflict, it does not mean that it came to exist in this world with the reason for conflict. All races and ethnic groups were born as innocent and free beings. Nonetheless, it is none other than we ourselves who make race and ethnicity the subject of conflict. This is the current stupidity of humanity which is regretful. Therefore, it is neither race nor ethnicity but human stupidity that should be eliminated from the human world. If this stupidity disappears from our human world, racial/ethnic groups will be able to sublime into the relationship to respect and reconcile with each other without conflict.

It is true that there are many resentments and hatreds resulting from the conflicts in the past between races and between ethnic groups. However, it is important to unconditionally forgive the past each other. Of course, we cannot change the past by forgiving each other, but we can change the future definitely with it. If we can't forgive each other, resentments, hatreds and conflicts will continue uninterrupted until the time of the extinction of humankind. This is even to bring the inducement for it. There must be various unforgivable past. However, we must forgive each other unconditionally now even if they are unforgivable past, for we must not increase the production of the unforgivable past to be remained in the future from now on, dragging the unforgivable past into the future. We must refuse the stupidity that the future will be ruled by the past. We should forgive the past each other and aim for interracial and interethnic respect and harmony to have human glory in the future.

By the way, the idea of forgiveness is not limited to race and ethnicity but just as important for inter-religions and inter-nations.

Is it, however, just an easy to mention but impractical theory that we will forgive each other and not fight by using force? Not so. There are at least two examples of how it could be done in relatively recent human history.

Former President Mandela claimed the sovereignty over blacks and was trapped in prison for 28 years himself under the Union of South Africa. However, when he was elected president and the country name was changed to Republic of South Africa, he chose the path to inter-racial reconciliation and implemented such policies that thoroughly forgive the past of all inhuman racial discrimination, grudges and hatreds, including past crackdowns and imprisonment and slaughter. Also, Mahatma Gandhi, the father of India's independence, did not fight by force at all but won the ending of the rule of the British Empire with disobedient resistance in a thorough nonviolence.

Nothing can reach the final solution by force. It can only be gained after mutual and true consent through dialogue because that's the human nature.

It is necessary to teach history in the field of education. However, it is not enough to just record and teach the evil deeds without decoration that race/ethnicity, religion or nation has done or has been done. By teaching the evil deeds and, on the one hand, by making it as a teacher, you must teach the reason and tolerance to forgive the past aiming for the happiness and long-term survival of humankind in the future.

2 Various Thoughts and Terms

01 Supreme Idea of the Human World

We can't answer the fundamental question that concerns ourselves, that is, "Wherefrom did we come, whereto do we go, wherefore are we here, and who are we?" In other words, we are ignorant and petty existence.

However, the doctrine that we humans should adopt is neither God-first principle nor a religion-first principle, but human first-principle. This does not mean its likes or dislikes comparing the three principles. Nor do I favor human-first principle. It is because this is only one that is theoretically correct. Even if we assume that God created humankind based on God hypothesis, this view will not change. This is as described below in "(1)-09 The supreme being is human himself."

Whoever and whatever we are, we can't deny ourselves. Happily, we should unconditionally 100% affirm ourselves. Therefore, the origin of all thinking lies in this point. Namely, it means that the starting point is nothing but human beings itself, not something else other than it.

(1) Nature of Human Life

We should unconditionally accept ourselves and its nature. This is because we can't deny ourselves.

The nature of us humans includes those, as shown below:

01 A carbon-based life form and microcosm made by stardust matter
02 Birth, old age, disease and dying life form
03 To preserve life and health, eat and ingest animals, plants, and minerals
04 To preserve life and species, perform reproduction acts
05 Having a selfish instinct
06 Having a body with five senses, and having desires and anxieties

related to it

07 Innocent and life as a free existence from anyone
08 Wishing for peace and freedom
09 The supreme being is human himself
10 Human nature is good
11 Prefer the preservation of species rather than extinction
12 Live a social life
13 Rejoice in intellectual and spiritual activity (inquire into the unknown, truth, etc.)
14 Enjoy art
15 Enjoy sensibility recognition on goodness and beauty in harmony with human life
16 Happy to play
17 Have emotions and sorrows
18 Others

(It would be noted that the 05~10 above are detailed in my book, "Thinking of God and Religion", though its English version is not available as of now)

(2) Supreme Idea of the Human World

Based on the preceding paragraph, assuming the items like those described below are universal in the human world, the writer assume them to be "Supreme Idea of the Human World."

Idea 01 Fully affirm the contents of the preceding paragraph, (1) Nature of Human Life

Idea 02 Construct the human world in harmony with human nature, not contradictory to it

Idea 03 We humanity want peace rather than war

Idea 04 We humanity hope to survive rather than perish and to construct the Utopia for us rather than hell on the earth, that is, in this Spaceship Earth

Idea 05 Construct the human world where it becomes possible that no single person is killed, basic human rights are respected, and all individuals live in freedom and soundness of mind and body throughout life

Idea 06   Construct the human world where it becomes possible that all individuals are blessed with healthy clothing, shelter and food, and enjoy their health and happiness together with living every day relaxedly, refreshingly and heartily

Idea 07   Others that are anything in harmony with 01~06 above.

(Note)   As for happiness, it is not clear what makes each person happy. So, happiness here means the happiness that each individual exists in the environment (a utopia) in which each one can pursue own happiness with freedom and in discipline.

(Note)

The origin of all judgements in our human world is not in God nor in religion but in human being itself. In other words, it should be the basis that all judgements, which are in harmony with human life form, are accepted, while all judgements, which are contradictory to the life form, are excluded. This means that not only good and evil, morality, ethics, goodness and beauty but also all other things related to us humans should be judged based on whether it is in harmony with or contradictory to the Supreme Idea of the Human World. It is noted that this Idea is assumed to be applicable to humans no matter what life forms humans will evolve into. (Further detail is in my book, "Thinking of God and Religion", though its English version is not available as of now)

02 Aliens

(1) Invasion by Aliens

We sometimes think of such a thing that although we humans have been fighting by dividing the human world on the earth with difference in nation, religion and race/ethnicity, yet we humans have a truce for the time being in order to fight a different fight cooperatively against aliens in case they may exist outside the solar system and come to invade earth (us humans).

I will think about this.

Aliens are life forms and so the attack by aliens may have to be classified artificial disaster, not natural disaster. But, here, artificial disaster is limited to the one brought by us humans, and the attack by the aliens is treated to be classified into natural disaster as it comes from the nature, the universe.

Now, is it likely that aliens come to attack us humans?

I think it unlikely even if aliens exist. The aliens' science is imagined extraordinary developed, compared to that of humans, taking it into consideration that they can reach earth by travelling the extraordinary distance in outer space naturally after they solved the space-time problem. Therefore, if aliens have the intention to invade us, we humans will instantly be wiped out regardless of whether we humans unite or not. In case the scientific power is too much different, there will be no space war between aliens and us humans. We can't win.

However, I imagine that aliens won't have such an intention to attack us humans. This is proven whereby aliens have been existing without self-destruction. In other words, since the aliens didn't make science disaster and have been controlling it appropriately and also their spiritual world is imagined extraordinarily developed, it could not be imagined that the aliens attack and harm us humans, who don't positively make negative intervention against aliens off earth. So, it would be thought that if we have a chance to come across aliens, it won't be an unhappy encounter. This could be easily understood if we think of exchanging aliens and humans. That is, if we humans visit other star, our visitation won't mean to kill or harm the dwellers that have the science inferior to humans'.

Let's assume that this view should not be right and we humans were attacked by aliens. There is no necessity or meanings to worry about, now that we have no means to fight against aliens at all. Because its attack, if made, must be rigorous as if the end of the universe or the destruction of the solar system befell, it is useless in worrying about the matter such as this.

We humans will be extinct.

In case I come to across aliens whose spiritual world should have been extraordinarily developed, I have many things to ask them. One of them is the concept of God and religion that we humans have. By all means, I like to know their view of it.

---

(2) Aliens

Speaking of whether aliens exist or not, it is more natural to think them to be existent rather than not to think them to be existent. Because there are countless stars in the universe, it is not natural to think that the star which can be a cradle of life is only one, earth. Relating to this, there is a view that if it is possible for one to exist in reality without being prohibited, it is rather forced to exist more than one or many.

If aliens exist, it is imagined that they are something within the wide range of it which looks like us humans and that which doesn't look like life form to our eyes. Also, we humans are a carbon-based life form, but aliens may be different type of life forms, for example, silicon-based.

Some people say that one of the characteristics of aliens is in its big head resulting from developed brain, but it is a single-hearted view as it can't be necessarily said so. For example, if the brain of the life forms on the earth is made up by vacuum tube while that of aliens is made up by transistor or integrated circuit with higher efficiencies compared to that of us humans, big size and weight of brain are not necessarily needed. Aside from brain, it seems that there is also an imagination that the aliens' internal organs may have been underdeveloped or degenerated. However, it is not necessarily so, as aliens may have strong physical body due to gravity and/or other conditions of the planet where aliens have been brought up.

Now, there is a view that aliens have been visiting earth since ancient time until today in the way that we humans have not been able to perceive it definitely and clearly. Assuming it is so, then, first, the science of aliens extraordinarily surpasses that of humans. This is because aliens have overcome the difficulties related to the distance between their native planet and earth. Even if their native planet is in the galactic system, the one-way distance to earth amounts to hundreds, thousands or 10s of thousands of light years. Moreover, if they come from outside the galactic system, one way distance to earth amounts to millions, 10s of millions, 100s of millions, or even 10s of billions of light years. Namely, even if aliens travel by the spaceship with the speed of light, it takes a vast time to reach earth. Incidentally, we humans appeared as Homo sapiens on the earth was only 10s of thousand years before. Therefore, if aliens have been visiting earth by overcoming the difficulties of the space-time problem, it goes without saying that the development of aliens' science extraordinarily surpasses that of humans.

We humans talk about aliens now and then mentioning to UFO (Unidentified Flying Object), so-called flying saucer, or various other matters that could look like aliens' footprints. That's interesting in its own way, but it is undeniable that it brings a confirmation bias. That is, because it is too great to desire the existence of aliens, we tend to seek out with its tinted glasses whatever seems to support it.

In the first place, it may be only we humans who think as of now that the space-time problem is extremely difficult or even impossible to solve, however, for aliens, to solve it may have been nothing difficult but very easy matter. If so, based on the premise that the space-time problem has been solved by aliens, it is not so bad for us humans to talk about aliens' visitation to earth, flying saucer, various matters that look like aliens' footprints and so forth. But even in this case, it goes without saying that we humans also need to solve the space-time problem by ourselves rather than leaving it to aliens. At the same time we talk about UFO and the like, if we think of the solution for this problem together, it is no doubt that aliens become more interesting topic than now and it may result in an unexpected contribution for us to obtain the solution to the space-time problem.

03 Cosmology (Cosmic View)

When we humans marvel at the infinity and wonder of the universe, are moved by the nature of the earth, and encounter the sophistication and charm of plants and animals, including us, we have the question as to how these came from and how they work.

If we call the answer to this question "cosmology," there are now two well-known cosmologies. One is the cosmology of God and the other is a cosmic view discovered by Buddha without the concept of God, however, neither of the two cosmologies is enough to satisfy our intellectual needs.

We humans defined God as "omniscient, omnipotent and complete system that created the universe and all things," but the existence of God is not known as of today. On the other hand, the cosmology without God found by Buddha starts from "there is such a universe" and it becomes like "the universe is like this and it works like such and such." This discovery is wonderful, but the scope of it covers only the partial information frame of, for example, birth, old age, disease and death, without mentioning the ultimate past as the way we came from and eternal future as the way we go to. Namely, since it is based on the premise that the realm of complete information is beyond thought, it is undeniable that there is a regret that it lacks completeness. In short, Buddha's discovery is only concerned with the intermediate range from nothingness to infinity. Under such a circumstance, however, the former was adopted in God religion and in some philosophy, and the latter was adopted in Buddhism.

By the way, the writer think there is another cosmology. It is a cosmology based on "Principle of Phenomenon." This is a broader concept than causality, of which detail is as described in the next paragraph.

04 Cosmology by Principle of Phenomenon

(1) Principle of Phenomenon

All phenomena are happening to happen, because they can't happen unless they are happening to happen. Therefore, it is self-evident that any phenomenon has a solution in which it happens. The writer call this "Principle of Phenomenon." This Principle is a broader concept than causality and can be expressed, as shown below:

$$\text{Principle of Phenomenon} = \text{Causality} + X + Y + Z$$

The X includes "En" (indirect conditions) in Buddhism and what is commonly called mechanism, the Y is that which we don't know the cause as of now, and the Z is a cause without cause. Consequently, the Principle of Phenomenon expresses "all phenomena are happening to happen" in an easy-to-understand manner without omission.

Expressed in this way, mystery is not mystery, paranormal phenomenon is not paranormal, and there is no magic, and it becomes very clear that these are all normal phenomena based on the Principle of Phenomenon. Since any phenomenon is happening to happen, otherwise it can't happen, it is self-evident that any phenomenon has a solution that it should happen.

The Y's "we don't know the cause as of now" means that the phenomenon exists, so we can think that the cause will be clarified soon or later. Example of this includes ① a model of two electrons spinning in opposite directions with the same magnitude, and ② what is called "emergence," that is, the characteristics which cannot be predicted or explained are created from the conditions that precede the process of biological evolution and the process of system development. (The detail of ① and ② is in my book, "Independence from God"/"Thinking of God and Religion", though its English version is not available as of now)

The best example of Z's "the cause without cause" would be that the cause of existence of God is God himself. Everything has its cause and if you go back in search of the cause, the cause will infinitely regress and not end. Under such a circumstance, it claims that the first cause that does not go back any further is God, so the existence of God is self-causing.

However, even if we acknowledge the divine hypothesis and that God has the power to cause himself, the existence of God is not a self-cause. This is because God must have already existed when he intended his existence of self-cause, as the cause is defined using time. That is, even if God can cause anything other than himself, there is no opportunity to exert self-causing power for God himself. Therefore, it makes no sense for God to have "self-causing power," and thus, it follows that "the existence of God is self-causing" is nothing but a fallacy.

Even God cannot apply "God is the cause of everything" to God himself. It looks that this has something to do with the Incompleteness Theorem (later in 05).

Thus, only what is known so far is that it does not hold that the existence of God is self-causing, so we cannot end the discussion of this topic at this point.

As for where the discussion goes for the cause of the existence of God, it can be considered separately as ① the existence of God has a cause but it has not been discovered by humans and ② there is no cause. We can think that the cause of the former will be discovered some day, since the existence of God has a cause which is temporary agnostic, not eternal agnostic. As against this, even though the language of the latter is clear as "no cause," its true meaning and content is unknown. However, it could be considered that the latter also has a cause and is temporary agnostic as well as the former.

By the way, now that we have come this far, we can think that Principle of Phenomenon is Causality in a broad sense.

Now, the Principle of Phenomenon is based on the premise that a phenomenon exists, but God has not been perceived or recognized as a phenomenon and its existence is unknown. If the phenomenon does not exist, there is no point in thinking about its cause (and so there is no such thing). However, although God has not appeared in front of humans until now, we can't say that he won't appear in the future either. Consequently, we can't simply eliminate the need for discussion, at this point in time, on the premise that the phenomenon exists.

By the way, if the existence of God is denied, it follows that the universe is not created by God and its cause is unknown. However, unlike God, now that the existence of the phenomenon of the universe is recognized, the cause is what we just don't know as of now, and we can expect that the solution to that phenomenon will be clarified sometime in the future.

In any case, Principle of Phenomenon is a broader concept than the causality of the cause and effect, and expresses that every phenomenon that is happening has a solution that causes it.

(2) Note

Because human intelligence is low (compared to the highest) and our experience and knowledge are limited, there are only few things we know, and there are an infinite number of unsolved and unknown things. Under such a situation, it goes without saying that it is important for us to make efforts to change unknown and unsolved things into the known. However, equally to or more importantly than that, we should receive the unsolved and unknown purely as what we don't know at this point. There is no other way but accept it.

The universe, the nature of the earth, miracles, mysteries, the supernatural phenomena, humans and all phenomena inclusive of such as animals and plants are happening to happen. Otherwise, nothing happens. So, in this sense, all phenomena are normal phenomena in the light of the Principle of Phenomenon. It's no wonder but natural that there are countless phenomena that can't be explained or understood by scientific law and other knowledge. However, any phenomenon itself has a solution to occur, so we can rather rest assured. It is useless for us to fear, worship, or conversely, despise what we don't understand as of now. Also, we must refrain from forcibly explaining them with fantasies and delusions and telling an irreverent and stupid theory of arrogance. In particular, regarding mystery, we should ask for its elucidation, and we must admit that not stepping into it and beyond is the abandoning scientific spirit. For what we don't understand as of now, we should be humble, natural, quiet, and having a sincere and academic attitude.

As for the existence or non-existence of God, the writer think it's okay for us to expect it as unknowable only for the time being, not unknowable forever, that is, it can be verified in principle and can be known someday.

> However, as a constraint from the fact that we humans are life forms that are composed of carbon-based fragments of stars, perhaps human intelligence has its limits and there may be unknowns and unsolved things that human beings will never know. (This is my translation of the meaning of the word by Stephen W. Hawking in "Uchu ni okeru Seimei" in Japanese, "Life in the Universe" in English, commentary/translation into Japanese by Katsuhiko Sato, published by NTT in Japan in 1993)

Even so, with regard to what we don't know today, we should keep the attitude that we might know tomorrow and we want to be happy to continue to study and think of it with courage. The only way for humanity to pursue the solutions to the unknown and unsolved until the end of humanity is only the way to go. As long as we humanity do not give up "thinking," we can't take any other way.

(3) Principle of Phenomenon Superior to Concept of God and Buddha's Cosmology

Since all things, including human beings, occur as phenomena, there must be solutions how they are occurring based on the Principle of Phenomenon. Therefore, to seek the truth of the universe, it follows naturally that we will seek the solution of the phenomenon. In this case, we cannot assume that the solution is God, because God can't even be a hypothesis of the solution, as God is only a pronoun of what we don't know. Although our current level of knowledge is insufficient for us to discuss to reach its solution, yet where the phenomenon exists, we can think of the solution to be temporary unknowable, not eternally unknowable. On the one hand, the existence or non-existence of God could also be considered as temporary unknowable, but there is no evidence of that as of now. Therefore, it is to be our expectation. When the solution as to how all things are occurring is known or when we get reasonably close to the solution, it may be possible for us to discuss or know what God is at that time, if we compare the solution with God.

However, it is not known when that will be.

05 Proof of Non-Existence of God's Word

The existence of God is not known as of today. On the one hand, under such a circumstance, even if we were based on the God hypothesis, there is no word granted by God (the Word in God religion). Therefore, any divine religious scripture is not a record of God's word but the word of human's creation, which is written in the name of God. The word of God is revelation, prophecy and teachings.

The proof of non-existence of the word of God is divided into two types due to difference in the attribute of God.

One of them (1) is based on the position of the attribute of God being "omniscient, omnipotent and complete system (A)," while the latter one (2) is based on the position of the attribute of God being close to A.

By the way, "omniscient and omnipotent" is a concept in contradiction, and the invalidity of "complete system" has been proven by Incompleteness Theorem. Therefore, strictly speaking, the upper limit that can be established for "omniscient and omnipotent" is a concept which is close to it, and "complete system" is also a concept which is close to it. (Further detail is in my book, "Thinking of God and Religion", though its English version is not available as of now)

I described, for the proof under (1), main proof (X) and one supplementary proof, and for the proof under (2), main proof (Y). For (2), there are many other supplementary proofs considered, but I omitted to describe them here. Also, in addition to the proofs for (1) and (2), I described one example for the proof under the attribute of God being common to (1) and (2).

(1) For the Attribute of God being "Omniscient, Omnipotent and Complete System"

Main Proof X

If God created the world, everything in the world inclusive of humankind must go according to the will of God. If so, after creating at will, that God teaches humankind must be unnecessary at all. Namely, the word of God does not exist because it is unnecessary.

This is called "Non-Existence Principle of the Word of God" in this book.

As stated above, the proof of non-existence of the word of God is simple and straightforward, and the above is necessary and sufficient. Therefore, any further proof would be redundant. But only this may look very unsocial, so I described one of the supplementary proofs below.

Supplementary Proof

If we define God as "omniscient, omnipotent and complete system that created the universe and all things," "How do we imagine God at this time?"

① God, who continues to create even universes other than the one in which we live (if they exist) from the eternal past to the eternal future (cosmic God A)
② God, who created and has been governing the universe in

which we exist (cosmic God B)
③ God, who created and has been ruling the galactic system, the solar system, and earth (Galactic God)
④ God in ③, who is concerned in all humankind (God of all humankind)
⑤ God in ④, who is concerned in some people (monotheistic religious God)

As above, since lower ranking God is subsumed and reduced to an upper ranking God, the only absolute God should be ①, or at least ②. In other words, the lower ranking Gods should be the children of God ①.

Therefore, there is no contradiction arisen among God ①~⑤.

Considering which God is the God related to monotheism in the human world, it will be God ⑤.

Now, God religion is said to be established with the word of God, but despite the word of the same God, it is different from religion to religion. Also, there are many instances that a religion is divided into religious sects due to different interpretation of the word. Because of this, there are various conflicts arisen between religions and between religious sects. Here, taking a look at God ④, an upper ranking of God ⑤, if we assume that God ④ has the intention for peace and happiness of all humankind, the conflicts among humans resulting from the different words of God ⑤ are contradictory to the intention of God ④. However, there must be no contradiction between God ④ and God ⑤.

Therefore, the word of God, which religions claim for, is not the word of God but the word of someone else or human word. Thus, it has been proven and concluded that the word of God does not exist.

(2) For the Attribute of God being "Close to Omniscient, Omnipotent and Complete System"

Main Proof Y

We humans first defined the attribute of God as "omniscient, omnipotent and complete system," but it turned out later that the definition does not hold, as discussed before. As a result, even if we assume the existence of God, the attribute of God now became a bit of a retreat to its maximum that is "close to omniscient and omnipotent, and complete system." It is thought that this will be involved in the proof of non-existence of the word of God.

In short, God who is lacking in perfection might make an inadvertent mistake. If so, as Nietzsche says, we humans might be God's failure. In this case, God came to have the necessity to newly give his teachings to humans, who act against his will, to modify it to his will.

For this purpose, it is thought that the need for God's word should arise. However, the proof of non-existence of God's word is the one to prove it contradictory for the word to exist, regardless of whether there is the God's necessity or not. That is, the proof is the one that God's word was not and has not been given to any religion from the beginning to date at all.

Religion here means many of self-proclaimed God religions that claim, as its feature, the existence of the only absolute God who created the universe and all things, to have religious scriptures with God's word, and to have belief in God and love with its religious doctrine.

Now that this God is said to be the only absolute God, the teachings preached by all of the God religions are the teachings of the same God. Consequently, it is required that all the teachings must perfectly correspond with one another, without even a slight discrepancy among them at all.

Nonetheless, the fact is not like this, that is, religious teachings are contradictory among them, that is, different from religion to religion. The conclusion drawn from this perception should be either one of the two below:

Conclusion (a)   The teachings of many religions are not the true teachings of the only absolute God but all fake, or

Conclusion (b)   One of the teachings of many religions is the real teachings of the only absolute God

Examination of the above conclusions—If God had the intention to give his teachings to humans, it must have been given equally and totally to all humans, otherwise his intention won't be attained. If God gave it to humans, the resultant must be in such a situation that there exists only one religion on the earth that preaches the teachings of God, and there exists no other religions that preach any other teachings.

Now, as in the conclusion (b), the situation that only one is real and all others are fake is a situation that the real teachings are not spread equally and universally among all humankind, and this contradicts God's will. However, even if it is said that God is a bit of a step back from perfection, he is still a being who can do whatever he intends to so long as he has the intention to do it. Nonetheless, the fact is that there are many religions with different teachings. From this, it is concluded that God has no intention of granting his teachings to humankind, and any teachings of any religion is not that given by God.

Based on the above discussion, conclusion (b) is denied and conclusion (a) turns out to be correct. The final conclusion thus reached is that all teachings of all religions are not the real teachings given by the only absolute God, that is, nothing but fake. This conclusion leads us to the proof that the relationship between God and religion, that religion claims, is fictitious.

Incidentally, under the monotheism, polytheism is subsumed in or reduced into the monotheism.

(3) Proof under the Attribute of God being Common to (1) and (2) Above

We humans don't know at this point in time "Wherefrom we came, whereto we go, wherefore are we here, and who are we?"

As for this question, it is inferred that we cannot know this answer to God. It is because God has not disclosed this answer to us humans until now, even if based on the divine hypothesis. If God has disclosed, we must have already known the answer. From the fact that God has not disclosed it to date, the inference that it will not be disclosed also in the future should be established. Although it is not known if God is timing the disclosure, God has been keeping silent.

The word of God to the human world does not currently exist.

06 Original Sin in the Bible

(1) Story of Adam and Eve

When I was a kid and first heard "the original sin," what came to my mind was that we were born with a sinful original sin because we humans cut off the life of animals and plants and eat them, even if we are an existence that cannot sustain its life without getting the nutrients. However, the original sin does not mean that but means the sin of eating the fruit of the tree of knowledge of good and evil (Is it meaningful?), breaking their promise to God.

But this story is strange. The strangeness is as follows.

If we put this story into the composition of the human world, it will be that parents disowned their children who disobeyed them and made a mistake. However, although this composition can be understood as a matter of the human world, it cannot be established between God and Adam and Eve. The writer will verify this below.

When God created Adam and Eve, God was able to take three options, as shown below:

① God could create Adam and Eve not to betray him
② God could create Adam and Eve to betray him
③ God could create Adam and Eve so as for them to decide whether or not they betray him

Now that Adam and Eve betrayed, it is clear that God had not taken Option ①. Next, even if God took Option ③, God, who could see the future, already knew that Adam and Eve betray him when he created them. Therefore, in this case there is no difference for God to take Option ② regarding what the result would be. In short, God created Adam and Eve so as for them to betray him.

Making it that way, God burdened Adam and Eve, who betrayed him, with the original sin. This is the first strangeness.

Next, as a confident criminal, God let humans, descendants of Adam and Eve, inherit the original sin, and then God forgave the liberation of humans from the original sin for the Jesus' death on the cross. This is the second strangeness.

Moreover, in Christianity, there is a Christian dogma called Trinity that means the unity of Father (God), Jesus (Son) and Holy Spirit as three persons in one Godhead. To put it in plainly, this means that Jesus is God Himself. Then, this brings such a composition that Jesus, God, on the cross played and showed himself and humankind his death, not death, so asked himself for releasing humankind from the original sin that he himself, God, intentionally had made humankind carry on the back, and then he himself, God, gave himself forgiveness to that wish.

What is this?

Did God reflect on his conduct that he intentionally let humans burden the original sin? This is the third strangeness. And, this thought occupied the origin of religion and based on that origin, the religious teachings were constructed. In Christianity, it is taught that everyone of humankind will be released from the original sin through believing in this story. Christianity calls the agreement made between God and Jewish people, through Moses, the Old Testament, and the new agreement made between God and humankind, through Jesus who died on the cross for the sin of humankind, the New Testament.

(2) Original Sin as God's Mistake

If God created the world, everything in the world inclusive of humankind must go according to the will of God. If so, that which Adam and Eve committed an act constituting the original sin should be as per God's will. In this case, there should be no need for God to cancel the original composition. Nonetheless, God later released the original sin of humankind, the descendants of Adam and Eve, through that Jesus was crucified and wished God's forgiveness. Now, then, why did God cancel it?

It follows that it was not God's will in the first place that burdened Adam and Eve (and their descendants) the original sin. In other words, it was God's mistake that he made humankind bear the burden with the original sin, therefore, the plot of the story of Adam and Eve could be that he corrected his own mistake.

As for why God, who is omniscient, omnipotent and complete system (let's say perfect system, God A), made such a mistake, if we consider God as close to perfect system, God B, not God A, we can explain it. For God B is not perfect, it cannot be denied that he made an inadvertent mistake. Although the story of Adam and Eve is strange, its strangeness disappears if we consider the creator was not God A but God B.

Incidentally, even if we assume that God created as he intended without mistake at all but he changed his mind later and cancelled the original sin, the creator will still be not God A but B, as he is lacking in perfection of consistency in this case. In this way, the creator of Adam and Eve was not God A but Go B, and we can consider in such a way that this God had no intention to let humankind bear the original sin in the first place.

(3) Plot of Fictional Story

There is a word, "truth is stranger than fiction." It seems to say something special but it is natural, so it is not surprising. This is because, whereas novel (fiction) requires the plot of the story that can convince the reader, facts don't have to be logical.

The Bible is also fictitious, therefore, it is necessary to make the story of Adam and Eve logical as a part of the Biblical story. For this reason, the story becomes essential for the construction of Christianity, but it is not accepted by other religions. For example, in Islam, which self-proclaims to be a religion that has evolved further from Christianity, the original sin of Adam and Eve, who were expelled from paradise, is said to have been forgiven later by God. If so, not only we now but also the descendants before Jesus was crucified had not inherited the original sin of Adam and Eve. In this sense, it was not necessary that Jesus was crucified. Despite the fact that both Christianity and Islam are the religions that have the same Old Testament (Judaism) as its important scripture, it follows that constructed were two hybrid religions with different religious components.

Changing the story, there is a relatively new religion in Japan called "Tenrikyo" which is a monotheism whose God is the only absolute God they call "Oyagami," literally means Parent God, commonly, Ancestral God. This religion has a kagura-style story, as shown below.

...... (kamiga) konoyono jitotentowo katadorite, fufuwo koshirae kitarudena, korega konoyono hajimedasi, ...

The above in Japanese means that God created earth, heaven and human couple, this is the beginning of the world.

Although both are fictitious, compared to the story of Adam and Eve, this one is simpler, brighter, and more friendly.

(4) Humanity is a Free and Innocent Being

To be an intelligent life form, we must refrain from adopting and claiming one of the things whose existence or truth is unknown. However, as against the Christian claim that we humanity were born bearing the original sin of Adam and Eve but were forgiven by Jesus being crucified, and God and humanity made a new covenant, I have an argument to defy that claim, breaking my wish to be an intelligent life form just once and as a foolish life form. It is that we are innocent and free beings from God and religion. In other words, the essence of my claim is in that we don't have to be bound by the spell of the New Testament with God, which is a false composition based on fiction based on the human word, that is, the original sin of the ancestors Adam and Eve which has nothing to do with God at all. Therefore, we should live proudly facing the blue sky without being sinners.

Now, it should be noted on this discussion that neither "the original sin" nor "innocent and free beings" has its firm ground on which the claim is based. However, if so, we can think that which we are innocent and free is not something given by someone else but the kind of thing that happens on us when we think that way.

However, it goes without saying that even though we are not sinners, we should always be modest and humble in all things and must not be arrogant.

07 Useless Religious Precept/Commandment

(1) Important Point of Religious Precept

Within religion, many precepts that are not in harmony with the human nature are preached. Therefore, we should not stick to the precept as what should be or immutable thing, and it is necessary to review it once and from time to time. The scriptures of God religion are not made up with the word of God, and Buddhist teachings are also all human thoughts and human word.

Therefore, there is nothing that prevents us from examining the precept many times. When any religion was established, it is considered in general that the things related to the culture and civilization at that time and place were reflected in the religious precept. However, it seems that there are many precepts that include various inconvenient and irrational things from the today's point of view. Now, with regard to the religious precept, therefore, what we humans should follow should be determined by us humans in the light of whether or not it is in harmony with the Supreme Idea of the Human World derived from the nature of us humans. It follows that it is not something that should be bestowed by God nor religion at all.

Whether it's religious precept or whatsoever, in general, this approach relating to the Supreme Idea of the Human World should be the important thing we humans to follow.

Below are some descriptions of something related to the precept.

(2) Meaning of Religious Precept

The dictionary says that precept is in general the standard of living in religion and consists of the work of the mind, that voluntarily tries to keep standards, and heteronomous criterion. The precept of Buddhism is close to this which is, in the first place, not a prohibited item but voluntary and autonomous effort target.

Therefore, only those who are ordained are penalized even if they break the precepts, and the most serious of these is expulsion from the order that is apart from being judged by secular law. Thus, the concept of breaking precept in Buddhism has a double structure, ethics as a Buddhist and order maintenance rules of cult.

On the other hand, since the precept of God's religion is based on the covenant with God (Judaism, Christianity) or God's commandment (Islam), it is different from dictionary explanation and Buddhist precepts. Failure to comply with any provision of the contract or the order will result in the punishment imposed by God. That is, we will be thrown into hell by God's final judgement.

(3) Content of the Precept

In the religious precepts, there are things related to ideological norms and life behavioral norms.

Ideological norms include things related to God that you have to believe in God and non-killing life (such as animals) in Buddhism, and behavioral norms are about morals, ethics and mental and physical health.

Out of these, as for ideological norms related to God that you have to believe in God, regardless of Judaism and Christianity, which are based on the covenant of God and human beings, or Islam, which requires that humans must absolutely obey God, there is no difference in the basic composition from the standpoint of the thought to reward good and punish evil. That is, those who follow the teachings of God will be welcomed into heaven or paradise, but those who cannot follow will be thrown into hell.

However, based on the recognition that the relationship between God and religion is fictitious, there exists no basis for humans to follow ideological norms and its precepts related to God that religion preaches.

Then, what about behavioral norms, which is the rules of conduct, preached by religions?

For God's religion, the basis for preaching the behavioral norms is thought to be even weaker than the ideological norms. This is because, in addition to the relationship between God and religion is fictitious, there is no such a thing as the code of conduct bestowed by God (God's highest good) for morals, ethics and mental and physical health (later 09). In other words, even if based on divine hypothesis, and if we assume the word of God, that does not exist, to be existent, it is impossible to include God's highest good, that does not exist, in the word and give it to the human world. Therefore, the precepts, preached by God's religion or not, turn out to be nothing more than human invention, not the word of God.

(4) Necessary Precept and Unnecessary Precept

We human beings are born as free beings who are not bound by God, religion and precept/commandment. However, for both our social life and mental and physical health as an individual, unlimited freedom is not allowed nor recommended. Therefore, even though we humans are basically free, we need to have some discipline that regulates our conduct for relationships with others and for oneself. If this is called a precept, then precept is necessary. Nonetheless, precept is not something that should be determined and be given to the human world by God nor religion.

In other words, since the code of conduct for life aims for a better human society and individual mental and physical soundness, regardless of relating to God or religion, practicing the code for good human behavior is highly recommended. Therefore, if a code that is considered appropriate for humans and the human world is discovered in religious teachings, we don't have to avoid it entirely just because it's in religion. All what we have to do is to take unbiased stance, that is, what is good is good and what is not good is not good. This is because all of the religious teachings are that which is devised by us humans if we look at its origin.

We here run in to the problem with regard to "What is the criterion for judging an appropriate code of conduct?" The criterion is, of course, us human beings. The specific criterion is the Supreme Idea of the Human World that originates from the living organism called human beings. In the end, if the precept/commandment is in harmony with the nature of us humans as a carbon-based life organism made by stardust matter, we accept it, but if it contradicts human nature, it follows that such precept/commandment becomes useless and we should exclude it from our human world.

There are many such precepts/commandments that are the shadows that religions cast on the human world. Below is the one out of them the writer picked up and tried to describe for a reference purpose.

(5) Dietary Precept/Commandment

There are many kinds of precept in religion and there is dietary precept in them. What is called dietary precept means prohibition of eating certain things.

However, any dietary precept in any religion is basically useless for us humans. The reason lies in ourselves and in God.

First of all, we human beings must naturally and unconditionally affirm ourselves. Based on this perspective, the precepts that contradict the life called human beings must be rendered useless.

In the dietary precept, there is the precept that prohibits to eat animals, for we should not take the life of living things. However, we humans are heterotrophic organisms that are unable to maintain its life and health if we cannot adequately ingest nutrients from minerals, plant and animals. We cannot survive if not dependent on other life forms (including plants). Therefore, providing such a precept is useless because it does not harmonize with the life form called human beings.

Now, in dietary precept, there is commandment ordered by God that eating animal X is allowed but eating animal Y is forbidden. This commandment is causing a funny and strange situation in such a way that in religion A, eating animal X is allowed but eating animal Y is forbidden, however, conversely, in religion B, eating animal Y is allowed but eating animal X is forbidden. Even if we assume God hypothesis and there were God's commandments, taking the attribute of God into consideration, the writer don't think that God does order such a funny thing to confuse the human world. In any case, since it is proven that there is no word of God even if based on God hypothesis, we don't have to worry about being bound by the commandment that is said to be ordered by God.

Now that the commandment is not the one ordered by God, it is clear that it is nothing but the commandment that we humans borrowed God's name and pretended to be God-given. It is considered that such a funny commandment and situation was caused because different people with different cultures and civilizations opened different religions by adopting the prejudice against animals (though there must be some reason for that).

Animals provide irreplaceable nutrients for humans. Basically, we humans can eat anything but humans (though until recently, there were societies with cannibalistic customs). We humans, who are nutritionally dependent organisms, cannot sustain our lives if we lose the proper nutrient balance due to the situation that we cannot depend on other life forms.

When we eat animals and plants, we have no other way we can do than we talk to them, "Please enter my body and become my blood and flesh and live with me."

08 Bonno (Worldly Passions, Desires, etc.), the Precious Treasure

The highest doctrine of Buddhism is said to be elimination of Bonno, open enlightenment and then reach the state of nirvana which is the state of tranquility and peace of mind.

Now, we human beings are born innately equipped with various

Bonno, that is, worldly passions, appetite, sexual desire, other various desires, attachment and so forth. However, since Bonno is first and the most important precious treasure itself for people to be people, it should not be eliminated or destroyed. When we leave Bonno, the workings of the mind disappear and people cease to be people. Here, what we need to be careful is the excessive attachment for some kind of Bonno(s), because it creates afflictions in our mind, that is, the cause of persistent pain or distress. Although attachment which is one of Bonno is an indispensable treasure for humans, yet we humans must take care to enjoy proper attachment lest we should get too obsessed with it. As described below, therefore, required is the recognition that Bonno is to live life with more taste taking advantage of it.

Consequently, Buddhism goes wrong at its entrance. In the first place, the highest doctrine of Buddhism cannot escape from the subject of criticism that it is itself the largest Bonno.

According to Buddhism, Bonno, which is all delusions, is mental effects such as desires and attachments that disturb and annoy the mind and body of human beings, and it stands on the recognition that there are many Bonnos that amount to 108 Bonnos or even 84,000 Bonnos.

Religion can start only from negative view, so Buddhism started on the premise that Bonno is also negative things. However, if Bonno is subtracted from us human life from, what remains will be empty human being who is no longer a human being. For this reason, Bonno is not unnecessary thing for humans but, on the contrary, it should be regarded as precious treasure that lets human being be alive as human being. Accordingly, the thought, which gives Bonno a negative image and destroys it, does not hold.

Bonno that humans are born with is initially not in the minus zone but in the plus/minus zero origin. It is considered optimum to take Bonno in such a way that from the origin, it has the possibility to progress to both plus zone and minus zone depending on the performance of the orchestra of many kinds of music instruments which can be called Bonno. Therefore, so-called Bonno should not be destroyed, and it is the best to take such an approach how to fly Bonnno to the plus zone (pleasure/comfort) by playing wonderful orchestra with many kinds of the music instruments and, conversely, how to avoid bad performance for Bonno so as not to fall into the minus zone (unpleasant/painful). In other words, we should aim for a wonderful performance by Bonnos' orchestra and it's not about not playing orchestra or disbanding.

We humans are living organisms made up of body and Bonno. We cannot deny ourselves and fortunately, we can only affirm ourselves. If the desires of our five senses are not satisfied, it doesn't make much sense for us to live with this special body. The state in which Bonno has been destroyed is the state in which the life form called humans has died. It is not living a happy life in this world, but already being surrounded by flowers as a resident of Buddhist altars or graves.

Human beings should live a happy life by utilizing the precious treasure of Bonno, that is, we shouldn't live a painful life that can't put it to use. It is important to recognize that the elimination of Bonno is the worst.

09 Non-Existence of God's Highest Good

If we say that the universal and absolute goodness for all things in the universe is God's highest good, no such a thing exists.

As for the system of good and evil, if minerals and plants can be excluded in this discussion, the rest will be intellectual life form (humans) and non-intellectual life form (animals). Now, if animals can also be excluded based on the assumption that they cannot understand good and evil, only humans remain as the object that the system is applied on to. In other words, in the whole universe, there exists the sole system of good and evil that can be applied only to humans.

In this perception, it can be considered that "good" is the act that harmonizes with the living organism called human, and "bad" is its contradiction. (If aliens exist and if their good and evil are not common to that of humans, the system will not be the only one in the universe)

Based on the above discussion, it is known that the good and evil of humans is not what should be given by religion as it should be in the name of God or Buddha, but it follows that it is what should be determined for us humans by ourselves and applied to ourselves.

However, because good and evil in the human world vary to a greater or lesser extent depending on the time and place (environmental condition), they are neither universal nor absolute. (It cannot be said that there are no universal things, and there are many things that are the same or similar, but, conversely, many are different and moreover, some good and evil are even reversed) Now, although religions preach that good and evil are universal and absolute, it is clear that it is not right as the teachings are not the same but different from religion to religion, that is, teachings among them are not absolute but nothing but relative. After all, since environmental conditions, that are the elements which are deeply involved in determining good and evil, differ and are not universal from region to region and from society to society, good and evil are not universal in the human world. In addition, and in the first place, in this world where everything flows, since both natural and artificial (man-made) environments change over time, there is no absolute good and evil in the sense of immutability.

With regard to the treatment of good and evil, which are not universal in the human world, even if a perfect match is not gotten, we have to aim to deepen mutual understanding through having constant dialogue while staring the lighthouse named Supreme Idea of the Human World. (The same goes for values)

As discussed, because there is no universal and absolute good and evil for all the groups that make up the human world, and because any good and evil at any point in time changes with the passage of time, it follows that "like a phantom" is the essence of good and evil. And this is natural thing, because, after all, what is called human being itself, who is the object of the application of good and evil, is like a phantom that flows and changes in many ways including evolution. Therefore, even God can't give something like universal and absolute highest good applicable to human being who is neither absolute nor immutable, namely, ever-changing being.

Furthermore, from another perspective, even if based on the God hypothesis and if there were God's highest good and evil, there is no word of God that has been disclosed to the human world. Accordingly, after all, for us humans, it follows that we have never known what is called God's highest good at all. God has not spoken, that is, has been keeping silent.

References: Omitted in the English Version

著者略歴

岡本　浩作（おかもと　こうさく）

1941年 徳島県生まれ
私立土佐高等学校卒業
米国ウッドベリー大学経営学修士（BBA、MBA）
米国ビバリーヒルズ大学経営学博士（Ph.D. in BA）
日米企業の役員を歴任

Author Biography

Kosaku Okamoto

Born in 1941 at Tokushima-pref., Japan
Graduated from Tosa Senior High School, Kochi, Japan
BBA, MBA, Woodbury University, Calif., USA
Ph.D. in BA, University of Beverly Hills, Calif., USA
Various executive posts of Japanese and USA enterprises

人類の選択→繁栄か、それとも、滅亡なのか？
Humanity's Choice → Prosperity or Destruction?

2023年8月10日　初版第1刷発行

著　　者　岡本　浩作
発行者　中田　典昭
発行所　東京図書出版
発行発売　株式会社 リフレ出版
　　　　　〒112-0001　東京都文京区白山 5-4-1-2F
　　　　　電話 (03)6772-7906　FAX 0120-41-8080
印　　刷　株式会社 ブレイン

© Kosaku Okamoto
ISBN978-4-86641-664-9 C0095
Printed in Japan 2023